Studies on the Reformation

Collected Papers in Church History
of Roland H. Bainton

Collected Papers in Church History

SERIES TWO

Studies on the Reformation

By Roland H. Bainton

Beacon Press   Boston

Published simultaneously in Canada by
S. J. Reginald Saunders and Co., Ltd., Toronto

Library of Congress catalog card number: 63-17527

Printed in the United States of America

Acknowledgments

Grateful acknowledgment is made to the following for permission
to reprint the articles comprising this volume: The American
Council of Learned Societies, from *Five Essays on the Bible*;
*Church History; Harvard Theological Review; The Lutheran
Quarterly; The Art Bulletin; The Germanic Review; Luther Today; The Yale Review;* The Lutheran World Federation; *The
American Historical Review; Journal of Religion;* E. J. Brill Ltd.,
from *Castellioniana, Quatre Études sur Sébastien Castellion et
l'Idée de la Tolérance; Het Boek;* Herald Press, from *The Recovery
of the Anabaptist Vision; International Journal of Religious Education;* and the *Andover Review Bulletin.*

Delio Cantimori, amico multos post annos fideli,
animae candidae.

Foreword

On a New England hillside within an enclosure bordered by walls of loose stone one will come upon a lilac in bloom. Beside the roots lies a broad flat stone at the threshold of an excavation kept from caving in by the remnants of a meticulously laid unmortared stone wall. Perhaps at one end of the cellar one will find the vestige of a brick chimney. On the slope below is a dilapidated apple orchard, unpruned, sprawling, the branches gnarled and broken. One should prowl only warily lest one tumble down a well only partly filled by rubble or not yet covered by the vigilance of selectmen. Once the well and the glebe sustained a teeming family. Now all are gone, leaving no memorial save ruins and a lilac bloom. Odd that all they built to live is crumbling and that alone retains its former semblance which was planted for sheer loveliness! One would not have the temerity to compare erudite articles to any blossom, yet they may perchance be worth refurbishing because addressed to life's ultimate concerns.

The essays in this volume, originating as byproducts of books, center around two foci, the radicals of the Reformation and Luther. I began with the radicals as the result of a personal concern. I was a conscientious objector in the first world war and was much agitated by the problems of conscience, civil and religious liberty, and the legitimate extent and limits of the constraints imposed by Church and state. The original plan was to bring out a volume on four heretics of the sixteenth century who fled from the Inquisition in four countries to the refuge of the Swiss cities, only there to fall foul of the Calvinist regime. The four were Castellio from France, Ochino from Italy, Joris from Holland and Servetus from Spain. A Guggenheim fellowship in 1926 made possible investigation in European archives. So much material came to light as to necessitate separate monographs. Castellio came out in 1935, Joris in 1937, Ochino in 1940, but Servetus not until 1953. The original plan of treating them in conjunction was achieved only by placing them in a larger setting in the book *The Travail of Religious Liberty*.

No essays resulted from the work on Ochino, though there

are several quotations from his writings in the essay on "The Parable of the Tares" and "The Immoralities of the Patriarchs" in the previous volume. In the case of Servetus I have not reprinted a grist of essays which were incorporated substantially in the biography but I did include in the previous volume a background essay on "Trinitarian Speculation," because the text of the notes did not go into the book. The Joris archives disclosed material bearing on the connections of Postell with members of the Joris sect. That paper appears here. In the case of Castellio I made a blunder in that I told almost nothing about him in the volume *Castellio Concerning Heretics*, since I had already published an essay about him in the Burr Festschrift. On the occasion of the commemoration in 1953 this material was revamped for the booklet *Castellioniana*. This version is included here.

My first study of Luther was a paper dealing with his attitude to religious liberty in 1929. It was written at a time when I felt intense resentment against him because he spoke so magnificently for liberty in the early 1520s and condoned the death penalty for Anabaptists a decade later. Having worked eight years on a biography of Luther in the 1940s, anger changed to sadness through the discovery that in this case, as often elsewhere, it is the saints who burn the saints. This essay has been thoroughly rewritten. The one on "Luther's Struggle for Faith" first appeared in the Festschrift for Gerhard Ritter. It was later incorporated into the biography of Luther *Here I Stand* (1950), but with the omission of the detailed examination of possible correlations between Luther's circumstances and diseases and his mental states. This portion only is reproduced here.

The article, "Congregationalism and the Puritan Revolution from the Just War to the Crusade," went only in part into the volume *Christian Attitudes to War and Peace* (1960) and for that reason appears here in full.

The present collections of papers thus aims at completeness for material not in books, and, with the exception of the abovementioned, those essays which have appeared in other of my volumes are not here included.

R. H. B.

Contents

List of Illustrations—*following page 142*

1. Self-portrait of Dürer
2. "St. Francis and Christ"
3. "Hus at the Stake"
4. Woodcut with Lucas Cranach self-portrait as Simon of Cyrene
5. "Luther Declaring the Word of God . . ."
6. Martin Luther as an Augustinian monk
7. Baldasare Cossa as a monk
8. A later representation of Baldasare Cossa

Abbreviations

Used in footnotes and bibliographies.

ACJ	*Acta et Commentationes Imp. Universitatis Jurievensis*
ARG	*Archiv für Reformationsgeschichte*
BR	*Briefwechsel* (Weimar Ausgabe, *Luthers Werke*). (*Correspondence*, Weimar edition, *Luther's Works.*)
CR	*Corpus Reformatorum*
DRA	*Deutsche Reichstagsakten*
EA	Erlangen Ausgabe (Erlangen edition, *Luthers Werke*)
EP	Epistle
PG	Migne, *Patrologia graeca*
PL	Migne, *Patrologia latina*
SVRG	*Schriften des Vereins für Reformationsgeschichte*
TR	*Tischreden* (Weimar Ausgabe, *Luthers Werke*). (*Table Talk*, Weimar edition, *Luther's Works*).
Trin. Err.	*De Trinitatis Erroribus* of Servetus
WA	Weimar Ausgabe (Weimar edition, *Luthers Werke*)
ZKG	*Zeitschrift für Kirchengeschichte*

I. Martin Luther and the Reformation

1. The Bible and the Reformation

The Reformation dethroned the pope and enthroned the Bible. This is the common generalization. In this form it is untenable. A book cannot replace a man. The real point is that the reformers denied that the pope is the infallible interpreter of the Bible and claimed that they were quite able to interpret better than he for themselves. The Catholic Church had never said that the Bible is not an authority or that the Bible can be dispensed with. The question was who should interpret what the Bible meant in cases of obscurity or with reference to new situations. There were differences of opinion on this score among Catholics themselves, and Luther only brought to a head the critical tendencies of the late Middle Ages. In an earlier period, the Bible, the tradition and the church as the custodian of both were not felt to be in conflict. But in the fourteenth century a rent appeared in the seamless robe. Early in that century, Pope John XXII was widely proclaimed by the Franciscans to be a heretic because he had asserted contrary to Scripture that Christ had property. William of Occam, the leader of the Franciscans, affirmed that the authority of the Church is derived from Scripture. The sectaries Wyclif and Hus went further and said that indeed the Church can never be at variance with the Scripture because the true church is that church which is in accord with Scripture. Such a church might be only a remnant, set over against the great institutional church which had departed from the norm. Then at the end of the century came the great schism, with Christendom divided between two popes, each asserting the other to be damned. Wyclif said that they were both right. In order to end the schism, the Conciliarists sought to make councils superior to popes. This did not mean, however, that any individual might interpret the Bible for himself, and when John Hus did so, he was

First published in *Five Essays on the Bible,* The American Council of Learned Societies, (New York, 1960).

burned by the Council of Constance. The point was simply that
the pope was not an infallible interpreter. Yet one canon lawyer at
the Council of Basel went further when he affirmed that "in matters touching the faith, the word of a single private person is to be
preferred to that of a pope, if that person is moved by sounder
arguments from the Old Testament and the New Testament."
Against all of these tendencies, the canon lawyers in particular
made more and more extravagant counterclaims, even to the point
that the only source of the doctrine was the living pope, who thus
displaced both the Scripture and tradition.

Luther epitomized two centuries of antipapal critique, and
with all the more vehemence because the Church met his attack
not by moderation but by heightening the most unbridled among
the papal pretensions. Sylvester Prierias, commissioned by Pope
Leo X to refute Luther, asserted: "Whoever does not rest on the
doctrine of the Roman Church and of the Roman Pontiff as the
infallible rule of faith, from which even Sacred Scripture draws its
strength and authority, is a heretic." Luther retorted: "If that be
so, what need or use is there of Holy Scripture? Why not burn it
all, and content ourselves with these unlearned lords at Rome, who
have the Holy Ghost with them, though as a matter of fact, the
Holy Ghost can dwell only in a Godly heart?" The Catholic argument soon came to be more sharply formulated: the Church must
be the lord of Scripture because the Church made the Scripture.
That is to say, the Church selected those books that should constitute the canon of Scripture. To this the reformers answered that
the Church did not make the Scripture. The Gospel made the
Church and the Church then selected those books which contained
the Gospel. Therefore, the Gospel is the lord of the Church.

This affirmation confronts us with the question: "What was
the Gospel if it was prior to the Church and made the Church?"
The term Gospel, by the way, was more congenial to Zwingli.
Luther preferred to talk of the Word, which made the Church. But
then what was the Word or the Gospel? By way of answer, we need
to take into account that Luther's distinctiveness lay in his recovery
of the historical element in Christianity. It is a religion of history.
There are religions of nature, which see God in the dying and
rising of the seasons and in the orderly course of the heavenly

[margin note:] Luther contradicts

bodies. There are religions of contemplation, which seek God from within. There are religions of morality, which see the disclosure of God in the deportment of man to man. And there are religions of history which find God revealed in the great crises of man's past. Judaism is such a religion and its holy days are commemorative. Christianity is such a religion. It rests on a deed of God in a time when a decree went out from Caesar Augustus that all the world should be taxed. To Christ the centuries lead up, and from Christ the centuries lead out. In him God the inscrutable became God the discernible. In him God the all terrible became God the all merciful. God was in Christ, reconciling the world unto himself. Therefore Christianity is forever anchored in the past.

There are various ways of obscuring the once-and-for-allness of God's redemptive act. One way is moralism, that man by his own goodness can at any time accomplish his salvation. Another is mysticism, that man in any age may start upon the ladder of ascents culminating in absorption into the ineffable One. There is the way of institutionalism, that the revelation of God at a point in the past is continued in the present through an institution as the source of an on-going disclosure. In late medieval Catholicism, this institution was increasingly focused on one man, the pope. Luther rejected naturalism, mysticism, moralism and institutionalism. Christianity, he held, rests on God's once-and-for all in Christ. This Word brought Scripture into being. Scripture itself is not the Word. Scripture is the manger in which lies the Babe, the Word. But Scripture is infinitely precious because it is the record of the Word. Scripture as the cradle of the Word provides a norm by which to judge the Church.

At the same time, the Word within Scripture may be used to judge Scripture. Luther treated Scripture with amazing freedom, with so much freedom indeed that one wonders why he did not disrupt the canon. Tradition at this point was presumably too strong for him. He regarded Esther as a hateful Jewish book and his strictures on the epistle of James are notorious. "An epistle of straw" he called it because of its emphasis upon works, whereas Paul had insisted that by no works can man be saved. And the Book of Revelation, to Luther, was not revealing. His canon within the Canon consisted of John's Gospel and the Pauline epistles proper. And only after these the Synoptics. In the Old Testament he liked Genesis because in it Abraham was saved by faith and the Psalms because David was so penitential, Habakkuk because it contains the verse "The just shall live by faith," and Jonah because the prophet had the faith to compose a Psalm while in the unventilated belly of the whale.

A recent Catholic interpreter of Luther has suggested that in setting up this scale he did not substitute a book for a pope but rather a dogma for both.[1] Curiously, while Protestants commonly accuse the Catholics of reducing revelation to propositions, here the charge is reversed. Luther, it is claimed, said not merely that man must be justified by faith, but that he must believe in the proposition of justification by faith. And in terms of this norm he demoted the pope and downgraded much of the Scripture. But as a matter of fact, justification for Luther was no mere proposition. To be sure, faith was directed toward the objective deed of God in history. But to be justified one must inwardly appropriate what God had done until the whole being was saturated and renewed by faith.

Yet the Catholic critique is right that Luther did take a very lordly attitude toward Scripture. At the same time, he rejected nothing and brought everything into line with what he took to be the core. There was a certain arbitrariness in this procedure of which not Luther alone was guilty but every exegete in that period, because no one was prepared to admit that the Scripture might contradict itself. Therefore, if the heart of Scripture were Paul's doctrine, that by no good deeds could man be saved, then all the passages in the New Testament with regard to heavenly reward would have to mean something other than appeared. And by the same token, Erasmus and the Catholics, who believed that man can contribute to his salvation through moral achievement, had to attenuate the rigors of Paul's doctrine. Luther actually came closer to a recognition of diversity and almost inconsistency in the Bible by his doctrine of levels than did any of his contemporaries.

One might have expected the great line of demarcation for him to have lain between the Old Testament and the New. It did

---

[1] George Tavard, *Holy Writ or Holy Church* (London, 1959).

for some Protestants, like the Anabaptists, who rejected the wars of Yahweh and took literally the ethic of the Sermon on the Mount. Luther on a different count might have used his distinction of law and gospel to repudiate Moses as law, but Luther did not. Law and gospel, said he, lie side by side throughout the whole Bible. That which relies on man's good works is law. That which relies on God's good grace is gospel. The Ten Commandments can witness to grace and the Sermon on the Mount can be treated as a new law. Therefore, the Old Testament is not to be rejected or relegated to a lower rank. Here one must recall that Luther interpreted the Old Testament in terms of the pre-existent Christ, who was speaking through Moses and through David. Thus, actually, the New Testament was a Christian book.

At the same time there was recognition of historical development in the Old Testament, not, however, a human development in which each generation learned something more and transmitted its accumulated wisdom. The development was rather of God, who was unfolding a great drama of redemption in the form of a symphony in which themes recurred without precise repetition but with reminiscence and anticipation, in varied forms leading up to the ultimate reconciliation. Thus, the theme of sacrifice is present in the murder of Abel and the attempted sacrifice of Isaac. Observe that this was not an exact anticipation of the sacrifice of Christ, because Isaac was not sacrificed. But the theme was there. So also in the persecution of the saints, the suffering of the beloved servant of the Lord, and to a degree in the examples in which God used the weak things of the world to confound the mighty and preserved his Church through the remnant of the hidden and despised. These are recurrent themes which linked the old dispensation with the new.

The modern reader will say that this unity was achieved by imposing upon the Old Testament a sense which was not there. But this is precisely the point at issue. Luther, following LeFevre, said that the plain historical sense of Scripture is what the writers of Scripture intended to say. Now if they intended to prophesy, then prophecy is the literal sense. If they intended to foreshadow Christ, then their clairvoyance is the historical meaning. This problem was not restricted to the sixteenth century. Even today

one who believes in a religious philosophy of history will interpret
the events differently from one who sees in the Old Testament only
the fortuitous clashing of nomads emerging from the Syrian sands.

Beneath the question of what the sacred authors meant is the
prior question of what they said, and this can be answered only on
the basis of philological study. At this point, there was almost no
line of cleavage between Protestants and Catholics in the sixteenth
century and there is even less today. The humanist scholars in that
period were in both camps. Erasmus died a Catholic; Melanchthon
died a Protestant. There is something symbolic in this, that whereas Luther reached the point where he would not talk to Erasmus,
Melanchthon on the contrary continued friendly relations with
both. But Luther was loyal to the method of Erasmus and asserted
roundly that God gave his revelation to the world in Hebrew and
Greek. Therefore our eternal salvation is absolutely dependent
upon knowledge of these ancient tongues, and many of the errors
of the popes, said he, were due to their ignorance of the sacred
idiom. Here Luther was not speaking *qua* Luther but *qua* Erasmus.
With great gusto Luther availed himself of the linguistic tools provided by Erasmus. And when the first edition of the Greek New
Testament appeared in 1516, the first ever printed, Luther was
lecturing on Romans 9. He brought the great tome into the class-
room and relied on it until the appearance of the next edition. For
his own translation he used the second edition of Erasmus of 1519.

In his scholarly principles, Luther was even more loyal than
Erasmus to sound humanist procedures, because he was less dependent upon authority. In his first edition Erasmus had omitted
the famous verse in I John 5, that there are three witnesses on
earth, the water, the spirit and the blood—this part is genuine—
and that there are three in heaven, the Father, the Son and the
Spirit—this much is spurious. Erasmus could find it in no manuscript and left it out. There was such an outcry that he agreed to
restore it in case it could be discovered in any manuscript. One was
found and manufactured for the purpose at Dublin. And Erasmus,
having sworn, was true to his oath and delivered the head of John
the Baptist on a platter. But Luther had not sworn, and at this
point he adhered to the first edition of Erasmus, though otherwise
he was following the second. Unhappily the spurious verse passed

from this second edition into the *textus receptus* and then into the King James translation. In the late nineteenth century, Pope Leo XIII declared it to be genuine, but forty years later a commission of the Church reversed his verdict. Today no Catholic would defend its authenticity.

Luther as a translator was astoundingly free. Some of his translations of the Psalms are almost paraphrases, superior to the original because so vibrant with Luther's own *de profundis*. An example of his freedom and power may be seen in his rendering of Luke 22:15, which is rendered in the King James version "with desire I have desired to eat this Passover with you." This is a literal carrying over of the Greek ἐπιθυμίᾳ ἐπεθύμησα which in the Vulgate appeared as *desiderio desideravi* and in the old German versions as *mit Begehr habe ich begehrt*. Luther leaped beyond them all and translated: *Mich hat herzlich verlangt, dies Osterlamm mit euch zu essen.*[2]

Rigorously exact philological work must be the basis for all Biblical exegesis. This Luther recognized. But when all is said and done, what does the Bible say? The common opinion is that Luther believed the Bible to be altogether clear, but that Erasmus found it obscure and therefore needed not only linguistic tools but also the authority of the Church as an interpreter. But this statement is not precise. Erasmus indeed said that the Bible is obscure, yet found it perfectly clear with regard to the love of God and the duty of man and the way of salvation. It was only Luther's paradoxes which he thought might better be left to the judgment day, and Luther indeed considered Scripture to be absolutely plain as to the essentials of salvation through justification by faith, but at many points he found God's inscrutable will in Scripture shrouded in thick darkness. And as for predestination, which is in Scripture, Luther said that by this teaching he had been cast down to the very abyss of desperation. For both Erasmus and Luther some passages were clear and some were obscure. They differed as to which was which.

And they differed above all as to how to tell the difference. The answer on all sides was that understanding must be given by

[2] Heinz Bluhm, "Luther's Translation of Luke 22:15," *Modern Language Notes* (June 1950).

the Spirit. The Catholics said that the Spirit was channeled through the pope. Luther deemed this doctrine to be the very height of individualism, namely, that we should commit "to one man, the Roman Pontiff, surrounded only by unlearned sophists, the exercise of the right of interpreting Sacred Scripture by virtue of the sole majesty of his sublimity and power against all intelligence and erudition." Luther maintained that any Christian, even Balaam's ass (provided of course he could bray in Hebrew and Greek) could be as inspired by the Spirit to interpret the Scripture as could the pope. Erasmus retorted by demanding tests for the Spirit. Luther replied that the test of the Spirit is Scripture. And Erasmus told him that this was to argue in a circle.

Then arose in Luther's own camp those who agreed with him to a most disconcerting degree. Luther, said they, is right that the Scripture must be interpreted through the Spirit. The Apostles wrote the Scripture in the Spirit. To understand the Scripture we must be in the same spirit as were the Apostles. But if we are in the same spirit as were the Apostles when they wrote the Scripture, then we do not need the Scripture. Away with the book! Away with the languages! Away with "the letter that killeth, in favor of the Spirit that giveth life." To which Luther retorted (remember that the Holy Spirit was portrayed as a dove), "unless you cite Scripture, I do not care if you have swallowed the Holy Spirit, feathers and all."

Luther now found himself in the middle, between the extreme papists who would localize the Spirit in the pope, and the inspired prophets who subordinated Scripture to their private revelations. Luther insisted that the Spirit does not operate apart from the written Word. God's deed in history must be appropriated by us afresh, but this will never happen apart from that which God has already given. Therefore, we must have the languages; therefore, we must study the text. Yet at the same time we shall not be able to understand them apart from the guidance of the Spirit.

And once again the question is raised: "How do we get the Spirit?" Is there anything we can do or must we simply sit and wait until the Spirit bloweth upon our hearts? Luther's only answer at this point was that man can prepare for the coming of the Spirit only by steeping himself in the Scriptures. He must read, meditate, contemplate, project himself into the Scriptures and then, and he knows not when, the Spirit will enlighten his mind.

How Luther did this is best exemplified by giving an example of the manner in which he treated a Biblical passage. Here in his own words, though greatly condensed, is his version of the sacrifice of Isaac:

Abraham was told by God that he must sacrifice the son of his old age by a miracle, the seed through whom he was to become the father of kings and of a great nation. Abraham turned pale. Not only would he lose his son, but God appeared to be a liar. He had said, "In Isaac shall be thy seed," but now he said, "Kill Isaac." Who would not hate a God so cruel and contradictory? How Abraham longed to talk it over with someone! Could he not tell Sarah? But he well knew that if he mentioned it to anyone he would be dissuaded and prevented from carrying out the behest. The spot designated for the sacrifice, Mount Moriah, was some distance away; "and Abraham rose up early in the morning, and saddled his ass, and took two of his young men with him, and Isaac his son, and clave the wood for the burnt-offering." Abraham did not leave the saddling of the ass to others. He himself laid on the beast the wood for the burnt offering. He was thinking all the time that these logs would consume his son, his hope of seed. With these very sticks that he was picking up the boy would be burned. In such a terrible case should he not take time to think it over? Could he not tell Sarah? With what inner tears he suffered! He girt the ass and was so absorbed he scarcely knew what he was doing.

He took two servants and Isaac his son. In that moment everything died in him: Sarah, his family, his home, Isaac. This is what it is to sit in sackcloth and ashes. If he had known that this was only a trial, he would not have been tried. Such is the nature of our trials that while they last we cannot see to the end. "Then on the third day Abraham lifted up his eyes, and saw the place afar off." What a battle he had endured in those three days! There Abraham left the servants and the ass, and he laid the wood upon Isaac and himself took the torch and the sacrificial knife. All the time he was thinking, "Isaac, if you knew, if your mother knew that you are to be sacrificed." "And they went both of them together." The whole world does not know what here took place. They two walked together. Who? The father and the dearest son—the one not knowing what was in store but ready to obey, the other certain that he must leave his son in ashes. Then said Isaac, "My father." And he said, "Yes, my son." And Isaac said, "Father, here is the fire and here the wood, but where is the lamb?" He called him father and was solicitous lest he had overlooked something, and Abraham said, "God will himself provide a lamb, my son."

When they were come to the mount, Abraham built the altar and laid on the wood, and then he was forced to tell Isaac. The boy was stupefied. He must have protested, "Have you forgotten: I am the son of Sarah by a miracle in her age, that I was promised and that through me you are to be the father of a great nation?" And Abraham must have answered that God would fulfill his promise even out of ashes. Then Abraham bound him and laid him upon the wood. The father raised his knife. The boy bared his throat. If God had slept an instant, the lad would have been dead. I could not have watched. I am not able in my thoughts to follow. The lad was as a sheep for the slaughter. Never in history was there such obedience, save only in Christ. But God was watching, and all the angels. The father raised his knife; the boy did not wince. The angel cried, "Abraham, Abraham!" See how divine majesty is at hand in the hour of death. We say, "In the midst of life we die." God answers, "Nay, in the midst of death we live."

Luther once read this story for family devotions. When he had finished, his wife said, "I do not believe it. God would not have treated his Son like that."

"But, Katie," answered Luther, "He did."

Here we see how Luther linked the Old Testament and the New by discovering in both the presence of Christ, how he steeped himself in Scripture until he virtually became Abraham, and how he brooded over the meaning of Scripture until his heart leapt into flame.

2. Luther's Struggle for Faith

Our interest in Luther's struggle for faith is not merely historical. We do not investigate this subject as we do Luther's views on monstrosities or the names for the gems in the Apocalypse, nor do we probe into his spiritual trials in order to collect additional specimens of abnormal psychology. If he was abnormal then the abnormal has become the normal. All of us today are engaged in a struggle for faith and our concern is not so much with the disease as with the cure. How was it that Luther, despite his travailing of spirit, could be so tremendous in his faith, so incredible in his courage, so astounding in his output? Luther's faith is our quest.

We must recognize—and we are glad to recognize, for it makes him closer to ourselves—that his groanings and travailings for the faith were lifelong. But this some scholars will not readily concede. They grant, of course, that Luther was subject to continual depressions, but insist that their character must have altered after the evangelical experience of 1513 when he came into the clear as to the faith. Boehmer claims that in the later years Luther was disturbed rather over his work, over the frivolities and turpitude of the rulers, over the ingratitude and sensuality of the masses, as well as over the more disconcerting thought that if he had been wrong he was taking so many souls to hell.[1] A certain warrant for this distinction can be found in Luther's own statement that in the cloister he had been troubled concerning the graciousness of God

This paper appeared in the *Festschrift für Gerhard Ritter zu seinem 60. Geburtstag* (Tübingen, 1950). Inadvertently, it was published earlier in *Church History*, XVII, 3 (September 1948), because the American editors were not aware that the German work was being held up pending approval of the French censors. Only the first half of the article is reprinted here because the second half was incorporated bodily into the biography of Luther, *Here I Stand* (New York, 1950). Whether Luther's evangelical experience is to be dated in 1513 has lately been subject again to debate, but the precise year does not matter for the present purpose.

[1] *Der junge Luther* (1929), 96.

but afterwards as to whether he had deceived others by his teaching.[2] This difference, however, is only one of degree, with the later torment the more intense. The question was still whether he had been correct in his insights as to the faith. But whereas formerly he had been involved only for himself, now he was responsible also for his converts.

We cannot escape the plain fact that Luther's evangelical experience of 1513 did not clear up his religious difficulties for the remainder of his days. The understanding of the text, "The just shall live by faith," which had come to him as a flash on the Damascus road, left no tangible relic to which one could return at will. Rather it was like a sunset which would return, but no man could say where or when. The testimony of the later years makes abundantly evident that the ancient doubts recurred. In the 1530s Luther questioned the very existence of God. "The devil so assails me that I do not know whether there is any God or not."[3] He questioned the justice of God. "Is it not against reason that all mankind should be subject to toil, sickness and death just because one man took a bite out of an apple?"[4] He questioned the graciousness of God. "The worst temptation is when Satan says, 'God hates sinners. You are a sinner. God hates you.'"[5] The devil can so beleager a heart, so terrify it that it will avoid God, become His enemy and blaspheme, for to a miserable conscience there is nothing other than that God, devil, death, sin, hell and all creatures are eternal unceasing enemies."[6] The year 1527 was for Luther a time of depression as severe as any he had ever known. To a friend he wrote in August of that year, "For more than a week I was close to the gates of death and hell. I trembled in all my members. Christ was wholly lost. I was shaken by desperation and blasphemy of God."[7] To lose Christ and blaspheme God, are not these the very assaults which plagued Luther in the cloister? Faith was no pearl to be mounted in a gold setting and gazed upon at will. Faith was ever the object of an agonizing search.

[2] *TR* 122.
[3] *TR* 518.
[4] *TR* 587.
[5] *TR* 141.
[6] *WA* XXXI, pp. 1, 147 (1530).
[7] *BR* 1126.

Who can read Luther's sermons in the later years on all the troubled spirits in the Bible without feeling that they are essentially autobiographical? With what feeling he portrays Adam when he crouches before the voice of God in the garden,[8] the agony of Abraham when commanded to sacrifice the son through whom should have been fulfilled the promise to become a great people,[9] the terror of Jonah as the monster which he did not yet know to be for his deliverance opened its cavernous jaws and the billows swept him into the belly of darkness,[10] the desolation of Job before the mystery of the inscrutable providence of God,[11] the anguish of the Virgin Mary when the child Jesus was lost and she believed herself to be rejected as his mother,[12] the dismay of the Canaanite woman when Christ compared her to a dog,[13] and supremely the agony of Christ in the garden and on the cross when he so identified himself with sinful humanity as to feel himself accursed and abandoned by God. Nowhere in all Christian literature will one find such poignant expositions of the words, "My God! my God! why hast Thou forsaken me?"[14]

In the case of one whose emotional upheavals were so intense and so persistent, one cannot blithely dismiss the possibility of abnormal psychology. The intensity was on occasion so great that he could consider suicide and feared to pick up a carving knife for fear of what he might do to himself.[15] As for persistence, we must recall that attacks of melancholia not only recurred after the evangelical experience but that they began before the entry into the cloister. Luther declared that after the receipt of his master's degree at Erfurt, and therefore during the six months prior to his entry into the monastery, he had been subject to continual melancholy.[16] Also we must recognize that if at times Luther was depressed, on

[8] *WA* XIV, pp. 136-140 (1523); XXXVII, pp. 454-455 (1534); XLII, pp. 127-129.

[9] *WA* XLIII, p. 202.

[10] *WA* XIX, pp. 194-229 (1526).

[11] *TR*, Nos. 3558b, 3669.

[12] *WA* XXVII, pp. 95-96 (1528).

[13] *WA* XVII, pp. 2, 201-202 (1525); XXI, pp. 110-112 (1528); XXXVII, pp 313-316 (1534).

[14] *WA* V, pp. 603-612 (1519-1521); XXXVI, p. 538 (1532).

[15] *TR*, Nos. 194, 1347, 2387; WA XL, pp. 1, 320; XXXIV, pp. 2, 203.

[16] *TR* 3593.

other occasions he was elated. In the cloister at times he had felt himself to be amid choirs of angels.[17] And in later life when Katie, to bring him out of a fit of despondency, would take him for a drive in the woods, he would begin to sing lustily.[18] He said himself that his moods were like April weather.[19]

To a modern psychiatrist, such fluctuations suggest manic depression,[20] and if such a classification appears extreme for one whose working capacity was never impaired—witness the prodigious output despite melancholy at the Wartburg—at least one is prompted to inquire whether the times of despondency may not have been due to some glandular or gastric deficiency.[21] Attempts have been made to trace a correlation between the moods and the maladies of Luther, but with very slight success. During the course of his life he suffered from constipation, insomnia, gout, hemorrhoids, stone, catarrh and ringing in the ears—quite enough to depress anyone. But there is no record of any of these in the cloister days when he suffered such agonies of spirit that had they lasted a tenth of an hour he could not have survived.[22] The attack of the stone in 1526 and the blood clot of January 1527[23] had cleared before the great depression of the summer of that year. And this depression itself was not preceded but was followed by ringing in the ears and coma. The sense of spiritual desolation which came first was, according to Luther, vastly worse than the succeeding malady, though that brought him to the gates of death.[24] At the Wartburg, again one wonders whether constipation and insomnia were the occasion or the aftermath of despondency coupled with superhuman industry.

Only slightly more successful is the attempt to link the emotional states to outward circumstances. However much prior de-

---

[17] *Luthers Werke, EA* XXIII, pp. 400f.

[18] A. Thoma, *Katherina von Bora,* p. 179 (1900).

[19] *TR* 956.

[20] H. T. Schou, *Sygdoms Betydning for det religioese sjaelelir* (1943), p. 53.

[21] H. T. Schou, *Religion and Morbid Mental States* (1926), see chapter on "Melancholy."

[22] *WA* I, pp. 557f.

[23] *BR* 1078.

[24] Report by Bugenhagen and Jonas, reprinted in Paul J. Reiter, *Martin Luthers Umwelt, Charakter und Psychose* (1941).

pressions may have contributed, the decision to enter the monastery was precipitated by the terror of death in a thunderstorm. The up-heavals in the cloister appear to have commenced with the terror of the Holy induced by the saying of the first mass. The great depression of 1527 was closely connected with the news of martyrdom among Luther's followers. He was distressed that his converts should suffer, while he, who was responsible for their faith, should be spared. Perhaps he was not worthy. Perhaps spiritual rather than physical torments were to be his portion.[25] As Luther came out of the coma he remarked to Jonas, "I was not worthy to shed my blood for Christ as many of my fellow confessors of the Gospel have done. Yet this honor was denied to the beloved disciple, John the Evangelist, who wrote a much worse book against the Papacy than I ever did."[26]

Again Luther's tranquil periods have some relation to outward events. He remarked that during the first year in the monastery the devil is very quiet.[27] Likewise he said that for some time after his marriage he was not troubled.[28] From this, one would infer that a change in outward circumstances was able for a time to allay his sense of spiritual insecurity, but when the newness wore off the malady returned. But the correlation between outward and inward was never close. The very nature of the dark night of the soul is that it may be induced by nothing at all. Luther was very fond of a passage in the book of Leviticus (26:36) which describes how a host may be put to flight by the stirring of a wind-blown leaf.[29]

The attempt to construct a cycle of Luther's ups-and-downs is equally futile. The Danish psychiatrist, Reiter, has made the attempt, but with how little success may be seen in that he places the years 1519 to 1521 on the curve of elevation. With regard to this, two comments are in order. The first is that during those years Luther was far from experiencing uniform exhilaration. After they were over, he was able in the retrospect of the Wartburg to recall

[25] *BR* 1107, 1126, 1128 and especially 1132.
[26] Reiter, *Martin Luthers Umwelt*, Vol. II, p. 578.
[27] *WA* VIII, p. 860.
[28] *TR* 141.
[29] Paul Th. Buhler, *Die Anfechtung bei Martin Luther* (1942), pp. 39f.

how often during those very years he had been plagued by the taunt, "Are you alone wise?"[30] The other comment is that if during that time Luther was highly elated the explanation is not to be found in any rhythm of his own but rather in the mood of an entire generation. Most of the leaders of Germany in that day were warbling with Hutten that it was a great time to be alive. Erasmus was exuberant because the sovereigns of Europe were embracing humanism and, he trusted, would unite their names and their hearts in loyalty to the gospels and in the service of peace. The election of Charles V inspired the most sanguine expectation. The year 1521 brought disillusionment for everyone. The outbreak of war between Charles and Francis shattered the dream of European concord cherished by Erasmus; the fiasco of Sickingen wrecked the hopes and the life of Hutten; the Edict of Worms rendered nugatory Luther's *Appeal to the Nobility of the German Nation.* If Luther was at times downcast we must bear in mind that Erasmus became a querulous old man. In neither case need we look for glandular or gastric deficiencies.

The source of Luther's depressions eludes us. Their form is more tangible. This is clear: they never assumed the shape of escape into a realm of illusion but only of an all too intense emotional reaction. He was always concerned with real problems, or at least they were real if his premises be granted. Anyone who considers the whole of religion to be unreal must, of course, say that he was concerned with unreality. Even so, it was not an unreality of his own constructing. He began with the religion and theology on which he had been reared and discovered there genuine difficulties to which others were not properly sensitive. His own emotional responses were too acute. He knew it, and when the assault was over, would say that the devil can turn a louse into a camel.[31] Yet, he came to feel that even such excessive upheavals were necessary to the discovery of valid solutions. "If I live longer," he said, "I would like to write a book about *Anfechtungen,* for without them no man can understand Scripture, faith, the fear or the love of God. He does not know the meaning of hope who was never sub-

---

[30] *WA* VIII, p. 483; cf. XXXVI, p. 475.
[31] *TR* 1289, 1113; *WA* XXVII, p. 96.

ject to temptations."[32] "David must have been plagued by a very fearful devil. He could not have had such profound insights if he had not experienced great assaults."[33] Luther verged on saying that an excessive emotional sensitivity is a mode of revelation. Those who are predisposed to fall into despondency as well as to rise into ecstasy may be able to view reality from a different angle than that of ordinary folk. Yet it is a true angle and when the problem or the religious object has been once so viewed, others less sensitive will be able to look from a new vantage point and testify that the insight is valid.

[32] *TR* 4777.
[33] *TR* 199.

3. Luther's Attitudes on Religious Liberty

Of all the papers in this collection only this one has been seriously revised since its appearance in 1929. I was then filled with no little resentment against Luther because I was fresh from the study of the radicals whom he suppressed, and it seemed to me inexcusable that he should have denied to them the liberty which he demanded for himself. In the interim, anger has given way to sadness that so often the saints persecute the saints. A more fundamental reason is a change in the entire temper of our times. Thirty years ago, liberty of thought and expression was an axiom of the Western world. Constraint was considered execrable. The intolerance of the main Protestant reformers of the sixteenth century was used by the Catholics to show that the Protestants were not in a position to cast any reproaches. The Protestants responded by seeking to extenuate or to salvage an unwitting contribution to liberty on the part of the reformers in that they broke the monolithic structure of the Church. The presupposition behind the universal belief in tolerance was commonly a higher evaluation of sincerity than of truth and an optimistic belief that in free encounter truth would triumph. The rise of fascism and communism disclosed that diabolical error is all the more diabolical if held with passionate sincerity. The liberals were confronted with the dilemma that, unless suppressed, the illiberals would triumph and exterminate the liberals, but, if suppressed, liberalism would destroy itself by adopting the weapons of the enemy. Perhaps this misgiving accounts for the falling off in historical writing about the problem of toleration. The literature which I surveyed in the article in 1929 still very nearly completes the roster. W. K. Jordan's work in four volumes

The original paper was first published in the *Harvard Theological Review*, XXII (1929), 107-149 under the title "The Development and Consistency of Luther's Attitude to Religious Liberty."

(*Religious Toleration in England*) might be regarded as an exception because it was not completed until 1940, but the first volume appeared in 1932. The only indisputable exception is the summation of previous studies integrated by independent research on the part of Joseph Leclerc (*Histoire de la Tolérance au siècle de la Réforme,* two volumes, Paris, 1955), written with the dispassionate spirit of one who gives the impression that for him the controversies of the sixteenth and seventeenth centuries belong to the past and the dilemmas of the twentieth century lie beyond the scope of his inquiry.

With regard to Luther, in former days the Catholics stressed the illiberal utterances and some of the Protestants stressed the liberal. But others—especially those in the Pietist tradition—distinguished an earlier liberal Luther battling for freedom against Rome and a later encrusted Luther suppressing the sectarians. This paper, as the title indicates, centers on the question of his development and consistency. The question is still worth raising but I have come to perceive that Luther's development mirrored that of an entire generation.

The sixteenth century in Europe was comparatively tolerant during its first quarter. The Inquisition had done its work, the medieval sects had been crushed, the marranos and Moriscos were under control in Spain. In that very land Erasmianism was the vogue in the 1520s, and throughout Europe a movement called *Evangelisme* flourished among Catholics. In that period the liberals were archbishops and cardinals. This tolerance was not deep-rooted, but arose from a sense of security. When this was shattered by the rise of Protestantism, all of the machinery of persecution was revived. Catholicism hardened and the liberals went to the stake, to prison or into exile. Protestantism, because attacking the great institution, was almost inevitably virulent against the Catholics and at the same time optimistic that on the basis of Scripture a new reformed Church could be erected, unified within itself. When however this confidence was shaken by inner rifts, the initial reformers were even more disconcerted than by the blows from Rome. Luther stood at the very center of this development. His own course was a sign, a symptom and in part also a cause of the wider sequence.

In the delineation of his attitude and development, one discovers a certain convergence of the topical and the chronological divisions. His three great opponents were the Catholics, the Sectaries and the Jews. They confronted him in precisely that order. His first attack was of course directed toward the Catholics against whom he fulminated for the rest of his life. The Sectaries emerged only after the opportunity came to establish the Reformation in Wittenberg in the 1520s. In that period Luther was optimistic as to the conversion of the Jews. Disillusionment at this point led him to rail at them in his later days.

But before undertaking this survey we must take note of some of Luther's presuppositions. He had never subscribed to the relativism of such Renaissance figures as Boccaccio, who told the story of the three identical rings signifying Christianity, Islam and Judaism, nor to the predilection of Erasmus for the pious heathen. Luther confessed that at one time he had been so zealous for the pope that he would have been willing to bring wood and straw to burn John Hus.[1] This view he came to renounce under the influence of the mystics from whom he learned that faith is inward and that suffering is a mark of the true Christian and of the true Church.

Faith is inward and God-given and therefore not to be forced by outward weapons in human hands. No one said this better than Luther in his tract, *On Civil Government*: "Faith is a free work to which no one can be forced. It is a divine work in the Spirit, let alone then that outward force should compel or create it.

"These poor blind folk do not know what a vain and impossible thing they undertake, for no matter how hard they command nor how strongly they rave, they cannot bring people any further than that they should follow with mouth and hand, but the heart they cannot compel."[2]

Again, religious experience, being inward, is also too intangible to be the subject of a judicial examination. "How does the senseless government know how to judge and conquer such a secret, spiritual, and hidden thing as faith?"[3]

---

[1] *WA* XL, p. 138. Cf. *WA* XII, p. 600.

[2] *WA* XI, p. 264 (1523).

[3] *Ibid.*, p. 264.

Likewise, "Heresy is a spiritual thing, which cannot be cut with steel nor burned with fire nor drowned with water."[4]

"To fight heresy is to fight the devil, as Paul says, 'Our warfare is not with flesh and blood but with the spiritual wickedness, the principalities and powers, the world ruler of this darkness.' "[5]

And, "Satan is a spirit who has neither flesh nor bone, so that one cannot touch him with steel or fist. We must tear him from the hearts with the Word of truth. That is our sword and fist which no one can withstand."[6]

Though for Luther the devil remained concrete and was not allegorized as by the mystics, even so, said he, force will not overcome the devil.[7]

For the mystic, the way of salvation is a *via dolorosa* of cross bearing so that he who persecutes cannot be a Christian and the true Church is bound to be persecuted.

"Christ said that one should not resist evil and injustice, but always give way, suffer, and allow oneself to be despoiled. We must pray for our persecutors, love our enemies, and do good to those who despitefully use us. These are our Christian rights, dear friends. Suffer, suffer, the cross, the cross, that is the Christian way and nothing else."[8]

"If one judges the tree by its fruits, it is evident who are the true Christians. We do not kill, banish, and persecute any one who teaches other than we or starts a sect. But the fruit of their [the papists'] faith is killing, burning, banishment, and persecution. It is clear enough that they are the devil's Christians."[9]

"We are persecuted in all places, slain, burned, and hanged for the sake of the Word. We are as the early Church, like Christ upon the cross. No one can deny that we do not shed blood, kill, hang, and revenge ourselves."[10]

---

[4] *Ibid.*, p. 268.
[5] *Ibid.*, p. 269.
[6] *WA* X, p. 167 (July 10, 1522).
[7] *WA* XVIII, p. 359 (1525).
[8] *Ibid.*, pp. 309-310 (1525).
[9] *WA* XIX, p. 263 (1526).
[10] *WA* LI, pp. 484-485 (1541).

"We must suffer, and leave vengeance to God. Otherwise we have an evil spirit in us."[11]

Some of these passages are from the later years, for Luther never forgot to talk in this fashion against the papists.

For the mystics, this suffering is not merely a passive endurance, but must issue in forgiving love. So Luther could write:

We must have love and do to one another through love what God has done to us through faith, without which love, faith is nothing, as Paul says to the Corinthians. There is need also of patience, for he who has faith and who trusts God and shows love to his neighbor in daily exercise cannot be without persecution. But persecution brings patience, for if I were not tempted and persecuted I should know little of patience, and patience brings hope. So through many temptations and persecutions faith increases more and more. Such a heart in which faith grows cannot rest, nor content itself, but must pour itself out and do good to its neighbor.[12]

The fate of the Christian will also be the fate of the Church for the true Church will always be on earth a remnant, since the word of God is that which goes counter to all the desires of the natural man[13] and those who receive it are bound to be stones rejected by the builders.[14] In the main, history moves in terms of the Augustinian conflict of the *Civitas Dei* and the *Civitas terrena*. "Every Abel has his Cain and every Isaac his Ishmael, every Jacob his Esau and every Israel his Edom, every David his Saul, and every Christ his Judas. 'All that will live godly in Christ Jesus shall suffer persecution.' "[15] When Luther was himself subject to persecution he gave this teaching a turn which Augustine would not have admitted. "I am not terrified," wrote Luther, "because many of the great persecute and hate me. Rather, I am consoled and strengthened, since in all the Scriptures the persecutors and haters have

---

[11] *WA* XLV, p. 409.
[12] *WA* X, Part 3 (1522).
[13] *WA* LVI, p. 423.
[14] *Ibid.*, pp. 56, 250.
[15] II Tim. 3:12; *WA* III, p. 304 (1513-1516). Consult Erich Seeberg, *Luther's Theologies* I, *Die Gottesanschauung* (Göttingen, 1929), pp. 133-141 and Walther von Lowenich, "Luther's Theologia Crucis," *Forschungen zur Geschiche und Lehre des Protestantismus,* 2te Reihe (Munich, 1929), pp. 151-166.

commonly been wrong and the persecuted right. The majority always supports the lie and the minority the truth."[16]

But over against these assumptions must be set others which go far to explain the polarities and sometimes discrepancies in Luther's thought and behavior. Faith is inward but it is directed to that which is outward. Faith is man's response to God's deed in the redemption of the world through Christ. Merely to believe in this deed as an historical fact is of no value, but to deny it as an historical fact is to renounce Christianity. The inward and the outward are conjoined in the assurance of the Christian.

"Augustine is not so to be understood, as if he would not have believed the Gospel had he not been moved by universal Christianity. That would be false and unchristian. Everyone must believe solely because it is God's Word, and because he inwardly finds it to be the truth, even though an angel from heaven and the whole world should preach against it."[17]

Luther, to be sure, was often disturbed as to whether he was right, yet at the same time continually reassured by the words of Scripture.

"I have been disturbed myself. Are you alone right? Has everybody else been wrong? Have so many centuries not known? But Christ confirms me with his sure and certain words."[18]

When reminded that other people who disagreed with him also believed that they were right, Luther replied:

"It may be said that the Emperor Charles is also certain that the papist teaching is true, and that he is consequently justified according to God's command in using all his might to wipe out our teaching as heretical from his kingdom. Answer: we know that he is not certain, and cannot be certain, because we know that he is wrong and opposes the Gospel."[19]

The faith of the Church for Luther was so concrete as to admit of creedal formulation. In 1533 he shared in the preparation of a test for university professors at Wittenberg whereby they should subscribe to the Apostles', Nicene and Athanasian creeds and to

[16] *WA* VII, p. 317 (1521).
[17] *WA* X, p. 90 (1522).
[18] *WA* VIII, p. 412 (Nov. 1, 1521).
[19] *BR* 614 (Sept., 1530).

the Augsburg Confession.[20] It is not so clear that the same test was applied to ministers,[21] but Luther would scarcely have objected. In 1534 he warned the authorities at Regensburg to beware of the sectaries. The Augsburg Confession should be the antidote.[22] In 1539 he was glad that Agricola had submitted to the Augsburg Confession and Apology. His teaching otherwise would be nothing and damned. The next year Luther joined the Wittenberg theologians in the statement: "Our opinion is set forth in the Augsburg Confession and Apology. From that we will not recede. If any one find it inadequate, ambiguous, or incorrect, let him ask us."[23]

Not only was Scripture the source for the concrete formulation for the faith, but tradition likewise.

"This testimony of the universal holy Christian Church, *even if we had nothing else,* would be a sufficient warrant for holding this article [on the sacrament] and refusing to suffer or listen to a sectary, for it is dangerous and fearful to hear or believe anything against the unanimous testimony, belief, and teaching of the universal holy Christian churches, unanimously held in all the world from the beginning until now over fifteen hundred years."[24]

Again, over against Luther's concept of the Church as a persecuted remnant must be set his view of the Church as a Christian society in correlation with the state, the school and all other agencies of the *Corpus Christianum.* The duality is not simply that of the Church invisible and the Church visible but also that between the Church small and persecuted and the Church large and influential. The sense of an integral Christian society was so strong with Luther that after the manner of the Middle Ages he could call

[20] *CR* XII, p. 7. Melanchthon, writing in 1553, said "about" twenty years ago. The reliability of the passage has been impugned. For a vindication see Tschackert, *Die Entstehung der lutherischen und der reformierten Kirchenlehre,* section 90.

[21] G. Rietschel, *Luther und die Ordination,* 2nd ed., 1889, made the assertion on the basis of this passage. But although Melanchthon referred to the example of the early Church in applying a creedal test to ministers, the contemporary situation had to do with the university. *Nolumus docentes a confessione nostra dissentire,* p. 6. *In hac Academia et coniunctis Ecclesiis,* p. 7. The reference to the churches may, however, imply the inclusion of the ministers.

[22] *BR* 2126 (June 30, 1534).

[23] *BR* 3436 (Jan. 18, 1540).

[24] *WA* XXX, p. 552 (1532).

upon the state as a Christian agency to correct abuses in the Church and to institute positive reforms. The one concept, if pressed, leads to the conventicle after the manner of the Anabaptists and the other eventuates in the state Church after the manner of later German Lutheranism. Both tendencies were in Luther and that is why he can be regarded in some sense as the father alike of Anabaptism and of Lutheranism.

Neither is one to forget that for Luther there was a dichotomy in God. Whereas to those redeemed in Christ God is a loving heavenly father, to the unregenerate He can be frightful. Here the Old Testament supplied abundant material, so much so indeed that the vindication of the honor of God could supersede love for the neighbor.

"It is a trifle for God to massacre a lot of peasants, when he drowned the whole world with a flood, and wiped out Sodom with fire. He is an almighty and frightful God."[25]

"On account of idolatry He often wiped out a whole race and city, land and people, kingdom and empire."[26]

Christ said that we should not be angry, but rather long-suffering and meek.

"Yes, but we cannot be meek against God's honor and command. It is written of Moses that he was the meekest man on earth, but nevertheless when the Jews prayed to the golden calf and angered God, Moses struck many of them dead and thus reconciled God again."[27]

"Love beareth all things, endureth all things, hopeth all things, but faith indeed or the Word bears nothing at all, but denounces, devours, or, as Jerome says, roots out, destroys, and dissipates."[28]

When some wish to "suppress the Gospel I am bound to obey faith more than love, for faith is above love. Faith I must defend with head, neck, and belly. When we have that we can come back to love."[29] If anyone hears a Jew mention the name of God, he

---

[25] *WA* XVIII, p. 302 (1525).
[26] *WA* XXVIII, p. 699, 16f. (Nov. 21, 1529).
[27] *WA* VI, p. 267 (1520).
[28] *BR* 451, p. 431.
[29] *WA* XV, p. 616 (1524).

"should report it to the magistrate or throw *Säudreck* on him; and let no one be merciful or kind in this, for God's honor is involved."[30]

"You say that I am not merciful in this [his attitude to the peasants]. I answer, mercy is neither here nor there. We are talking about God's Word."[31]

"Don't talk to me about peace and unity, if thereby one loses God's Word."[32]

" 'Love your enemies.' Yes, but God's enemies must be my enemies."[33]

With these presuppositions in mind, we can now turn to the course of Luther's development, and first, as to the treatment of the Catholics. In the period between the posting of the indulgences in 1517 and the condemnation at Worms in 1521, Luther was certainly guilty of some incendiary utterances. In 1520 he declared:

"If we punish thieves with the yoke, highwaymen with the sword, and heretics with fire, why do we not rather assault these monsters of perdition, these cardinals, these popes, and the whole swarm of the Roman Sodom, who corrupt without end the church of God, why do we not rather assault them with all arms and wash our hands in their blood?"[34]

Luther was not allowed to forget this passage and it was cited against him at the Diet of Worms. When first reproached he explained that he did not mean what the words seemed to imply.[35]

"Emser lies again when he says that I wish the laity might wash their hands in the blood of the priests. I wrote, '*If* we burn heretics why do we not rather attack the pope and his followers with the sword and wash our hands in their blood.' Since I do not approve of burning heretics not of killing any Christian—this I well know does not accord with the Gospel—I have shown what they deserve *if* heretics deserve fire. There is no need to attack you with the sword."

[30] *WA* XLIII, p. 537.
[31] *WA* XVIII, p. 386 (1525).
[32] *WA* XXXIV, p. 387 (1531).
[33] *WA* XXXII, p. 400 (1530-1532).
[34] *WA* VI, p. 347.
[35] *WA* VII, p. 645 (1521).

There were however some other sayings in this period with a sinister ring. "The nobles," he wrote, "should go to Rome and smite with the sword all who, like Sylvester Prierias, make Scripture subject to the pope, and declare that the pope should go unpunished though he take the whole world to the devil."[36] Again, in the *Address to the German Nobility* Luther urged that the papists be severely punished "because they have blasphemously abused the ban and the name of God and want to make us participators by consent in their blasphemy. We are bound before God to withstand them. Paul treats as worthy of death those who do such things and those who suffer them to be done."[37]

But these sayings were unguarded outbursts. Luther's sober opinion is revealed in the following quotation.

"All predict a revolution like that in Bohemia and that there will be an attack on our clergy. I am not to blame, for I tried to get the German nobility to put bounds to the Romanists not with the sword but with counsels and edicts, which they easily could, for to make war on this unarmed crowd of clergy is like fighting women and children."[38]

In December 1521[39] Luther wrote:

It looks as if it might come to revolution, and the papists, monks, bishops, and clergy be slain and driven out. But no revolution is to be made for God. Scripture gives the pope a very different end. He is to be 'destroyed without hand,' (Dan. 8:25) that is without the sword and bodily force. The Lord Jesus 'will slay him with the Spirit of his mouth' (II Thess. 2:8). But because it is God's affair is no reason why the magistrate should not do his part and with the sword anticipate a portion of God's anger, just as Moses allowed three thousand of the people to be slain. Not that one should now slay the papists, which is not needful, but that one should forbid them with words and restrain them by force from what they do against the Gospel. One can do more than enough with words and letters, so that neither hewing nor stabbing is necessary.[40]

After the Diet of Worms Luther's situation altered. Already

[36] *WA* VI, p. 585 (1520).
[37] *Ibid.,* p. 431.
[38] *BR* 378 (Feb. 27, 1521).
[39] *WA* VIII, p. 673.
[40] *Ibid.,* pp. 676-677, 680.

while still in hiding at the Wartburg, he was called upon to give advice with regard to the progress of the reformation at Wittenberg. His general position was that the clergy might institute reforms, the magistrates might suppress abuses, but the mob should say its prayers. Luther had occasion to formulate his judgment on all of these points while still at the Wartburg. When, in October 1521, the Augustinians discontinued the mass, Luther commended their courage, while reminding them to show consideration for the weak;[41] but when, on December 3, a mob of students and citizens broke into the parish church, snatched the mass books from the altars, and expelled the priests with stones, Luther was not at all pleased, and after his return to Wittenberg expressed himself strongly.[42] It was well enough to have abolished the mass, but it should have been done in orderly fashion, that is, by the magistrate.[43] Luther did not propose its restoration,[44] but had he seen the papists celebrating he would have preached against them instead of dragging them by the hair.[45] Private masses should be given up, but:

"Don't tear the priests from the altar. Tell the people to withdraw financial support, and with such preaching the masses will in time fall of themselves."[46]

"Show consideration to the weak."[47]

"There are people who pray to the sun, moon, and stars. Shall we therefore pluck them out of heaven? Wine and women make fools of many. Shall we therefore prohibit wine and despatch women?"[48]

---

[41] *WA* VIII, pp. 411, 476. The preface was ready November 1, 1521. On the whole question of the suppression of the mass at Wittenberg see Karl F. F. Müller, *Luther und Karlstadt* (1906). Tiling, 'Der Kampf gegen die Missa Privata in Wittenberg im Herbst 1521,' *Neue kirchliche Zeitschrift* 20, 1909 and Nikolaus Müller, *Die Wittenberger Bewegung 1521 und 1522* (2nd ed., 1911).

[42] *WA* X, pp. 1-64 (March 9-17 as reported by Aurifaber), reworked by Luther himself in *Von beider Gestalt des Sakraments zu nehmen, WA* X, pp. 11-41 (April 1522).

[43] *Ibid.*, p. 9.

[44] *Ibid.*, p. 17.

[45] *Ibid.*, p. 18.

[46] *Ibid.*, p. 32, condensed.

[47] *Ibid.*, p. 20.

[48] *Ibid.*, p. 33.

"In a word I will preach, speak, write, but I will force and drive no one, for faith must be willing and unconstrained."[49]

"Christians fight only with the Word against the devil's teaching and work. First take hearts and consciences away from him and then all will fall of itself."[50]

Yet Luther did not intend this counsel to apply indefinitely and he began very quickly to inveigh against the house of idolatry in the castle church at Wittenberg, and to hope the Elector Frederick would be the Frederick Barbarossa who should deliver the Lord's sepulchre.[51] There followed repeated appeals to the prince himself to put in his hand.[52] Let him at least suppress those masses for which he was financially responsible,[53] a request which implied that he might suppress others as well. He was to act not merely as patron, but as magistrate.

But Frederick would not act; so Luther directed his appeals to the clergy of the castle church. Weakness had received sufficient consideration, he declared. The Gospel had been set forth so clearly that boys, girls and blockheads could understand. His conscience would not suffer him to be silent for the credit of his ministry. Then follows a threat of the ban.[54] The clergy asked for grace until the coming of the new dean. On his arrival Luther again wrote: "Enough patience. You cannot plead that the prince commands or does not command to do or not to do. I am talking to your conscience. What has the prince to do with such matters?"[55]

A flagrant inconsistency, according to Paulus, for had not Luther just been appealing to the prince?[56] The discrepancy, however, is only verbal. The prince might check an abuse whether the clergy liked it or not, but the clergy might institute a reform whether the prince liked it or not. Luther did not recognize the right of the prince to hinder the reform, and when the elector

---

[49] *Ibid.,* p. 18.
[50] *Ibid.,* p. 37.
[51] *WA* VIII, p. 475.
[52] *BR* 441 (Nov. 22, 1521); *BR* 558 (Dec. 19? 1522); *BR* 556 (Jan. 2, 1523).
[53] *BR* III, p. 2.
[54] *BR* 586, p. 35 (March 1, 1523).
[55] *Ibid.,* 634.
[56] Paulus, *Protestantismus und Toleranz,* p. 5. *See* p. 240.

feared that he had not done enough at Wittenberg,[57] Luther told him bluntly that he had done altogether too much.[58] There were further negotiations with the clergy and the elector.[59] Luther in a sermon on August 2, declared that he would not use force, but nevertheless waxed so hot that Roth stopped taking notes,[60] and on August 19 he wrote to the clergy telling them that all fee-masses should be abolished, whether the people recognized them as a sacrilege or not.

"Not all the prophets of Baal under Josiah believed their rites to be impious, but Josiah paid no attention to that. It is one thing to tolerate the weak in non-essentials, but to tolerate in matters clearly impious is itself impious."[61]

Some changes were made with the consent of the elector, but in November Luther heard that the mass had been given in one kind only, contrary, as he believed, to the agreement. He at once informed the clergy that they were possessed of the devil. They must stop this game, else he would make them act, whether they liked it or not. Let them answer yes or no before Sunday.[62] The dean and two of his adherents tearfully informed the elector that they feared a tumult of the people: they would however follow his orders.[63] But Luther received no answer; so on Sunday week (November 27), despite an appeal from the prince to practice what he preached,[64] Luther preached what he practiced, calling on princes and other magistrates to stop this dreadful blasphemy. "If it is allowed by God to punish a reckless scamp who blasphemes in the market-place, it is also permitted to drive this horrid antichristian blasphemy out of your town."[65]

As a result, representatives of the university and city authori-

---

[57] *BR* 454 (Feb. 1522).

[58] *Ibid.*, 455 (March 5, 1522).

[59] *BR* 634 (July 11, 1523), *Nachgeschichte,* pp. 113-114.

[60] *WA* XII, p. 645 f.

[61] *BR* 648 (August 19, 1523).

[62] *BR* 794 (November 17, 1523).

[63] Veit Ludwig von Seckendorf, *Commentarius historicus de Lutheranismo* (1694, Vol. I, p. 276).

[64] C. A. H. Burkhardt, *Dr. Martin Luthers Briefwechsel* (1866), p. 76 (November 24, 1524).

[65] *WA* XV, p. 774.

ties urgently besought the clergy to abolish the mass, informing them that a priest who celebrated it was worthy of death.[66] Since this gentle suggestion went unheeded, the same dignitaries announced that they would have no further communion with the clergy, if they did not stop. The mob smashed the windows of the dean's house,[67] but the mass continued until the clergy declared themselves convinced.[68] This has been described as suppressing the mass by force. Immoderate pressure would be a more precise term.

We may sum up Luther's attitude to the Catholics during this period by saying that in his sober moments, at least, he objected to taking their lives. He was opposed to mob violence, would have the magistrate confine himself to the elimination of abuses, and would leave the work of positive reformation to the clergy. At the same time Luther indulged in incendiary utterances likely to inspire the very lawlessness which he deplored.

Luther came to be even more ready to condone constraint when Frederick the Wise was succeeded by his brother John who was more disposed to stringent measures on behalf of the evangelical cause. Luther was not slow with suggestions.

"If the endowed clergy at Altenberg request the restoration of their former unchristian ways, turn them down. Although I know your Grace is well informed and well inclined through God's grace, yet I cannot refrain from reminding your Grace."[69] To Spalatin Luther wrote: "You ask whether the prince should suppress the abominations, since no one is to be forced to faith, and the power of princes extends only to externals. Answer: our princes do not compel to faith, but merely suppress external abominations. Princes should prohibit public crimes such as perjury, manifest blasphemy of the name of God, and the like, without considering whether the culprits believe or not, or whether they curse in private."[70] Only two years before, Luther had complained that the Catholics attempted to judge anything so inward as faith, while

---

[66] Walch, *Luthers sämmtliche Schriften* 19, 1453.
[67] Seckendorf, *loc. cit.*
[68] *BR* 802 (Dec. 2, 1524).
[69] *BR* 904 (July 20, 1525).
[70] *Ibid.,* 946 (Nov. 11, 1525, condensed).

recognizing that *de occultis non judicat ecclesia*.[71] His own formula, that no one can be compelled to faith, was now attenuated. In *The Eight Sermons* he had urged consideration for the weak, but now one must beware lest the plea of weakness be merely a cover for wickedness.[72] The mass must be abolished, not gilded with a glittering reformation.[73] The prince should see to it that the endowed clergy at Altenberg either stop entirely or else conduct their rites in private. One reason was that the prince was the financial patron, but another was that in one place there could be but one preaching lest there be disturbance of the peace.

"If they appeal to conscience, that will not help. Conscience must be instructed from Scripture. If they object that they are forced to faith, that is not the point. Public offence alone is forbidden them. They may stay in the land, and in the privacy of their rooms pray to as many gods as they like."[74]

In his later years Luther was guilty of virulent and indecent fulminations against the papacy. He wished that there were more English kings to kill cardinals,[75] and was pleased with a rumor that bishops had been executed in Denmark.[76] The year before his death he raked together such a pile of "Gutter-muck" in the tract *Against the Papists at Rome,* that he was himself compelled to halt: "I must stop, *ich mag nicht mehr in dem lästerlichen, höllishen Teufelsdreck und Stank sudlen.*"[77] He could afford to stop, after having already expressed the hope that the princes would rise up, destroy the papal state, tear out the tongues of pope and cardinals, and nail them to the gallows like seals on a bull.[78] And after having stopped he still went on to say that if he were the emperor, he would tie up together the blasphemous pope and cardinals and take them not more than three miles from Rome to Ostia, where he would not drown them, as Paulus states, but give them a bath of

[71] *WA* II, p. 264.
[72] *BR* 1061 (end of 1526).
[73] *WA* XIX, p. 443.
[74] *BR* 978 (Feb. 9, 1526).
[75] *BR* 2276 (ca. Dec. 3, 1535).
[76] 1536. See Paulus, *op. cit.,* p. 18.
[77] *WA* XLIV, p. 263.
[78] *Ibid.,* p. 243.

half an hour in the Tyrrhenian sea, a precious bath of salvation; and that, he guaranteed, would clean them up.[79]

At the same time one must remember that there was nothing personal in Luther's attack. He railed at Henry VIII, yet on hearing that he was inclined to the reform sent a conciliatory letter and likewise in the case of Duke George. But when such hopes proved illusory, Luther started again to blast. Some of his bluster was deliberately adopted for effect.

"Almost all condemn me for being so biting. But I see that things which are handled quietly in our day soon fall into oblivion and nobody cares. The present age takes it ill, but the judgment of posterity will be more favorable. Paul called his adversaries dogs, concision, ministers of Satan. But these terms are hackneyed and don't get under any one's ribs any more."[80]

But in the end one must remember that Luther was so adverse to violence as to endorse the territorial principle of one religion only in one region lest the existence of two should endanger the civil peace. This meant that his followers would have to abstain from missionary endeavors in Catholic lands[81] and that such areas could come over to the reform only if they did so as a whole, with and under the authority of the prince. It meant also that minorities would not be tolerated, but there was this gain for liberty that all such could emigrate with household and goods. It was the refusal on the part of the Catholics to recognize this as a two-way arrangement which provoked the famous protest at Speyer. The principle of territorialism was clearly enunciated in the following passage written in April 1526. "No one can be a papist without being at least a murderer, robber, and persecutor, for he must approve of the burning, banishing, and persecution. If one judges the tree by the fruits, it is abundantly clear who are the true Christians. We do not kill, banish, and persecute anybody who teaches other than we do. We fight with the Word of God alone. If they don't want it, we let them go *and separate ourselves from them* and let them cleave to any belief they like. We do the best we can toward them and let

[79] *Ibid.*, p. 283.
[80] *BR* 328 (Aug. 19, 1520).
[81] *WA* XXXI, p. 211.

them live among us. Whom do the papists treat like that? They fight only with the sword like the Turk."[82]

In the case of the sectaries who arose in Wittenberg in the 1520s one might have supposed that Luther would have steadfastly refused to introduce any constraint against them because he had earlier so unequivocally declared himself against the coercion of heretics. In the *Defense of the Ninety Five Theses* he had the papists say: "It pleases us not to destroy heresy and error, but to burn heretics and those who err. We are guided rather by the counsel of Cato than of Scipio for the destruction of Carthage, and go counter to the will of the Spirit, who wrote that the Jebusites and Canaanites should be left in the land of promise to give the Israelites exercise in war. This refers to the heretics."[83]

In the *Address to the German Nobility* we read: "If heretics were to be overcome with fire, the executioners would be the most learned doctors on earth. We need not study any more, but he who could get the better of the other might burn him."[84] Two years later Luther hoped that Frederick would not imbrue his hands in the blood of the Zwickau prophets.[85] The tract, *On Civil Government* of 1523, set forth in thorough-going fashion the spiritual and inward character of faith, which cannot be judged or forced by outward means. Constraint merely leads the weak to deny their convictions. It would be better to let them err than to force them to lie.[86] In 1524, writing to the elector with regard to Müntzer, Luther advised him to let the spirits fight it out. If some are lost, *c'est la guerre*. "They are not Christians who besides the Word resort to fists, be they filled to overflowing with ten Holy Ghosts."[87]

The only disputed point in this period is the banishment of Carlstadt from Saxony in 1524, of which Luther approved. Barge calls this a brutal transgression of liberty of conscience.[88] Karl Müller replies, and I think rightly, that in Luther's eyes Carlstadt

---

[82] *WA* XIX, p. 263 (April 1526).
[83] *WA* I, p. 624-625 (June 1518).
[84] *WA* VI, p. 455 (Aug. 1520); *ibid.*, p. 392.
[85] *BR* 452, p. 444 (Jan. 17, 1522).
[86] *WA* XI, p. 263.
[87] *WA* XV, pp. 218-221 (Aug. 21, 1524).
[88] Hermann Barge, *Andreas Bodenstein von Karlstadt*, 2 vols. (1905), Vol. 2, p. 139.

was not expelled as a false teacher, but as a disturber of the peace
like Müntzer.[89] The fact that Luther was mistaken in his charges
does not affect the ground upon which he based his opinion.[90]

The year 1525 brought a number of significant changes.
There was the case of Thomas Müntzer whose fiery religious radicalism was associated with social revolution. There was the replace-
ment, already mentioned, of Frederick the Wise by the more
stringent John. Perhaps even more important was Luther's abandonment of any attempt at a concrete realization of a Church of
believers. In 1520 he had defined Christianity as an "assembly of
believers including all who have true faith, hope, and love. Though
separated a thousand miles in the body, they are still an assembly
in the Spirit."[91] Again, in 1523, Luther wrote that "the world and
the mass of men are and remain unchristian, though they have all
been baptized and are called Christians. But Christians live far
from one another so it is impossible that a Christian regime should
extend over the world or even over a country or a large group."[92]

The effort to form a nucleus of heartfelt believers began in
1522, when Luther allowed those who wished communion in both
kinds to receive it apart from the rest.[93] When the time came that
all were required to communicate in both kinds, Luther desired to
separate the true believers into a place apart.[94] In 1526 he went still
further and recommended that earnest Christians meet alone in a
house for prayer, reading, baptism and the sacrament. Non-Christians should be excluded with the ban.[95] This was not precisely the
Anabaptist separatist congregation, because Luther's group existed
within the territorial church as leaven, a *collegium pietatis,* and
did not exclude governmental interference with the larger group.[96]
Nevertheless, where the magistrate was unfavorable, as in Bohemia,
Luther recognized that such a congregation might become sepa-

[89] Karl F. F. Müller, *Luther und Karlstadt* (1906), p. 178.
[90] *WA* XVIII, pp. 93, 138 and notes.
[91] *WA* VI, p. 292.
[92] *WA* XI, p. 251.
[93] *BR* 465 (March 26, 1522).
[94] *WA* XII, p. 485 (1523).
[95] *WA* XIX, p. 75.
[96] Stressed by Heinrich Hermelink in *Zeitschrift für Kirchengeschichte* (1908), p. 311.

ratist.[97] This is the justification for those who say that the Anabaptists took up an ideal which Luther had dropped,[98] for he did drop it. The last mention was in 1527, in a letter in which he expressed the hope that these devotional groups would be increased by the Visitation,[99] as if the prince could create assemblies of sincere believers.

The abandonment of the attempt was marked by the liturgy of 1526 which, said Luther, "was not intended for Christians, who worship in the Spirit, but for non-Christians and those who need to be strengthened."[100] In other words he had relinquished the hope of gathering the ardent and had turned to the education of the masses. There should be neither a sect nor a cell, but the Church should coincide with the community and all those baptized in infancy should be accounted Christian. The final step was the institution of the Visitation by the prince in order to give tangible form to the evangelical Church. This was in 1527. Luther may have looked upon this measure as a temporary expedient and not as a permanent role for the magistrate. And he may not have been happy when the prince referred to *his* visitors.[101] In the preface to the supplement to the *Visitation Articles,* Luther said that the prince had been called upon for this service "out of Christian love, for as civil magistrate he was under no obligation."[102] But Luther went on to say: "Although the prince is not commanded to rule in spiritual matters nevertheless as civil magistrate he must not suffer division, sectarianism, and sedition," and should accord to the recalcitrant the treatment which Constantine meted out to the Arians, and that was banishment.

This at first was as far as Luther would go. He was by no means so swift to condone the penalty of death as was Zwingli, who sanctioned its use against the Anabaptist Felix Manz in Zürich in 1526. At least two years afterward, in 1528, Luther wrote: "You ask

[97] *WA* XI, p. 411 (1523).
[98] Walter Koehler in the *Deutsche Zeitschrift für Kirchenrecht* (1906), pp. 217-218; and in *Christliche Welt* (1907), p. 376.
[99] *BR* 1091 (March 29, 1527).
[100] *WA* XIX, p. 73.
[101] "Unsere verordenten Visitatores," Sehling, op. cit. I, p. 375.
[102] *Ibid.,* p. 150.

whether the magistrate may kill false prophets. I am slow in a judgment of blood even when it is deserved. In this matter I am terrified by the example of the papists and the Jews before Christ, for when there was a statute for the killing of false prophets and heretics, in time it came about that only the most saintly and innocent were killed. I cannot admit that false teachers are to be put to death. *It is enough to banish.*"[103]

Yet six months earlier the elector had suppressed the writings of the Anabaptists and Zwinglians and all unauthorized assemblies, even for a wedding or a baptism, on pain of imprisonment.[104] Luther made no protest.

There was however in the *Visitation Articles* of that same year a survival of the older liberalism in that the weak might be allowed for a time to receive the sacrament in one kind only, since no one is to be forced to faith.[105] And to the death penalty Luther still strenuously objected.

"It is not right and I am deeply troubled [he wrote with regard to the Anabaptists] that the poor people are so pitifully put to death, burned, and cruelly slain. Let every one believe what he likes. If he is wrong, he will have punishment enough in hell fire. Unless there is sedition one should oppose them with Scripture and God's Word. With fire one will get nowhere."[106]

The very next year appeared the imperial edict of the diet of Speyer, whereby the Anabaptists were condemned to fire and sword without previous ecclesiastical examination.[107] We have no immediate comment from Luther, but he was tightening up. In August he recommended that everybody should be compelled to attend church on the ground that politics and household economy are taught in the decalogue and catechism. Those who wish to live in the land must learn the laws.[108] By the beginning of March 1530 Luther gave his consent to the death penalty for the Anabaptists,

[103] *BR* 1294. The Weimar editors think this section was interpolated into a letter to Link of July 14, 1528 from a later reply to Brenz but earlier than the commentary on the 82nd Psalm of 1530.

[104] Wappler, *Inquisition und Ketzerprozesse*, Anhang 1, No. 1, cf. pp. 8-11.

[105] *WA* XXVI, pp. 185, 214 and note.

[106] *Ibid.*, p. 145.

[107] April 23, 1529. Wappler, *op. cit.*, p. 56.

[108] *BR* 1467 (August 26, 1529). Cf. *WA* XXX, pp. 349, 461.

but on the ground that they were not only blasphemers, but highly seditious.[109] Those who rush into the temple and blaspheme should, on a second offense, receive the penalty of sedition. Here blasphemy seems to constitute the sedition.[110] In August he was pleased with the rumor of the execution of Campanus.[111] In *The Exposition of the Eighty-second Psalm* in the same year blasphemy was put on a par with sedition.[112] Nothing was said definitely as to the punishment, but death was almost certainly intended, for Luther had long recognized it as the current penalty for blasphemy.[113] A direct appeal was made to the example of Moses, who commanded blasphemers to be stoned.[114] Luther was no longer deterred because the Jews persecuted the true prophets. That was no reason for not stoning the false.[115] The executioner should dispose of unauthorized preachers even though orthodox.[116] It is not likely that the unorthodox would fare better, however authorized.

The distinction between heresy and blasphemy may appear to have been of little moment because what before was called heresy now was called blasphemy. The rejection of an article of faith clearly grounded in Scripture and universally accepted like the Apostles Creed was blasphemy.[117] True, but heresy might be only private conviction whereas blasphemy requires public proclamation. And although to deny either is not religious liberty, yet to admit of one is something of a gain. Significantly in England, penalties for heresy ceased much sooner than for blasphemy. One may say that Luther's distinction prolonged the legislation against blasphemy, or better one may say that it hastened the removal of penalties for heresy.

[109] "Seditiossimi." *BR* 1532 (end of Feb. 1530). Luther to Menius and Mykonius commending their plan to write against the Anabaptists. When the work appeared, Luther wrote a preface, *WA* XXX, p. 211 f. Neither Menius nor Luther was specific as to penalties. Menius' tract is in the Wittenberg edition of Luther's works, Vol. 2, pp. 299b-301a (1551).

[110] *BR* 1578 (June 1, 1530).

[111] *Ibid.*, 1672 (Aug. 3, 1530).

[112] *WA* XXXI, p. 207.

[113] *WA* VI, p. 229. Cf. Völker, p. 91 and Paulus, p. 36, note 4.

[114] *WA* XXXI, p. 209.

[115] *Ibid.*, p. 213.

[116] *Ibid.*, p. 212.

[117] *Ibid.*, p. 208.

Any doors which Luther might have left open in the second period from 1525 to 1530 were closed by Melanchthon in the memorandum in 1531. Rejection of the ministerial office was described as insufferable blasphemy, and destruction of the Church was considered sedition against the ecclesiastical order, punishable like other sedition. Luther added his assent, "for though it seems cruel to punish them with the sword, it is more cruel that they damn the ministry of the Word, have no certain teaching, and suppress the true, and thus upset society."[118]

The second memorandum composed by Melanchthon and signed by Luther in 1536 is of extreme importance in making clear what was involved. The circumstance was that Philip of Hesse who steadfastly refused to go beyond banishment and imprisonment in matters of faith, invited the theologians in a number of localities to give him advice. One of the most severe among the replies was that which came from Wittenberg. In this document the Anabaptists were declared to be seditious and blasphemous, but in what did their sedition consist? The answer was: not by reason of armed revolution, but on the contrary, by reason of pacifism.

They teach that a Christian should not use a sword, should not serve as a magistrate, should not swear or hold property, may desert an unbelieving wife. These articles are seditious and the holders of them may be punished with the sword. We must pay no attention to their avowal 'we did no one any harm', because if they persuaded everybody there would be no government. If it be objected that the magistrate should not compel anyone to the faith the answer is that he punishes no one for his opinions in his heart, but only on account of the outward word and teaching.

The memorandum goes on to say that there were other tenets of the Anabaptists touching upon spiritual matters such as their teaching about infant baptism, original sin and illumination apart from God's Word.

What now would happen if children were not baptized, if not that our whole society would become openly heathen? If then one holds only the articles in spiritual matters on infant baptism and original sin and unnecessary separation, because these articles are important, because it is a serious matter to cast children out of Christendom and to have two sets

[118] *CR* IV, pp. 739-740. Wappler, *Inquisition,* pp. 61-62; Paulus, pp. 41-43.

of people, the one baptized and the other unbaptized, because then the Anabaptists have some dreadful articles, we judge that in this case also the obstinate are to be put to death.[119]

Luther signed.

This document makes it perfectly plain that the Anabaptists were revolutionary, not in the sense of physical violence, but in the sense that their program entailed a complete reorientation of Church, state and society. For this they were to be put to death.

Luther himself took the initiative in treating absence from Church as blasphemy, to be met with the threat of banishment and excommunication.[120] In 1536 he had come to regard imprisonment and death as preferable to banishment, which simply spread the infection elsewhere,[121] and in 1538 he himself revised the *Visitation Articles*, omitting the passage which gave consideration to the weak.[122]

As for the Jews, Luther included them, as he did the Catholics and the Protestants, under the principle of territorialism, but their territory was Palestine. Let them go back. Luther was a Zionist. In the 1520s he saw no problem because he was then hopeful that by patience and instruction they might all be converted. Here are some of the passages from that period:

"If I were a Jew, I would suffer the rack ten times before I would go over to the pope."[123]

"The papists have so behaved toward the Jews that a good Christian would rather be a Jew than one of them, and were I a Jew I would rather be a sow than a Christian."[124]

"What good can we do the Jews when we constrain them, malign them, and hate them as dogs? When we deny them work and force them to usury, how can that help? We should use toward the Jews not the pope's but Christ's law of love. If some are stiff-necked, what does that matter? We are not all good Christians."[125]

[119] *WA* L, p. 12.
[120] *BR* 2075 (1533).
[121] *BR* 3034 (June 7, 1536).
[122] *WA* I, p. 625 (1518).
[123] *TR* 2912a.
[124] *WA* XI, p. 314.
[125] *Ibid.*, p. 336.

But his sanguine hopes were not realized and when toward the end of his life he heard that the Christians in Moravia were being induced to embrace Judaism, he came out with a sulfurous blast: "Burn the synagogues; take away their books, including the Bible. They should be compelled to work, denied food and shelter, preferably banished. If they mention the name of God, report them to the magistrate or throw *Säudreck* on them. Moses said that idolators should not be tolerated. If he were here he would be the first to burn their synagogues. If they want to follow Moses, let them go back to Canaan. I would rather be a sow than a Turkish emperor or a Jewish Messiah, for a sow fears neither hell nor the devil."[126]

Luther probably did not realize that he was recommending for the Jews a return to the earlier situation in Europe when they had tilled the soil until driven by Christians from the land into commerce and from commerce into usury. This only can be said by way of extenuation for his virulence that if in this period there was nothing comparable in England, France or Spain it was because the Jews had long since been expelled from these lands.

In assessing the entire situation one must of course remember that Luther was not writing in the midst of a religiously pluralistic society in which diversity of religions has long since been shown to be compatible with public order. He lived in the era of hot war when no one was as yet ready for co-existence. Luther was at war with himself and, alongside some of the savage blasts, one should set a statement from his last decade taken from the commentary on Genesis:

The cross and condemnation are infallible signs of the true Church. 'Precious in the sight of the Lord is the blood of his saints.' All histories show that the true Church has always endured suffering at the hands of the false. There can be no doubt, therefore, today that the pope's Church is that of Cain, but we are the true Church. As Abel did not harm Cain so we not only do not harm, but rather endure vexation, condemnation, and death from the Church of the pope. It is not only useful but exceeding joyous to have this most certain means of judging between the two Churches, between the purple harlot disguised as the true Church and the other despised, suffering, hungry, thirsty, and oppressed, as Christ re-

[126] *WA* LIII, pp. 417-552, especially p. 536.

called in Matthew 25 that he was hungry. Then follows the judgment between the full and the hungry, the sheep and the goats, between Cain and Abel in which God will declare that he approves the Church which is suffering and hungry and condemns the Church which is hypocritical and bloodthirsty.[127]

This picture does not appear unrealistic when applied to the situation of the Lutheran churches as over against the papacy and the empire, but Luther strikes us as naive in his claim to have been persecuted also by the sectaries by reason of their odious accusation that he was worse than the papists.[128]

Luther's basic contribution to liberty was in the shift of attention from heresy as belief to the social concomitants of heresy. When in practice these proved to be unreal the way was open to abolish the penalties.

[127] *WA* XLII, pp. 188-189.
[128] *WA* XL, p. 681.

Selected Bibliography

ALLEN, J. W., "The Political Conceptions of Luther," *Tudor Studies* (1924), pp. 90-108. Practically the same article in *Political and Social Ideas of Some Great Thinkers of the Renaissance and Reformation*, ed. F. J. C. Hearnshaw, pp. 171-191.

BORNKAMM, HEINRICH, *Luthers Geistige Welt* (1953), the chapter on "Der Staat."

BRANDENBURG, ERICH, "Martin Luthers Anschauung von Staat und Gesellschaft," *SVRG*, No. 70 (1901), pp. 1-30.

BRIEGER, THEODOR, "Die kirchliche Gewalt der Obrigkeit nach der Anschauung Luthers," *Zeitschrift für Theologie und Kirche* (1892).

CRANZ, FERDINAND EDWARD, "An Essay on Luthers Thought on Justice, Law and Society," *Harvard Theological Studies* 19 (1959).

DIEM, HAROLD, *Luthers Lehre von den zwei Reichen* (1938).

DREWS, PAUL, "Entsprach das Staatskirchentum dem Ideale Luthers?" *Zeitschrift für Theologie und Kirche*, Ergänzungsheft (1908).

EVANS, AUSTIN P., *An Episode in the Struggle for Religious Liberty* (1924), pp. 98-126.

FAULKNER, J. A. "Luther and Toleration," *Papers of the American Society of Church History*, 2nd series (1914), pp. 131-153.

FOERSTER, ERICH, "Fragen zur Luthers Kirchenbegriff aus der Gedankenwelt seines Alters," *Festgabe für Julius Kaftan* (1920).

HERMELINK, HEINRICH, *Der Toleranzgedanke im Reformationszeitalter* (1908).

——— "Zu Luthers Gedanken über Idealgemeinden und von weltlicher Obrigkeit," *ZKG* (1908), pp. 267 ff.

HOLL, KARL, *Gesammelte Aufsätze*, 1 *Luther:* "Luther und das landeskirchliche Kirchenregiment" (1923), pp. 326 ff.

KATTENBUSCH, F., "Die Doppelsichtigkeit in Luthers Kirchenbegriff," *Theologische Studien und Kritike* 100 (1928), pp. 197-347.

LITTELL, FRANKLIN H., *Landgraf Philipp und die Toleranz* (1957).

MEINECKE, FRIEDRICH, "Luther über christliches Gemeinwesen und christlichen Staat," *Historische Zeitschrift* (1920), pp. 1-22.

MÜLLER, KARL F. F., *Gemeinde und Obrigkeit nach Luther* (1910).

POINCENOT, E., *Les Idées de Luther sur la Repression de l'Hérésie* (Thèse, Paris, 1901).

RIEKER, KARL, *Die rechtliche Stellung der evangelischen Kirche Deutschlands* (1893).

SOHM, RUDOLF, *Kirchenrecht* 1 (1892), pp. 461 ff.

TÖRNVALL, GUSTAF, *Geistliches und weltliches Regiment bei Luther* (1947).

WAPPLER, PAUL, *Inquisition und Ketzerprozesse in Zwickau zur Reformationszeit* (1908).

——, *Die Stellung des Landgrafen Philipp von Hessen zur Täuferbewegung* (1910).

4. Luther and the *Via Media* at the Marburg Colloquy

Any reformatory movement possessed of the least stability is bound to be a *via media* between extremes. On the one side will be the body whom the reformers are seeking to reform, and on the other an unstable fringe; and should that fringe in time become stable it would find itself confronted by another and more radical periphery. A group which thus stands in the middle is advantageously situated to operate as a reconciler of extremes. Sharing in a measure the view of each, it can seek to interpret the one to the other; but the median position has also its disadvantages for the mediator, because an advance in one direction commonly produces a recoil in the other. Should the middle join hands with the right, then the door is closed to the left, and vice versa. To prevent a partial unity at the expense of a complete schism, the middle party commonly avoids going too far in either direction, and thus the supreme achievement of the *via media* is that it succeeds in remaining the *via media*.

These generalizations admit of abundant illustration from the period of the Reformation. All of the moderately stable groups conceived of themselves as occupying a median position. This was true of Erasmus. "The wise navigator," said he, "is one who steers a middle course between two evils."[1] For himself he would avoid Catholic obscurantism on the one hand and Lutheran schism on the other. He long continued both to defend and attack Luther, because he wished to make clear that he had neither succumbed to Catholic reaction nor endorsed Protestant secession.

Luther likewise after 1522 found himself in the middle of the way between the Catholic Church, which had placed him under

First published in *The Lutheran Quarterly*, I, 4 (November 1949).

[1] *Erasmi Opera*, X, 1251, 1257-1258.

the ban, and the radicals in his own ranks who were striking at his work a worse blow than any he had ever received from the papacy. Those who were having recourse to violence in smashing images, those who abandoned the written word in favor of the word within—not to mention dreams and visions—those who discarded the doctrine of the real presence in the sacrament or abandoned the sacraments altogether, these were enemies no less formidable than the papists, and the more detested because they had sprung from Luther's own loins. "Between the two," declared Luther, "we must stay in the middle of the road," *auff der rechten mittelstrasse bleyben.*[2]

And curiously some of the Anabaptists whom Luther branded en masse as fanatics discovered such diversities within their own ranks that they too were found to be in the middle way. To the right were all the state churches—Catholic, Lutheran, Zwinglian and Anglican. To the left were the revolutionaries, the eschatologists, the polygamists and so on. The Anabaptists of the sober sort, like the Mennonites, were thus also a *via media.* Strangely some of the spiritual reformers who could accommodate themselves to the outward rites of any church, so long as the spirit was not quenched, declared themselves to have found a middle road between Catholicism and Lutheranism.[3]

The strength and weakness of the middle way as a vantage point for mediation is well illustrated by the position of Luther at the colloquy of Marburg. There Luther and Melanchthon were dealing with the Swiss sacramentarians. The Catholics were not present, but they were certainly not forgotten, and whatever was done with reference to the Swiss was bound to affect what could be and would be done toward and by the Catholics. All of this must be borne in mind if one would understand the position taken by Luther.

He is commonly regarded as having manifested throughout a position of dogged intransigence. He began by drawing a circle in chalk upon the table and writing within it the words "This is

---

[2] "Von beider gestalt des Sakraments zu nehmen" (1522), *Clemen Ausgabe,* II, 322.

[3] John Horsch, *The Mennonites in Europe* (1942), p. 158.

my body," and he ended by saying that the Swiss had a different
spirit and he could not accord them a handclasp fraught with theological implications. These particular details are all correct, but
they were selected for recital in order to illustrate the outcome and
they leave out of account the highly illuminating course of the
discussion.

The documents published by Walther Koehler in the anniversary year 1929[4] make it plain that Luther as a matter of fact was
not so intransigent throughout. In fact, he and his party took the
initiative in proposing a formula of concord. They confessed that
the discussion had opened their eyes and they were prepared to
repudiate all of their previous works against Zwingli and Oeko-
lampadius as irrelevant because based on misunderstanding.
Zwingli, as a matter of fact, had advanced from the view that the
Lord's Supper is only a memorial to the position that Christ is
spiritually present. Luther had always insisted that whatever the
nature of the physical presence, it is of no benefit without faith.
Hence any magical view of the sacrament is excluded. The discovery of these approximations to each other's positions offered
hope for agreement, and the Lutherans came forward with the
declaration "that Christ is truly present, that is substantively [they
did not say substantially], essentially though not quantitatively,
qualitatively or locally." The Swiss rejected this statement as not
sufficiently safeguarding the spiritual presence, and also because
they could not understand how anything could be present some-
where without being there locally. They were not satisfied by
Luther's explanation that the categories of geography do not apply
to the presence of God. Agreement had failed.

But then Philip of Hesse proposed that, despite the disagree-
ment, inter-communion should be practiced. "Luther for a moment
consented, only to recoil when Melanchthon interposed out of
consideration for Ferdinand and the Emperor."[5] This is the statement of Martin Bucer, the reformer of Strassburg, who was a par-
ticipant in the discussion at Marburg and sent a report at the very

---

[4] Walther Koehler, "Das Marburger Religionsgesprach," *SVRG*, XLVIII
(1929).
   [5] *Op cit.*, pp. 139-140.

time to his friend Ambrose Blaurer. Bucer was well informed and reliable. There is no reason to question his statement. It is highly significant because what it says is that Luther was willing to practice inter-communion without doctrinal agreement, but that he recoiled from this position when Melanchthon pointed out to him where the Lutherans would place themselves in the eyes of the Catholic authorities, the emperor and his brother, the ruler of Austria, in case there were a union with the Swiss.

Bucer of course implied that the motives of Melanchthon were political, that he was endeavoring to secure toleration by disclaiming the more radical co-believers. But this is scarcely fair to Melanchthon. The point is that he still entertained a hope of reunion with Rome and he did his best the following year at Augsburg to achieve it. Then the roles of Melanchthon and Luther were reversed. At Marburg Luther wanted to yield to the Swiss, but Melanchthon would have none of it. At Augsburg Melanchthon was on the point of yielding to the Catholics, but Luther would have none of it. He wrote to his colleague, "In personal relations I am the more yielding and you the more stalwart. In public relations it is the reverse."[6] This was not quite the way to put it, but Luther was thinking of the small conference at Marburg where he dealt face to face with the Swiss as compared with the great Diet of the Empire where Melanchthon was negotiating with the Catholics in a less personal way. But the real point was that Luther wished to move to the left and Melanchthon declined because he perceived that to do so would close the door which he desired to keep open to the right. Luther already despaired of any reconciliation in that direction, and told Melanchthon at Augsburg that there was no hope of agreeing with the pope unless he should abolish the papacy. Luther's judgment was vindicated by events, and after the negotiations with the Catholics had failed the conversations were renewed with the Swiss, issuing in the Wittenberg Concord.

All of this is very interesting for the light which it may throw upon the tactics to be employed by Church unity movements. Conceivably, there might in the long run have been more to be gained by renouncing the right wing and joining up with the left at Mar-

[6] *BR* 1611.

burg. Still more interesting and significant is Luther's momentary
readiness to sanction communion other than on the basis of doctrinal unanimity. He was there endorsing the Anglican principle that
men may join in a common act of worship even though they may
place upon it different constructions.

5. The Man of Sorrows in Dürer and Luther

On two occasions Dürer portrayed himself in the guise of the Savior. The first was in 1500 when the composition of the picture and the modification of the features unmistakably suggest the traditional portrayal of Christ. The second was in 1522 when, wracked with malaria and sensing the approach of death, he drew his wasted body in the nude with the instruments of the passion, the whip and the scourge, in his hands (Fig. 1).* Professor Panofsky very properly inquires how so humble and pious an artist as Dürer could have resorted to a device which many less religious men would have considered blasphemy. The answer is found in the theme of the imitation of Christ and further in the concept that genius derived its creative power from God and might be depicted with a resemblance to God.[1]

This interpretation is sound but admits of amplification and illustration. To the theme of the *imitatio Christi* should be added that of the *conformitas Christi*. The former was an endeavor on the part of man to follow Christ, the latter was a gift conferred by God of likeness to Christ. The proponent of the one was Thomas à Kempis; the exemplar of the other was St. Francis, to whom was granted in his own body conformity to the Savior through the gift of the stigmata. Very early the claim was advanced by Fra Salimbene that St. Francis was in all respects conformable to Christ. The theme received a most detailed development at the hands of Fra Bartolomeo da Pisa, who in 1390 composed a work entitled *De conformitate vitae beati Francisci ad vitam Domini Jesu*. Every feature of the passion of Christ was here asserted to have been reduplicated

First published in *The Art Bulletin*, XXIX, 4 (December 1947), under the title Dürer and Luther as the Man of Sorrows."
* All figures in Chapter 5 follow p. 142.
[1] Erwin Panofsky, *Albrecht Dürer* (Princeton, 1945), I, 43.

in St. Francis. Like his Master, he was subject to sale, betrayal, the
agony in the garden, the binding, mockery, scourging, crowning
with thorns, stripping of raiment, crucifixion, piercing with a lance
and the offer of vinegar. The conformity could, of course, be maintained only through allegory. As an example, take the way in which
even the superscription on the cross was transferred to Francis. He
too was *Jesus Nazarenus Rex Judaeorum*. He was *Jesus* by reason
of the conformity, *Nazarenus* through asceticism, *Rex* through
mastery over the passions, and *Judaeorum* as the leader of an elect
people.[2]

How soon such ideas affected the iconography of St. Francis
is difficult to determine with precision. In modern portrayals, such
as that by Fritz Kuntz, the features of St. Francis and Christ in the
same picture are practically interchangeable (Fig. 2). But whether
Giotto, in portraying the saint with a somewhat aquiline and
bearded countenance, was consciously producing a conformity to
the traditional likeness of Christ would be difficult to establish.[3]

A curious parallel is to be observed in the iconography of
John Hus, who in modern times has been portrayed after the guise
of Christ in the garden of Gethsemane (Fig. 3). Such treatment of
Hus entailed a decided break with the earlier iconography in which
he was shown beardless and rotund. By the time of the sixteenth
century, especially in German woodcut, the face had become elon-
gated and bearded. That any deliberate imitation of Christ was
already at work would be too much to affirm, though the possibility
is not to be excluded because Hus already in the sixteenth century
was given a high place in the heavenly hierarchy. There is a picture
of him at the stake dating from 1510 to 1514. The face is still beardless and rotund. The smoke clouds billow from his pyre to form a
wreath in which God the Father appears in the apex, and immediately below, cherubim placing a crown upon the head of this
same Hus quite after the manner of the Coronation of the Virgin.[4]

[2] Ernst Benz, *Ecclesia Spiritualis, Kirchenidee und Geschichtsphilosophie
der Franziskanischen Reformation* (Stuttgart, 1934), 115. Cf. George Goyau, "Les
étranges destinées du livre des Conformités," in *Saint François d'Assise* (Paris,
1927).

[3] Both the Kuntz and the Giotto pictures are reproduced in Vittorino
Facchinetti, *San Francesco d'Assisi* (Milan, 1921), pp. 402, 414.

[4] Reproduced in *Mistr Jan Hus* (Prague, 1915).

Whether these developments were already sufficiently overt in art to have asserted an influence upon Dürer is questionable, and in any case such exaltation of the canonized dead would scarcely have prompted the living to treat themselves in the same fashion.

Literary parallels are more definite. The accommodation of a martyrology to the Gospel narrative of the passion of Christ is discoverable as early as the second century in the Martyrdom of Polycarp. An example in Franciscan history occurred in 1389 when one of the Fraticelli was burned at the stake. A sympathizer at once composed the story of his martyrdom by employing such phrases as these: "Now when even was come, the chief of the Pharisees sent for Fra Michele."[5] In Dürer's century a much more extensive use was made of this device in a narrative of the trial of Martin Luther at the Diet of Worms. The whole story was recorded in what might be called almost a parody of the Gospel. One scarcely knows whether to use the word "parody," which suggests levity. This document does at certain points remind one of the parodies of the Mass in the Middle Ages, or of the Lord's Prayer and the Apostles' Creed in the polemic of the Reformation. The satirical is suggested by the use of the word "courtesan" for the courtiers of the pope, and the reference to the Roman *Trias*. These allusions suggest an author in the circle of Ulrich von Hutten, who had already composed a lampoon with the title *Trias,* because the enormities of Rome were arranged in triplets. Yet Hutten, though a satirist, was passionately in earnest. The real mood of this assimilation of the passion of Luther to the passion of Christ can be gauged only by reading. For that reason the document is here translated in full.

A few preliminary words are necessary as to the persons mentioned. The High Priest of Mainz called Caiaphas was Albert of Hohenzollern, the Archbishop of Mainz. Though the first to denounce Luther to Rome he was later induced by Erasmus to adopt a mediatory role. Carraciolo and Aleander were the papal nuncios at the Diet of Worms, the former in matters political, the latter in matters religious. Aleander was often taunted with being a Jew and hotly rejected the appellation. Chièvres was a minister of Charles V and had been instrumental in arranging to have Luther brought

[5] *Storia di Fra Michele Minorita,* ed. Francesco Flora (Florence, 1942).

to Worms. The Saxon was Luther's patron, Frederick the Wise. He was neither so pusillanimous nor so bold as he is here represented. The Cardinal Gurk was Matthew Lang, the Bishop of Gurk, Archbishop of Salzburg, and Cardinal. He was an Austrian and an abettor of the Hapsburgs. Though no friend of heresy, he counseled giving Luther a hearing to avoid tumult. Glapion was the confessor of Charles V, who attempted a compromise solution that Luther flatly rejected. John Eck was an official of the Archbishop of Trier, and is not to be confused with another John Eck who debated with Luther at Leipzig. Eck of Trier examined Luther at Worms. The Cardinal Sitten was Matthew Schinner, a Swiss, at first favorably disposed to Luther. The Bishop of Liège was Eberhard von Lüttich, who was credited with a very stinging list of grievances against Rome. The Archbishop of Trier was Richard von Greiffenklau, to whose arbitrament Frederick the Wise had long sought to have Luther's case referred. After the public hearings at Worms the plan was carried through, and Trier presided over a committee which gave Luther several private examinations. Hutten was an inflammatory German knight who threatened to use the sword on Luther's behalf. Carlstadt was Luther's older colleague on the faculty of the University of Wittenberg and his associate at the Leipzig debate. Hutten and Carlstadt were included along with Luther in the papal bull of condemnation. The "Sect of Bern" is a reference to a hoax perpetrated by the Dominicans at Bern, who attempted a bogus stigmatization on the person of recruit named Jetzer. Exposure sent several of the Dominicans to the stake.

In full imitation of biblical language the narrative proceeds:

Luther with his disciples went forth over the River Rhine and entered into Worms, where Caesar was holding a diet. Knowing that he was come, the High Priests and Pharisees assembled into the palace of the High Priest of Mainz, called Caiaphas, and consulted with the scribes how they might violate his safe conduct, and take him by subtlety and burn him. But they said, not during the Diet lest there be an uproar among the people. While then Luther was in the house of the Knights of St. John, Carraciolo called Pedico, and Aleander the Jew sought to betray him with the kiss of peace. But Luther, knowing all things that should come upon him, went forth and said unto them, "Whom seek ye?" They answered unto him, "Dr. Luther." Luther said unto them, "I am he." They inquired whether he wished to come to Carraciolo and Aleander the Jew, or whether they should come to him. Luther answered, "I sat daily with them teaching in the temple and they laid no hand on me. Now therefore I do not wish to speak to them, because they have been excommunicated by me, except they wish to engage with me in public disputation." And when they heard this they went backwards and fell to the ground. Then came one from the court of the governor named Capra (Chièvre). To the papists he said, "What will ye give me and I will deliver him unto you?" And they consigned to him a large sum of ducats together with certain great prebends, benefices and dignities for his nephew who also betrayed him.

The third hour the disciples of Luther came to him saying, "At what hour wilt thou that we prepare for thee to eat the supper?" And Luther answering said, "The fifth," and the disciples did as Luther had commanded them and prepared the supper. Now when even was come he sat down with his disciples and friends, and as he did eat he said, "Verily I say unto you, there are those in this city who for money will betray me, and many of you will be offended in me, for it is written, 'I will smite the shepherd and the sheep will be scattered.'" Then one answered, "Though all should be offended in thee, nevertheless the Saxon will never be offended." But Luther said to him, "Before two days he will deny me thrice." But they said, "Though we should die with thee, yet will we not deny thee." Luther answered, "You will be with me in tribulations, even to the sacrifice."

The next day about the fourth hour there came the imperial marshal, Ulrich von Pappenheim, with a great company with swords and staves, sent by the governor to the princes of the empire, and they led Luther to the judgment hall. But the papists did not enter the judgment hall, that Luther might have no opportuniy of disputing with them, but that he might be condemned without just cause. There was there also Annas, the Cardinal Gurk, together with the Cardinal of Mainz. It was this Annas who counseled that it were better that one man should die for the papists than that their wickedness should be made manifest and Roman wickedness should fail. The Saxon, indeed, followed afar off and came into the judgment hall, and having entered sat down with the others that he might see the end. The High Priests and the papists then sought false testimony against Luther, that they might condemn him and burn him with fire, but they found nothing. When then many witnesses had accused him falsely there came in two tongue-thrashers, John Rabula (Glapio) and John Eck, the official of Trier, and they testified, "He said that the Council of Constance erred and that the pope is Antichrist, who however can commit no sin." Then arose Caiaphas of Mainz, the Chief Priest, and said, "What sayest thou to these things that are testified against thee? I adjure thee by the living God, confess them to be true." Then Luther, undismayed, answered, "Thou hast spoken. Verily I say unto thee, I am able to prove from the testimony of scripture that which is written in my books, and unless I am convinced by sacred scripture or manifest reason, I will not recant. If I have spoken evil, bring testimony of evil. Instruct me better, for I am ready myself to cast my books into the fire. But if I have taught well, why do they kill me? Why not listen, why not answer?" Then Caiaphas of Mainz waxed hot and said, "He has blasphemed! What need have we of any further witnesses? Ye have heard his blasphemy. What think ye?" And they all condemned him to be guilty of death. Then they spat upon the earth and would not hear him further, because they could not controvert him. But some cried out, "He hath a demon!"

Now the Saxon was sitting with them and there came to him the Priest of Liège and said, "Art thou a Lutheran?" And he denied it in the presence of them all, saying, "I do not know what you say." As he was going out of the door the Cardinal Sitten said to those about him, "He harbored Luther in his territory." But he denied it in the presence of them all, saying, "I know not the man." And those standing about after a pause said to the Saxon, "Truly you are a Lutheran, for your words have often shown it." Then he began to declare that he had been too occupied with other matters to pay any attention to the man. And it was evening and morning, the second day. Then the Saxon remembered his word, that before two days he would deny him thrice, and going out he declared that he would defend him before all men.

When morning was come the High Priests and the papists took counsel against Luther, that they might burn him with fire. Then they took him and turned him over to the Archbishop of Trier, and he inquired of him, "Art thou a doctor of the gospel and the truth?" And Luther said, "Sayest thou this thing of thyself or did the Romanists tell it thee of me?" And the Archbishop said, "Am I a Romanist? They who cannot endure the gospel truth and the words of Paul delivered thee to me. What hast thou done?" Luther answered as a Christian, "My writings are not concerning this world but concerning God. If the papists had regarded the gospel truth and the words of Paul they would not have delivered me to thee." And Trier asked, "Art thou a doctor of evangelical truth and of St. Paul?" And Luther answered, "Thou hast said. To this was I born, and for this came I into the world, that I should restore to their pristine purity the words of the gospel and of St. Paul, because the papists have distorted them to their own use and for the Roman curia, to the great detriment of the German nation. If the German nation will follow and observe my words, she will be free from the fangs of the Romanists and the courtesans." And when he was accused by the High Priests and the Romanists he answered nothing save as a Christian. Then Trier said to him, "Wilt thou submit thy writings to the judgment of Caesar and the Diet?" But Luther so answered in all things that the Archbishop of Trier marveled greatly, and he said to Luther, "What is the wickedness of the Romanists and the papists?" And when he had said this from that hour he sought to free him, for he knew that he had been delivered through envy of the High Priests and papists. And the Archbishop of Trier said, "I find in him no cause of death. Will you that I release him?" But they cried out the more, "No! If he is released the whole Roman curia together with the papists and the courtesans will be reduced to poverty. There is no other way to sustain the Roman *Trias*."

When then the governor was seated on his tribunal, there came to him his wife, that is the German nation, saying, "Have nothing to do with this just man. For this night I have suffered much concerning him, and if he is burned then all German liberty will be consumed with him." Then the princes and the priests persuaded the governor to destroy Luther, and the governor said, "What shall I do with this truly Christian man, who teaches the true evangelical doctrine and desires to liberate the German nation from the snares and nets of the Romanists and courtesans?" And they all said, "Burn him!" And the governor said, "Why? What evil has he done?" But all the more they cried out, "Burn him! Burn him! Beware, if you release him you are no friend of the Roman pontiff, who will give you aid against France. Besides, we have a law, and according to this law he should die because he has written evil of the Roman Antichrist and all the courtesans." Then said the governor, "Take him and burn him according to your law." They answered, "In the German Empire it is not permitted to us to burn anyone. If we had him in Rome we could easily poison him." Then the governor saw that it did no good and that a great tumult was made among the people, that is among the Romanists, because they displayed much money and great dignities. Having then taken water and washed his hands in the presence of the people, he said, "I am innocent of the blood of this Christian man, as you see." And all the clergy and the Romanists answered, "His blood be upon our heads!"

Then the governor delivered to them the books of Luther to be burned. The priests took them, and when the princes and the people had left the Diet they made a great pyre in front of the High Priest's palace, where they burned the books; and they placed on the top a picture of Luther with this inscription, "This is Martin Luther, the Doctor of the Gospel." This title was read by many Romanists and courtesans, because the place where Luther's books were burned was not far from the bishop's court. Now this title was written in French, German and in Latin. Then the High Priests and the Romanists said to the governor, "Write not, 'a doctor of evangelical truth' but that he said, 'I am a doctor of evangelical truth.' " But the governor answered, "What I have written, I have written." This was done by some of the order of the preachers and of the Sect of Bern and of the heretics.

And with him two other doctors were burned, Hutten and Carlstadt, one on the right hand and one on the left. But the picture of Luther would not burn until the soldiers had folded it and put it inside a vessel of pitch, where it was reduced to ashes. As a count beheld these things which were done he marveled, and said, "Truly he is a Christian." And all the throng present, seeing those things which had come to pass, returned beating their breasts. The following day the chief priests and the Pharisees, together with the Romanists, went to the governor and said, "We recall that this seducer said he wished later to write greater things. Make an order therefore throughout the whole earth that his books be not sold, lest the latest error be worse than the first." But the governor said, "You have your own guard. Go publish bulls as you know how, through your false excommunication." They then went away and put forth horrible mandates in the name of the Roman pontiff and of the emperor, to which they made additions *ad lib.*

To this day they have not been obeyed. They will see him whom they have transfixed.[6]

Even after reading this document the man of our time may still be in doubt as to how to interpret it. But this we know, that contemporaries were not shocked, neither Catholics nor Protestants, for in 1536 the Catholics employed the same device with Charles V in the role of Christ, and in 1546 the Lutherans did the same for the Saxon prince, John Frederick.[7] Still more revealing is it to observe how Luther and his friends, without knowledge of this document, had in varying degrees employed the same theme. Luther himself began to draw the analogy between his trial and that of Christ when, after the interview at Augsburg, Cardinal Cajetan endeavored to persuade Frederick the Wise either to deliver Luther to Rome or at least to banish him. Luther wrote to the elector on November 19, 1518: "I cannot suffer that such a wise prince as you should be made into a Pilate, for when the Jews brought Christ before Pilate and were asked what evil he had done they answered, 'If he were not an evildoer we should not have brought him to you.' In just the same way the noble legate has brought Brother Martin with hateful words before the prince, and the prince has asked, "What evil has he done?' "[8] To another, Luther wrote on November 25, "Cajetan advised that I be sent to Rome . . . even so

---

[6] Text and notes in Otto Clemen, *Beiträge zur Reformationszeitalter* (Berlin, 1900-1903), III, 10-15.

[7] Fritz Behrend, "Das Leidensgeschichte des Herrn als Form in politisch-literarischen Kampf besonders in Reformationszeitalter," *ARG* XIV (1917), 49-64. See p. 53.

[8] *BR* 110, p. 243.

did the Jews deal with Christ before Pilate, wishing him to credit them even before the crimes had been named."[9] On January 14, 1520, Luther commented to a friend, "As Christ was formerly crucified on account of the Jews, even so am I on account of communion in both kinds."[10] In his recital of the interview with Cajetan, Luther recorded, "My writings to this day have been in the house of Caiaphas, that they might find false witness against me, but they have found nothing."[11] On the way to Worms Luther received an ovation at Erfurt. To a friend he commented, "I have had my Palm Sunday. I wonder whether this pomp is merely a temptation or whether it is also the sign of my impending passion."[12]

The same imagery was used by Luther's friends. When his fate after the interview was still uncertain, Staupitz wrote to him, "As Christ was formerly crucified in such hate, so now I do not see what there is in store for you save the cross. Deserted, let us follow the deserted Christ."[13] The imperial mandate calling for the sequestration of Luther's books was promulgated on March 27, which was Wednesday in Holy Week. Lazarus Spengler called attention to the coincidence, adding, "Damit Luthers Passion dem Leiden Christi ähnlich werde."[14] As Luther came from his hearing at Worms a voice from the crowd called out, "Blessed is the womb that bare thee" (compare Luke 11:27).[15] Even Frederick the Wise, to whom in our document was assigned the role of Peter, remarked that the lords temporal and spiritual were to Luther not only as Annas and Caiaphas, but also as Pilate and Herod.[16]

In the time of Luther and of Dürer, heaven yet lay so close to earth, and the concepts of the *imitatio* and the *conformitas Christi* were so vivid that no sense of sacrilege attached to portraying either one's friends or oneself in the guise of Christ. These ideas found pictorial expression in Luther's circle. In the second edition

[9] *BR* 113, p. 256.
[10] *BR* 239.
[11] Walch ed., XV, No. 225, col. 614.
[12] *BR* 395, p. 206.
[13] *BR* 119.
[14] *DRA,* Jüngere Reihe II, No. 210, p. 891.
[15] Julius Köstlin, *Martin Luther* (Berlin, 1903), I, 412.
[16] Paul Kirn, "Friedrich der Weise," *Beitrage zur Kulturgeschichte des Mittelalters und der Renaissance,* XXX (1926), 142.

of Luther's *Passional Christi und Antichristi* of 1521, Lucas Cranach introduced a new woodcut of Christ staggering under the weight of the cross and Simon of Cyrene stepping forward to carry it in his stead. To Simon the cross bearer have been given the features of Cranach himself (Fig. 4).[17]

An even more striking example is to be found in a Reformation woodcut of the year 1545 (Fig. 5) in which Luther is portrayed in the pulpit declaring the word of God as committed to him by the Holy Trinity through the inspiration of the Holy Spirit which as a dove hovers about his head. Below the pulpit three scenes are depicted. The first is the baptism of an infant. The second is the celebration of the Lord's Supper in both kinds, that is, both the bread and the wine are dispensed to the laity. The third scene is that of the congregation gathered about the pulpit listening devoutly to Luther's sermon. Among them stands the Elector John Frederick, his head twisted backwards that his features may be unmistakable. Upon his shoulder rests a heavy wooden cross.[18]

Such examples enable one to comprehend how fully the men of that generation moved in a perpetual Passion play in which each and all might take the role of Christus. The morbid emphasis on the *via crucis* as the sole way of discipleship among some of Luther's followers led him to protest on countless occasions against self-imposed crosses. Let one not seek the cross but rather be found by it, he would stay. Then the misfortunes and vexations of life came to be interpreted as examples of the cross; and here, perhaps, we are closest to Dürer's depiction of disease as a cross. The perfect parallel occurs in one of Luther's letters in which, after an acute attack of constipation, he remarks, "Even so does Christ not leave us without relics of His holy cross."[19]

That Dürer was acquainted with the religious atmosphere which could discover in Luther a conformity to Christ is no mere conjecture. At the close of the Diet of Worms on May 17, 1521,

---

[17] *WA* IX, Beilage, Taf. 11a. Georg Stuhlfauth, "Selbstbildnisse und Bildnisse Lucas Cranach d. Ä. (1472-1553) und Lucas Cranach d. J. (1515-1586)," *Theologische Blätter*, XI (1932), p. 239.

[18] Max Geisberg, *Die Reformation in den Kampfbildern der Einblattholtzschnitte* (Munich, 1929), No. XXXV, 7.

[19] *BR* 429.

Dürer committed to his diary this prayer: "Oh Lord, who desirest before Thou comest in judgment that as Thy Son Jesus Christ had to die at the hands of the priests and rise from the dead and ascend to heaven even so should be made conformable to Him Thy disciple Martin Luther, whose life the pope seeks with money treacherously against God, but whom Thou wilt quicken."[20]

[20] "Dürers Briefe, Tagebücher und Reime," hrsg. Moritz Thausing, *Quellenschriften für Kunstgeschichte,* III (1872), p. 121. Only after this note was in print was I successful in obtaining access to the work of Hans Preuss, *Martin Luther der Prophet* (Gütersloh, 1933), which in two sections deals with parallels between Luther and Christ. Preuss points out for example that when Luther preaching at Erfurt on his way to Worms calmed an audience frightened by the sagging of a gallery, the town chronicler recorded, "This beginning of signs did Luther, and his disciples came and ministered unto him." Preuss shows that Catholics did take exception to this treatment of Luther but the offense lay rather in the adulation of a heretic than in the theme itself which as late as 1862 was used to compare the sufferings of Pius IX to those of his Lord.

6. The Joachimite Prophecy: Osiander and Sachs

Hans Sachs must have been both astonished and intrigued when the ardent Lutheran minister of the St. Lawrence Church in Nürnberg came posting to the shoe shop with a fantastically illustrated book discovered in the library of the Carthusian cloister. Another copy had been found in the Ratsbibliothek. What it was all about Pfarrer Osiander himself did not quite know, but he was perfectly sure that the work consisted of prophecies about the popes accompanied by portentous woodcuts of venerable antiquity. He could hardly overlook the recent printing of the book itself, for the copy from the Carthusian cloister with the notes of Hans Sachs is still extant and bears the imprint, "Bologna, 1515." It had been off the press scarcely more than a decade. But the content was old. The title read: *Joachimi Abbatis Vaticinia circa Apostolicos viros et Ecclesiam Romanam.* The Abbot Joachim, explained Osiander, wrote in the year 1278. His predictions in all likelihood had been subsequently altered to make them less unpalatable to the Church, but the illustrations themselves would have survived unchanged and could now be reinterpreted in accord with the original intent of the prophet, which meant of course that the pictures could be utilized for the polemical pamphleteering of the Lutheran reform. Osiander proposed to re-edit the work with his own elucidations. Would not Hans Sachs supply each cartoon with a pair of his piquant couplets? The shoemaker bard, who had already lauded the Wittenberg nightingale, consented to this more daring venture.

At Nürnberg, in the year 1527, there issued from the press of Güldenmunde a work entitled: *Eyn wunderliche Weyssagung von dem Babstumb wie es yhm biss an das endt der welt gehen sol in*

First published under the title "Eyn Wunderliche Weyssagung, Osiander-Sachs-Luther" in the *Germanic Review*, XXI, 3 (October 1946).

figuren oder gemäl begriffen gefunden zu Nürmberg ym Car-
theuser Closter vnd ist seher alt. Eyn vorred Andreas Osianders.
Mit gütter verstendtlicher ausslegung durch gelerte leut verklert.
Welche Hans Sachs yn teutshe reymen gefast vnd darzu gesetzt hat.
ym M.D. xxvii Jar.

One of the pictures is of especial interest because it represents
Martin Luther. The entire page is herewith reproduced (Fig. 6).*
We have before us an Augustinian monk, in his right hand a tooth
edged sickle, in the left a rose. Beside him on the right stands an
amputated leg, on the left some odd object which might be a fragment from a Corinthian column. Osiander knows what it all
means. "The monk?" "*Ich mein ja es sei der Luther.*" The amputated leg refers to the words of the prophet Isaiah, "All flesh is as
grass" (40:6). The odd object to the left is a branding iron and sig-
nifies the fire of Christian love which both consumes and kindles.
Hans Sachs in his couplets further celebrates "*der Held Martinus
Luther.*"

The booklet speedily found its way to Wittenberg, and quite
took the fancy of Doctor Martinus. The identification of himself
with the reaper monk struck him as entirely appropriate but he
could not make out why he should be holding a rose.[1]

Obviously Osiander and Sachs had not fully comprehended
the import of the book which fell into their hands. If we examine
the Bologna imprint which they utilized perhaps we may do better.
The page on which they thought to see the figure of Luther is here
fully reproduced (Fig. 7). As a matter of fact it does not help us
greatly. Only a few details are different. The monk of course does
not wear Luther's habit and the branding iron is simply the letter
"B." The explanation below speaks of one who will last only for
three years and then as an old man will be taken to hell.

To solve the riddle we must consult other editions of the
Vaticinia Joachimi. It comprised a collection of thirty pictures
with brief prophetic annotations applying to the popes from Nich-
olas III (1277-1280) to Paul II (1464-1471). The first fifteen prophecies were attributed to the Calabrian monk of the late twelfth century, the Abbot Joachim of Fiore, and the remainder to a certain

[1] Letter of May 19, 1527.
* All figures in Chapter 6 follow p. 142.

Anselmus episcopus Marsicanus. Some of these prophecies can be
traced back to the threshold of the year 1300. The collection as a
whole obviously could not have antedated the latter half of the
fifteenth century.[2]

The name of the Abbot Joachim, whether genuine or spurious, is the password to the portals of medieval sectarianism. It was
he who revived the eschatology of the primitive Christian community. The Church of the Middle Ages, following St. Augustine, had
projected the return of the Lord into the indefinite future and
centered attention rather on the *dies irae* confronting each individual soul.[3] The Calabrian restored the sense of the imminent end
of the historical process. For him, history was divided into three
periods: the age of the Father, the age of the Son and the age of
the Holy Spirit. The second period was nearing its close. The new
era of the Spirit was about to be ushered in when the Church on
earth would give way to the *ecclesia spiritualis.* The new era would
be prepared by a forerunner, a *homo spiritualis,* to arise from
among the monastic orders. The radical sectaries of the late Middle
Ages avidly appropriated these predictions and further elaborated
the ideas in spurious documents attributed to the Abbot Joachim,
such as the *Evangelium Aeternum* of the Spiritual Franciscans.
The name of Joachim in consequence became suspect in ecclesiastical circles. Nevertheless, the Church could not escape his spell. The
prophecies issued in his name exercised a Circean charm in the
period of the Renaissance, so devoted to the revival of ancient
augury. The Bologna imprint of the *Vaticinia* which lay before
Osiander and Sachs had been issued by a Dominican and was dedi-
cated to the Cardinal Giulio de' Medici. The preface related these
predictions to the art of the augurs.

In many editions the prophecies are assigned to particular
popes in chronological order and the name accompanies the picture. In a north Italian manuscript edition of the late fifteenth cen-

---

[2] Herbert Grundmann, "Studien über Joachim von Floris," *Beiträge zur
Kulturgeschichte des Mittelalters und der Renaissance,* XXXII (1927), 196-198.
J. C. Huck, *Joachim von Floris* (1938), pp. 212-217.

[3] Wilhelm Kamlah, "Apokalypse und Geschichtstheologie: die mittel-
alterliche Auslegung der Apokalypse von Joachim von Fiore," *Historische Studien,* CCLXXXV (1935).

tury there stands above the monk, whose identity we are seeking, the inscription: *Dominus Baldasar Cossa legatus Bononiae deinde Johannes papa XXIII.*[4] This puts us in a position to explain the amputated leg. As A. Warburg has pointed out, it is the armorial device of Pope John XXIII. His name was Cossa and the word for haunch in Italian is *coscia*.[5] With such a lead the explanation of the letter B becomes simple. It is the initial of the Christian name of Baldasare Cossa. We have before us, then, the pope who was deposed by the Council of Constance.

But why does he appear as a monk whereas all the other popes in the series are shown in pontifical dress wearing the tiara? Baldasare Cossa, the ex-pirate and condottiere, was not the man to suggest the cowl. I venture the suggestion that this monk is not the pope at all. He is rather the monastic forerunner of the original Joachimite prophecy, the *homo spiritualis,* who should prepare the way for the inauguration of the new dispensation. To do so he must purge the Church and cut down the malodorous pope who had so defamed the name of John that for five centuries and a half no pope ever assumed it again.

The sickle as the instrument of the purge has ample Biblical warrant. In the Book of Revelation the figure like unto the Son of Man bears in his hand a sharp sickle and the angel cries, "Thrust in thy sickle and reap." (14:14) But this sickle is not sharp. What is the meaning of the jagged edge and why should he who is to purge the papacy bear a rose in his hand? A. Warburg, with erudite acumen, notes the resemblance of this tooth-edged sickle to the one borne by the pagan deity of classical antiquity, Saturn, who used it to cut down lilies and roses. But what is he doing here? Observe again the prophecy applied to Pope John XXIII. His days are numbered. He is to last but three years. Now Saturn is the Latin equivalent of the Greek Chronos, the god of time, often symbolized by the hourglass. As with his jagged sickle he reaps even the rose so will he cut down the unworthy pontiff. Here we have an as-

[4] Hermann Julius Hermann, "Die Handschriften und Inkunabeln der italienischen Renaissance. 2. Oberitalien." *Beschreibendes Verzeichnis der illuminierten Handschriften in Österreich,* Bd. VIII, Teil VI (1905), p. 187.

[5] A. Warburg, "Heidnisch-Antike Weissagung in Wort und Bild zu Luthers Zeiten." *Gesammelte Schriften,* II (1932), pp. 520-521 and 652-653.

tounding combination in one figure of the reformatory monk of
the Joachimite prophecy, the avenger of the Apocalypse, and the
grim reaper of the pagan pantheon. And all of this turns into
Martin Luther.

The Church of Rome had good reason to feel that this illustration called for some modification. An edition of the *Vaticinia
Joachimi* printed in Venice in the year 1600 during the time of the
Counter Reformation has rendered this *homo spiritualis* perfectly
innocuous. He is no longer a monk but a pontiff, wearing the tiara
(Fig. 8), still wielding the sickle though no longer jagged, still holding the rose, still accompanied by the amputated leg and the letter
B. The connections alike with Saturn and Pope John XXIII had
long since been forgotten. The artist depicted better than he knew
when he portrayed the reformatory pope as the god of time eradi-
cating the vestiges of one of the most unsavory pontiffs of the Great
Schism.

7. Luther on Birds, Dogs and Babies

Gleanings from the "Table Talk"

The topic "Luther on Birds, Dogs and Babies" has been given the subtitle "Gleanings from the *Table Talk*." Many more extensive examples could have been gathered had a wider range of his works been encompassed, and twice in this paper I have cited his letters. But otherwise I have relied on the *Table Talk* alone, because of a subsidiary interest in displaying the nature of this source and the way in which it may be properly employed. It has been used all too indiscriminately by Luther's foes to provide examples of his none-too-fastidious speech, and by his friends in order to spice his already salty biography. The trained historian looks somewhat askance at the *Table Talk* because it reports Luther only at second hand, and a comparison of the variant versions discloses discrepancies. Nevertheless, it is not for that reason to be rejected, but rather to be used with caution. At no point is it more likely to distort less than in those instances where Luther was commenting on some immediate and simple daily occurrence—something going on in the room or out of the window—rather than recalling his own remote past or discussing an intricate point of theology.

I have chosen to discuss gleanings from the region of the immediate and obvious: namely, Luther's comments on birds, dogs and babies. In all he found some theological lessons. He did in everything for that matter, from the heavens above to the frogs in the Elbe—the latter were, of course, his Catholic opponents. Birds, dogs and babies have this in common: all three display a simple and unsophisticated faith. But this does not exhaust the subject. Luther's fertile and inveterate homiletical bent could discover

First published in *Luther Today*, Luther College Press (Decorah, Iowa, 1957).

manifold and often startling analogies in the animal and the infant world.

In his use of dogs and birds, he was of course in the medieval tradition. Bestiaries, so-called, were among the usual equipment of the medieval preacher. There is a difference, however, because the pulpiteer of the Middle Ages delighted in fantastic allegories and did not disdain legendary lore—as, for example, the resurrection of the phoenix, the pelican nourishing her young from her own breast, not to mention the unicorn. Luther restricted himself to the animals before his eyes. Very seldom would he introduce even a literary allusion. The contrast here is striking with Melanchthon, who would tell a story about a bird in order to illustrate the Latin proverb, *Crede parum, tua serva et quae periere relinque,* which means, "Believe little, look after what you have, and don't hanker after what you have lost." Melanchthon related that a captive bird cried to its snarer, "Oh, let me go and I will show you a gem worth many gulden." "You will fool me," answered the captor. "Oh, no," replied the bird. "Come with me and see the gem." The bird was released, perched then on the branch of a tree, and quoted, "Believe little, look after what you have, and don't hanker after what you have lost." This was the gem worth many gulden.[1] Luther only once to my knowledge employed a quotation about a bird. It came from the lives of the Desert Fathers. A young monk came to an old one and confessed himself beset by many unsavory desires, and the old father said to him, "You cannot stop the birds from flying over your head, but you can keep them from nesting in your hair."[2]

Luther did on occasion invest the birds with human characteristics, as in his famous letter from the Coburg, the authenticity of which is doubted by the Weimar editors because the original is lost and there are difficulties about the date; but the style is certainly *echt.* Luther himself, unable to attend the Diet at Augsburg, imagined himself in the midst of a Diet of Birds. "Beneath my window is a grove like a small forest where the jackdaws and crows are holding a Diet. They ride in and out and make a continual racket day and night as if they were all swaggering drunk. Young and old

[1] *TR* 7051.
[2] *TR* 7075.

jabber together till I marvel how voice and wind can hold out so long. I wonder whether there are any such nobles and knights left among you, because they appear to have gathered here from all over the world.

"I have not yet seen their Kaiser, but the nobles and other big brass parade and strut before our eyes. They are not in lively uniforms, but all dressed alike: simply, in black, with grey eyes. They all sing the same song, but with a pleasing variety between the young and the old, the big and the little. They care nought for a palace or a hall because their hall is vaulted by the fair broad heaven, their floor is just the field carpeted with beautiful green branches, and their walls are as wide as the ends of the earth. They care nothing for horses and armor because they have feathered chariots with which to escape a snare. They are mighty lords. But what they are deciding I do not yet know. So far as I can find out from an interpreter, they are planning a mighty campaign against wheat, barley, oats, and all manner of grain. So you see, we are here at a Reichstag and we watch with delight as the princes and lords and estates of the Reich sing so lustily. We are especially delighted to see them strut like knights, polish their bills, and throw down the defenses so that they may be victorious over corn and malt. We wish them all luck—that all of them put together may be impaled on one spit."[3]

This example, of course, is from the *Letters*—but now for the *Table Talk*. One is amazed at the variety of lessons derived by Luther from birds, and one is refreshed by his complete lack of sentimentality. He marvels at God's astounding creation and man's blindness to the wonder of the ordinary. How we gape if someone brings a hen or an egg from Calcutta! But Christ said simply, consider the lilies, consider the birds.[4] "No one can calculate what God spends to feed them, even the ones that are no use. I would estimate that it costs more than the annual income of the king of France to feed the sparrows, not to mention the ravens, crows, and jackdaws. Who, then, among men should be anxious about the body, wherewithal it shall be clothed?"[5]

[3] *BR* 1555.
[4] *TR* 3390.
[5] *TR* 2123.

Luther was not for that reason too tender toward all birds. "A law should be passed," said he, "to exterminate all sparrows, crows, and magpies." "But," objected Dr. Jonas, "the Master said, 'Your heavenly Father careth for them.' " "That's just it," retorted Luther. "God feeds them and they poach on our fields instead of having harvests of their own, even though God has provided for them in winter."[6]

These unworthy birds served Luther, however, as an illustration of justification by faith without the merit of works. Asked why Christ refers to sparrows, which are pestilent and odious birds, the Doctor answered that if Christ could have thought of any more obnoxious fowl, he would have done so in order to show that, like these birds, we receive all things without any merit on our part.[7]

The birds, perhaps curiously, served alike to illustrate timorous unbelief and confiding faith. Once two birds flew into Luther's garden to make their nest; but when he and others entered, they always took to flight. "Ah, dear birds," exclaimed Luther, "do not fly away. I wish with all my heart that you might build your nest and have your house here. I do not mean to harm you. The trouble is, you do not believe it. Just so, we do not believe in God although he is merciful and with all his heart wishes us well. He does not mean to slay us; indeed, for our sakes he suffered his only-begotten Son to die upon the cross."[8]

But on another occasion Luther saw in the birds an example of trust. "One evening Dr. Martin Luther saw a little bird settle for the night on the branch of a tree and said, 'This bird has had its supper and will sleep now in peace with no concern for the morrow or for lodging.' As David said, 'He that dwelleth in the secret place of the most high shall abide under the shadow of the Almighty.' The bird sits blissful on his bough and lets God take care of him. Alas, if Adam's fall had not corrupted all, what a wonderful creature of God man would have been, endowed with all knowledge and wisdom! How blessed would have been his life without toil, misfortune, and sickness! He would not have been plagued by

[6] *TR* 1641.
[7] *TR* 4644.
[8] *TR* 1637.

the fear of death and would have delighted in all God's creatures. What a joyous change there would have been in all things, just as now in this vale of misery, God gives us in many creatures a fore-taste of the resurrection."[9]

Luther's comments on dogs have no note of disparagement, for he was fond of his dog Toelpel. The dogs, like birds, illustrated for him the marvel of God's creation. "Look at that dog," said he of Toelpel. "There is nothing wrong with his whole body. He has glistening eyes, stout legs, beautiful white teeth, and a good stom-ach. All such gifts of the body God bestows on an unreasoning ani-mal."[10] "God makes common his best gifts. This is clear in the case of dogs. They are most useful and valued. Eyes are very precious and all living creatures have them. The tiniest birds have the clear-est eyes, sparkling like jewels or drops of purest dew. They can spot a fly across the room, which we old sausages can never do in this life."[11]

But for all their endowment, dogs are subject to men. Luther noticed little Martin tousling the dog and remarked, "This child preaches God's word in very deed because God said, 'Man shall have dominion over the fish of the sea and over the fowl of the air and over every living thing that moveth on the face of the earth' (Genesis 1:28). Just see how this dog will take anything from that child."[12]

Toelpel taught Luther the lesson of unwavering persistence in prayer. The dog was eyeing a piece of meat which he expected from the Doctor's hand, and the eyes were riveted with steady, un-flickering gaze. "Ah," said Luther, "if only I could pray the way that dog looks at meat. All his thoughts are on that morsel; he thinks, wishes, and hopes about nothing else, but my heart fails because it can not hold to prayer without wandering."[13]

Luther could not believe that so faithful a beastie would be excluded from life eternal. Asked whether he expected to find dogs in heaven he answered, "Certainly, for there the earth will not be

[9] *TR* 4110.
[10] *TR* 869.
[11] *TR* 2849a.
[12] *TR* 1638.
[13] *TR* 274.

without form and void. Peter said that the last day would be the restitution of all things. God will create a new heaven and a new earth and new Toelpels with hide of gold and fur of silver. God will be all in all; and snakes, now poisonous because of original sin, will then be so harmless that we shall be able to play with them."[14]

Luther's comments on children, like those on birds and dogs, are forthright, affectionate, unsentimental, and highly varied. To begin with, he counted it a blessing to have children. "I am richer than all the papist theologians in the whole world . . . I have three children born in wedlock, and that is more than any papist theologian has."[15]

The arrival of a baby was greeted alike with joy and a touch of facetiousness. We read in the *Table Talk* that "in the year 1533, on January 28, in the first hour of the night there was born to Dr. Martin Luther a son Paul. His godparents were Duke John Ernest, Hans Loeser, Dr. Jonas, Philip Melanchthon, and Margarete Lindemann. When Loeser called, Luther said, 'See, I have thrown a stone into your garden. Today a new pope is born. I want you to help the little fellow. I have called him Paul because I owe so much to the Apostle. If the lad wants to be a soldier, let Loeser take charge; if a scholar, then Jonas and Melanchthon; but if he wants to work, I'll apprentice him to a peasant.' "[16]

Four years later, on the birth of a daughter, Luther wrote to her prospective godmother: "Grace and peace in Christ. Noble lady and dear friend, I beg of you a favor for God's sake. He has given to my dear Kathy and me a little heathen girl. Won't you please be godmother to make her into a Christian, that through your help she may come from the old birth in Adam to the new birth in Christ by Holy Baptism? . . . I commend you to God. Amen. P.S. I haven't dared to go out in this wind."[17]

The arrival of a child always introduces for parents a new order of existence. Luther sometimes commented without inhibition on the annoyance, trouble and anxiety caused by babies. The

[14] *TR* 1150.
[15] *TR* 2579.
[16] *TR* 2946b.
[17] *TR* 3541.

Table Talk records: "On New Year's Day in 1533 Dr. Martin Luther's baby cried and could not be quieted. The Doctor and his wife for an hour were extremely sad and anxious. Afterwards Luther said, 'These are the trials of marriage which make everyone shrink from it. We are afraid of the ways of women, of the bawling of infants, of the upkeep of a home and of the annoyance of bad neighbors. We want to be free and unfettered.' "[18]

To little Martin, Luther said, "What have you done that I should love you so? Why do you deserve to be the heir of all my goods? You have to be diapered, I have to hire a maid, you have to be nursed, and if you don't get all this, you bawl through the whole house."[19] When Luther was fondling the babe, his lap was soiled and he reflected, "Oh, how much does our Lord God have to put up with in us, much more than a mother with a child!"[20]

Vastly more distressing to parents is it when the child does not turn out well. "Dear God," ejaculated Luther, "how Adam must have loved Cain, his first-born! And he rewarded his father by becoming a homicide. Pfui!"[21]

Luther had learned like St. Augustine that our Lord commends a child, not because of its disposition, but because of its dependency upon parents and its trust in parental bounty. Luther was charmed and heartened by the simplicity of childhood faith. Children of course know no more than adults about the life to come. The ignorance of the child before birth is a symbol of the ignorance of us all. "As little as the child in the womb knows what is ahead, so little do we know of life eternal."[22] But children believe. When Anastasia was four years old, she was talking confidently about Christ, angels and eternal joy in heaven when Luther said, "My dear child, if only we could hold fast to this." "Why, Father," she asked, "don't you believe it then?" "Children accept it all," Luther said, "without question, and that is why Christ commended them as our teachers."[23] On another occasion Luther's little son was prattling about heaven and what a wonder-

[18] *TR* 2867b.
[19] *TR* 3141.
[20] *TR* 3203b.
[21] *TR* 2963a.
[22] *TR* 3339.
[23] *TR* 660.

ful time he would have eating and dancing. There, said he, rivers run milk and buns grow on trees. Luther commented, "The life of children is most blessed and best. They have no earthly cares, they do not see the churches rent by the radicals, they feel no pangs of death and hell, they have only pure thoughts and joyous fantasies."[24]

The Doctor found solace in a baby's unconcern, and when he saw little Martin nursing, exclaimed, "Child, your enemies are the Pope, the Bishop, Duke George, Ferdinand, and the Devil, and there you are, blithely sucking."[25] Luther was pleased that children are insouciant of the problems of their support. He asked his little son how much he cost his father during the year, and the lad answered, "Food and drink don't cost anything. Only apples and pears."[26]

Luther found himself a child with his children and even a pupil of his bairns. Before God he was no more than they, and with the same simplicity and trust he must come into the presence of the Heavenly Father. "I am abashed," he remarked, "that no matter how much I may be a doctor, I still have to go to school with Hans and Magdalene, for who among men can understand the full meaning of this word of our God, 'Our Father who art in heaven'? Anyone who really believes these words will be bound to say, 'He is the God who holds the heaven and the earth in His hands. Because He is my Father and I am His son, who can harm me? I am the lord of heaven and earth and all that is therein. The Angel Gabriel is my servant and Raphael is my watchman and the angels, in every need, my ministering spirits. My father who is in heaven has given them charge over me lest I dash my foot against a stone; and while I am affirming this, my God suffers me to be thrown into prison, to be drowned, or beheaded.' Then faith falters and in weakness I cry, 'Who knows whether it is true?' There is no harder word in Scripture than the word *Thy* in the petition, '*Thy* will be done.' "[27]

And therefore it is that *Doctor* Martin Luther must go to school with Hans and Magdalene.

[24] *TR* 2507b.
[25] *TR* 1631.
[26] *TR* 2531.
[27] *TR* 2047.

8. Luther's Life in Review

I. *A Critique of Heinrich Boehmer's* Road to Reformation

Heinrich Boehmer was a very accomplished Luther scholar and this work, though devoid of critical apparatus, rests upon his careful investigations and a full acquaintance with the work of others. He wrote vividly, nicely balancing concrete detail and the presentation of ideas, without impediment to movement and dramatic effect. A more readable account of Luther through the Wartburg period could scarcely be named. The translation is admirable, idiomatic, with no trace of the Germanic—a sheer delight.

The book is divided into two parts: the first from the beginnings up to the indulgence controversy; the second from the ninety-five theses through the exile at the Wartburg.

In the first part, the most crucial question is the nature of Luther's religious struggle. Boehmer asserts that one of the chief sources of distress was the problem of predestination of which Luther had been persuaded by the reading of Augustine's *City of God.* Whether Augustine was or need have been the source is questioned by Adolf Hamel, who says that until Luther had himself come into the clear, he interpreted Augustine in the sense of the *Moderni*; and that as far as predestination is concerned he did not need to understand Augustine because he could find the doctrine in Paul or in Biel.[1] Much more serious is the objection of Erich Vogelsang that predestination cannot have been the problem prior to the evangelical experience because Luther at that time had not abandoned belief in free will and did not commit himself to predestination until the lectures on Romans at the earliest in 1515.[2]

First published as a book review in *Church History*, XVI, 3 (September 1947). *Road to Reformation* was published by the Muhlenberg Press (Philadelphia, 1946).

[1] *Der junge Luther und Augustin* (2 vols., 1934-1935).
[2] "Der angefochtene Christus bei Luther," *Arbeiten zur Kirchengeschichte,* XXI (1932), 32f.

The whole subject has been thoroughly canvassed in an unpublished study by John von Rohr who concludes that, strictly speaking, Vogelsang is correct. Nevertheless, Boehmer has not missed the heart of the problem which was what man may expect of God. The doctrine of predestination holds that human destiny is already settled. Distress arises if one believes or fears the determination to have been adverse. There was another view of the matter, prevalent among the Occamists in whom Luther was steeped, a view if anything even more disconcerting, which holds that man's fate is not only not settled but is not even predictable, because God is wholly unconditioned and may not see fit to confer a reward even upon meritorious works. Predestination is comforting to those who believe themselves to be of the elect, but the view of God as altogether capricious is perfectly terrifying. Luther's essential problem, then, was not missed by Boehmer, even though the form may have been somewhat different. And perhaps Boehmer is entirely right, for need one assume with Vogelsang that concern over predestination could not arise until after a belief in free will as a factor in salvation had been completely abandoned? Sick souls seldom observe strict logic.

A very serious problem is to explain why Luther, after the resolution of his difficulties in the *Turmerlebnis,* should have continued to be troubled by spiritual depressions throughout his life. For such experiences Luther used the word *Anfechtung.* There is no exact English equivalent. One may say temptation, anxiety, distress, depression, horror, desperation. Why, if the light broke in 1513, did Luther continue to be assailed? Boehmer answers that the *Anfechtungen* of the later time are to be sharply distinguished from those of the former. The first disturbances were as to his faith, the second as to his profession. The later attacks were due "primarily to worry over his work, grief over the frivolity and moral shortcomings of the evangelical princes and lords, and disillusionment over the ingratitude and sensuality of the masses. At times it was also the thought which he calls the greatest and severest trial: 'You alone are the cause of this state of affairs' " (93). This sharp differentiation between the *Glaubensanfechtungen* of the early period and the *Berufsanfechtungen* of the later appears to me thoroughly unsound. Luther suffered from both varieties throughout his life. He was never free from struggles for faith. The insights which so comforted him in 1513 were not a solid deposit to which he could invariably refer. He was not suffered like Jacob to escape with only one wrestling with the angel and much of the vehemence of Luther's polemic arose from the struggle to convince himself. For documentation of these assertions consult pages 13 to 15 above and the following treatments:

Buehler, Paul Th., *Die Anfechtung bei Martin Luther* (Zürich, 1942).

Bornkamm, Heinrich, "Christus und das erste Gebot in der Anfechtung bei Luther," *Zeitschrift für systematische Theologie,* V (1928), 453-77.

Gerke, Friedrich, "Die satanische Anfechtung in der ars moriendi und bei Luther," *Theololgische Blätter,* XI (1932), 320-31.

——"Anfechtung und Sakrament in Martin Luthers Sermon vom Sterben," *Theololgische Blätter,* XIII (1934), 193-204.

Hasenzahl, Walter, "Die Gottverlassenheit des Christus," *Beiträge zur Förderung christlicher Theologie,* XXXIX, I (1937). Has a section on Luther's interpretation of Psalm 22, 2 throughout his entire life.

Jacob, Günther, "Der Gewissensbegriff in der Theologie Luthers." *Beiträge zur historischen Theologie,* IV (1929), especially the sections on *Tod und Gewissen* and *Satan und Gewissen.*

Stange, Carl, "Luthers Gedanken über die Todesfurcht," *Greifswalder Studien,* VII (1932).

Stomps, M. A. H., "Die Anthropologie Martin Luthers," *Philosophische Abhandlungen,* IV (1935), the section on *Angst.*

Wolf, Ernest, *Luther's Prädestinationsanfechtungen* (Diss. Rostock, 1925).

——"Staupitz und Luther," *Quellen und Forschungen zur Reformationsgeschichte,* IX (1927).

Boehmer then hints at another distinction. He suggests that the later *Anfechtungen* were physically conditioned, the earlier perhaps connected with a psychic defect. The whole question is here raised as to psychic abnormality in Luther and the possible correlation with physical deficiencies. The entire subject has never been satisfactorily handled. Recently an attempt has appeared in two volumes by a Danish psychiatrist, Paul J. Reiter.[3] The first, on

[3] *Martin Luthers Umwelt, Charakter und Psychose* (2 vols., Kopenhagen, 1937-1941).

the *Umwelt,* is useless. The second is not to be so readily dismissed. The conclusions, to be sure, do not commend themselves and the picture of Luther savors in spots all too much of Grisar. Nevertheless, the results of previous studies on Luther's physical ailments are gathered up and no little material assembled by way of direct citation from Luther as to the occurrences, frequency and character of his spiritual depressions. A discriminating investigator will find in this book much useful data.

On the question of the date of the *Turmerlebnis,* there is a careful survey on the progress of opinion by Hermann Wendorf,[4] who recommends exceeding caution because of the difficulty of dating the various portions of the manuscripts of the lectures on the Psalms. On the whole he thinks there is very much to be said in favor of Boehmer's view.

The second part of Boehmer's work deals with the indulgence controversy and the prosecution up through the exile at the Wartburg. With a masterly hand Boehmer threads his way through the intricate connections. The picture of Luther is essentially sound, but I am not satisfied with the treatment accorded Frederick the Wise, Erasmus and Hutten in their relations to Luther.

With regard to Frederick, Boehmer says: "If Spalatin had not continued to encourage him and if his other advisers . . . had not been 'good Lutherers,' Elector Frederick would probably have dropped the 'Herr Doctor,' who was so difficult to manage, at the first opportunity which presented itself" (158). There is no telling, of course, what Frederick would have done without such encouragement. He certainly cannot be turned into Frederick the Confessor after the manner of Kalkoff, but neither was he quite so pusillanimous as Boehmer's judgment implies. Frederick had a deep sense of his obligation to act as a Christian prince and to secure justice for his subjects. He was resolved that Luther should not be condemned without a fair hearing. What constituted a fair hearing was his problem and the major source of his hesitations. On two occasions he was deeply troubled to know whether Luther

---

[4] "Der Durchbruch der neuen Erkenntnis Luthers im Lichte der handschriftlichen Überlieferung," *Historische Vierteljahrschrift,* XXVII (1932), 124-144, 285-327.

had not been fairly heard and properly condemned. The first was after Luther's interview with Cajetan, the second was after the examination at Worms. A few crucial facts with regard to Frederick's relations to Luther are overlooked by Boehmer and deserve to be recorded.

When the prospect of a citation to Rome first confronted Luther, he wrote: "Our prince, *quite unsolicited* has undertaken that under no circumstances I be taken to Rome."[5] Frederick arranged the interview with Cajetan at Leipzig. After it was over, he was not only under pressure, but also in a quandary to know whether the condition of a fair hearing had been met. He was even more dubious at this point than appears from Boehmer's account, because of the misdating of the letter from Staupitz at Salzburg tendering to Luther an invitation to join him and adding, "The prince is in accord." Boehmer, following the Enders edition, dated this letter on September 14, and identified the prince with Archbishop Matthew Lang; but the Weimar edition pointed out that Lang would never have tolerated Luther in his domains. The letter is to be dated in the first half of December 1518, and the prince is Frederick the Wise[6], who was indeed so ready to have Luther in exile that on December 1 the journey to France or to the open sky would have been commenced, had not word come from the Elector to stay.[7] Precisely what had happened to occasion this change of front we shall never know. Luther declared years afterwards that the prince had already in mind a plan to hide him,[8] but a few weeks after the event Luther wrote, "At first the prince would have been willing not to have me here."[9] Two years later Frederick declared that he would have accepted Luther's offer to leave had not word come from the papal nuncio that Luther would be less dangerous under surveillance than at large.[10] At any rate, on December 18, Frederick announced a firm stand. He would neither send Luther to Rome, nor banish him, unless he were convicted of heresy.[11]

[5] *BR* 64. Italics mine.
[6] *BR* 119.
[7] *BR* 116.
[8] *TR* 1203.
[9] *BR* 121.
[10] Walch ed., Vol. XV, 437, p. 1403.
[11] *BR* 250.

So matters stood throughout the period of the Leipzig debate and until after the election and coronation of the new Emperor, Charles V. Frederick met him in Cologne on November 4, 1519, and there secured the promise that Luther would not be condemned without a hearing *(nisi auditus)*. This is a very important point, quite overlooked by Boehmer. It was not a promise that Luther might come to Worms, let alone that he would be heard in the presence of the Diet. It was simply the assurance that he would be heard. From that the rest developed. Our authority for this statement is Erasmus, who was in Cologne at the time.[12]

After the public hearing at Worms, on April 18, 1521, Frederick was again in doubt. Spalatin said that the prince was very much troubled to know whether Luther had or had not been convicted from the Scriptures *(Annales,* 30ff.). On the day after the hearing, Aleander heard the report that all six of the electors were ready to pronounce Luther a heretic.[13] That would, of course, include Frederick the Wise; but when on the following day the electors presented their report to the Emperor, declaring themselves in accord with the prosecution of Luther as a notorious heretic, of the six only four signed. Among the dissenters was Frederick the Wise.[14] From that point forward, there is no need to demonstrate that the Elector hid Luther at the Wartburg and later afforded him protection in Wittenberg against the Emperor, the Diet of Nürnberg, Duke George and the devil.

One point in connection with the promise extracted from the Emperor at Cologne has been not a little discussed, but is passed over completely by Boehmer; and that is the legal ground on which Frederick based his plea for a hearing for Luther. Some have assumed that he took his stand on articles 17 and 24 of the imperial constitution to which Charles had to subscribe as a condition of his election. The former article provided that no German subject of whatever rank should be taken for trial outside of Germany. The second declared that "no one of high estate or low, elector, prince or any other should be outlawed without cause and

[12] *Ep.* No. 1166, ed. Allen, p. 399.
[13] *DRA* II, 867.
[14] *Ibid.,* 596, note 3.

without a hearing (*on Ursach auch unverhört*)."[15] The assumption
has been made that Frederick himself was responsible for the insertion of these clauses in the constitution in order to provide protection for Luther. The objection to this view is that the object of
the legislation was to protect the German princes from outlawry
for failure to meet the financial demands of the Church and in no
sense to immunize a mere monk from the penalties for notorious
heresy. The most decisive point is that neither Frederick nor Luther in any extant document ever made appeal to these clauses of
the constitution. The most that can be said is that Frederick harped
on the word *unverhört*.

The trend of scholarly opinion has been to dissociate the
Emperor's promise to Frederick at Cologne from any obligation
under these articles. The following notes on the progress of opinion may be of interest:

Paul Kalkoff applied the articles to Luther: *ZKG,* XXV (1904), 545.

Hans von Schubert thought Frederick might have been responsible
for the insertion of article 24. *Reich und Reformation* (1910), 12-14.

Kalkoff held that the Emperor would not feel that the clause covered Luther's case. *Wormser Reichstag* (1922), 179-80.

Elizabeth Wagner severely combatted the view that the articles
would be held to afford Luther protection. *ZKG,* XLII (1923), especially
341-2, 347.

Von Schubert felt that the Emperor's consultation of the estates
rested on article 24. But that is a different point from the promise at
Cologne. *Lazarus Spengler* (posthumous, ed. Hajo Holborn, 1934), 286.

Kalkoff, "Dass der Kurfürst dabei [art. 17 and 24] auch an Luthers
Schicksal gedacht hat, lässt sich natürlich nicht beweisen, aber noch weni-
ger bestreiten," *ZKG,* XLIII (1924), 185.

Paul Kirn excludes articles 17 to 24 as affording protection to
Luther. *Friederich der Weise* (1926), 138.

The relations of Hutten and Luther are given scant attention
by Boehmer. At this point he appears to be still under the influence of Kalkoff, who vigorously discounted the connection. A study
of Hajo Holborn's *Ulrich von Hutten* (English, 1937), would have
served at this point as a wholesome corrective. The contention, of
course, is sound that in actual practice Luther repudiated Hutten's

[15] *Ibid.,* I, 871, 873.

program of violence. Yet one cannot well deny that in the summer of 1520 Luther's utterances at times had an incendiary ring reminiscent of Hutten. Take the famous passage in which Luther said: "It seems to me that if the Romanists are so mad, the only remedy remaining is for the emperor, the kings and princes to gird themselves with force of arms and attack these pests of all the world and fight them not with words but with steel. If we punish thieves with the yoke, highwaymen with the sword and heretics with fire why do we not rather assault these monsters of perdition, these cardinals, these popes and the whole swarm of the Roman Sodom, who corrupt youth and the Church of God? Why do we not rather assault them with arms and wash our hands in their blood?"[16] When taxed with this passage, Luther afterwards explained that the stress was on the *if*—"*If* we burn heretics, etc."[17] Boehmer prints the passage with the "ifs" in italics in the first place, but if the passage be read as it originally stood, one can understand why the curialists so harped upon it and why a reference to it was inserted in the Edict of Worms among the counts on which Luther was condemned.

With regard to Erasmus, Boehmer says that on the appearance of Luther's *Babylonian Captivity*, Erasmus was "moved to believe that there was no longer any prospect of reconciling Rome and Wittenberg" (325). That is correct. Erasmus said that this work had made the breach irreparable.[18] Boehmer adds that Erasmus was thoroughly disillusioned and alienated from Luther. Similarly after the burning of the bull and the canon law, Erasmus "now considered the breach between Rome and Wittenberg irreparable and abandoned the tumultuous monk forever" (375). The first half of these statements is correct, but not the second. Erasmus saw no hope, but kept on trying. Even after he had commenced the *De Servo Arbitrio* as a reply to Luther, Erasmus inserted in the *Familiar Colloquies* the *Inquisitio Fidei*, which was a plea for tolerance for Lutherans. A study on this subject has appeared from the pen of Craig Thompson.[19] And Erasmus continued to support Luther

---

[16] *WA* VI, p. 347.

[17] *Ibid.*, VII, pp. 645-646.

[18] *Ep.* No. 1203, May 14, 1521.

[19] Craig Thompson, "Inquisitio de Fide," *Yale Studies in Religion*, XV (1950).

covertly by attacks on Rome, even after the public rupture. The
peak of the anti-clerical, anti-monastic utterances in the *Familiar
Colloquies* was not reached until February, 1526.[20]

The treatment of Cajetan by Boehmer is fortunately not in
the vein of Hutten, who painted him as a rascal. Kalkoff in this
instance had done good work in rehabilitating Cajetan as an upright churchman. But Boehmer does follow Luther's judgment
who said that Cajetan was no more fitted to handle his case than an
ass to play on a harp. As a matter of fact, Cajetan was shrewd and
Luther blustered so much because he was trapped. Cajetan confronted him with the bull of Clement VI, *Unigenitus,* and claimed
that it contains the doctrine of the treasury of the merits of Christ,
the Blessed Virgin and the saints which, through the power of the
keys conferred upon Saint Peter and his successors, can be utilized
to release souls from purgatory.[21] That is what it says, but Luther
tried to escape its plain meaning by the quibble that in the text the
merits of Christ are not declared *to be* a treasure. The statement is
made only that by his merits Christ *acquired* a treasure.[22] Luther
was cornered, because if he admitted the construction which Cajetan very properly placed upon the words, either Luther must renounce his own position or else he must repudiate the decretal of
the Pope and impugn also the canon law in which it was incorporated. For so radical a step Luther was not yet ready. But on the
following day, Luther took the step. Cajetan had scored. Surely
this was not the work of an incompetent.[23]

A few minor matters in Boehmer's treatment call for correction. The description of what took place in the meetings of the consistory at Rome when the Lutheran case was considered is much
more detailed than the facts warrant. Boehmer at this point relied
uncritically on Kalkoff who had reconstructed the scene in a tissue
of fact and conjecture.[24] Boehmer states that the cardinals, in the
sessions of May 21, 23 and 25, 1520, were unanimous in endorsing

[20] Preserved Smith," A Key to the Colloquies of Erasmus," *Harvard Theological Studies,* XIII (1927), 39.

[21] Walther Kochler, *Dokumente zum Ablasstreit* (1934), No. 10.

[22] *BR* 99.

[23] *BR* 99-110.

[24] "Zu Luthers römischen Prozess," ZKG., XXV (1904), especially 110ff.

the condemnations already pronounced by the universities of Louvain and Cologne against forty-four articles extracted from Luther's works. "The remaining sections of the Bull, composed by the jurist Accolti, were also for the most part allowed to pass without adverse comment. Only against the statement that the appeal to a general council was the rankest piece of heresy which Luther had committed was any objection raised by any of the cardinals. This opposition came from the aged Spaniard, Bernardino Carvajal, though it was merely a *pro forma* objection. The only points on which the discussion appears to have spun itself out to any length were the questions whether all the heretic's writings should be condemned to the flames, or only those in which one or another of the forty-four condemned articles appeared; also whether, as Cajetan especially recommended, the exact degree of reprehensibility should be indicated in the case of each article; and, lastly, whether the heretic should once more be formally admonished to recant, as Accolti recommended, or, as Pucci proposed, be formally and immediately anathematized. But nothing of any consequence resulted from the discussion" (350-51).

This statement affirms both too little and too much. There was a debate in the consistory as to whether Luther should be condemned outright, as the theologians desired, or given an opportunity to defend himself, as the jurists demanded, pointing out that although God knew Adam to be guilty, He said, "Adam, where art thou?," thus giving him an occasion for defense. The source of this statement is Sarpi.[25] Sanuto said that some feared the issue of a bull enumerating Luther's errors would serve only to increase the scandal in Germany.[26] But who said what, we are by no means in a position to say. That Accolti voiced the demand for a trial is altogether probable. He was a jurist and he is credited with having said of Tetzel, "*O ribaldo! O porcaccio!*," and to have given *uno bono rabbuffo* to Prierias.[27] We do not know a thing about what Pucci said, only that he completely endorsed the bull of excommunica-

[25] Aloys Schulte, "Die römischen Verhandlungen über Luther," *Quellen und Forschungen aus italienischen Archiven und Bibliotheken* (1904), 32-52.

[26] *Martin Luther und die Reformationsbewegung in Deutschland . . . aus Sanutos Diarien* (1863), 3.

[27] *BR* 122.

tion after it had been adopted.[28] The outcome was a compromise,
according to which Luther should neither be condemned outright
nor given a hearing, but should be given sixty days in which to
make his submission.[29]

Then there were discussions among the theologians. Eck said
that he had a debate with Egidio of Viterbo over Luther's doctrine
of baptism and original sin.[30] Boehmer's affirmation that there was
opposition to the condemnation of conciliarism and that the chief
dissenter was Carvajal, is more than we know. The author of the
Acta Academiae Lovaniensis, presumably Erasmus, charged: *Con-
stat Romae rem actam sine ordine, vehementer obsistente Card. S.
Crucis* [Carvajal] *et aliis multis.*[31] But there is no statement here
that conciliarism was the point at issue. That is merely a plausible
conjecture, resting on the fact that Carvajal had been a conciliarist
under Julius II.

We do not know that Cajetan recommended indicating the
exact degree of the reprehensibility in the case of each article.
What we do know is that on another occasion Cajetan warned
against indiscriminate condemnation.[32]

Perhaps all this may appear to be quibbling, because the
whole reconstruction is plausible, but when the narrative leaps
from fact to conjecture, would it not be well to give the reader
some inkling of the change?

Boehmer states, quite without qualification, that Rome, in
order to secure the adherence of Frederick the Wise to the papal
candidate for the Empire, was willing to confer upon Luther a
cardinal's hat (58). Kalkoff had blithely made this assumption,[33]
and Boehmer probably drew from him. The case is by no means so
clear. What was said to Frederick by Orsini, the papal representative, was this: "If the King of France is elected, his Excellency

[28] Balan, *Monumenta,* No. 40.
[29] Clearly brought out by Karl Müller, *ZKG,* XXIV (1903), especially
80-81.
[30] Kalkoff, *ZKG,* XXV, 116.
[31] Wallace Ferguson, *Erasmi Opuscula* (1933), p. 322; 1; 55-56.
[32] Horawitz und Hartfelder, *Briefwechsel Beatus Rhenanus* (1886), 166.
[33] *Luther und die Entscheidungsjahre der Reformation* (1917), 111ff.

[Frederick] may make one of his friends a cardinal."[34] Frederick took this to mean that he might name Luther, and evidently passed on the word, because Luther declared that he did not wish a cardinal's hat.[35] But when the Archbishop of Trier asked Aleander whether it was so, he branded the rumor as a downright lie.[36] Among modern scholars, Strack found himself unable to credit the curia with such an *Ungeheurlichkeit*.[37]

At the Leipzig debate, according to Boehmer, "Luther brought with him a small bouquet of pinks and, when his opponent began to thunder, smelled them with gusto" (285). Luther repudiated this story as a slander.[38]

Boehmer has misread the letter of Scheurl to Luther reporting on the statements of Miltitz, who did not affirm that the *pope* said of Tetzel *"O porcaccio!"* nor that the *Pope* gave *uno bono rabbuffo* to Prierias. This is all ascribed to Cardinal Accolti, who made the former remark *to the pope (Pontifici declarasse)*.[39]

The translators have made a slip on p. 236. For "Gerondist" read "Gersonist."

None of these comments is meant to detract from the reputation of a splendid book. Research is not stagnant and none was readier in his day to revise his own work than Boehmer.

II. *A Critique of Erik H. Erikson's* Young Man Luther

Professor Langer, in his recent presidential address before the American Historical Association, affirmed that the next dimension of history to be explored is that of psychological depth and that psychiatry should be applied to the understanding of the movements and the men of the past. The claim is valid that what-

First published as a book review in the *Yale Review* (Spring 1959). *Young Man Luther* was published by W. W. Norton & Co. (1958).

[34] *DRA* I, 824.
[35] *BR* 309, 135.
[36] *Aleander und Luther*, ed. Brieger (1884), 40.
[37] "Luthers grosses Selbstzeugnis" (*SVRG*, CXL, 1926), 64 note 1.
[38] *BR* 205.
[39] *BR* 122.

ever casts light upon the present should be thrown upon the past. Yet one must recognize that the task is one of extreme difficulty because the dead cannot be summoned for examination. Luther is a very intriguing person from this point of view, and has already attracted the attention of psychiatrists because he was a genius subject to intense emotional upheavals. The task essayed before is here essayed again by Erik Erikson, who is much better equipped than any before him to undertake it. He is a trained psychiatrist with clinical experience. He is acquainted by reading with the inner history of men who may be compared with Luther in stature, such as Darwin, Freud and Shaw. Erikson is not narrowly addicted to his own discipline and recognizes the soundness within limits of several approaches. The social status of Luther's father as a miner rather than a farmer is duly appraised. The emotional environment is not overlooked and attention is paid to the preoccupation of Luther's age with the cult of death. The author recognizes the possibility of metaphysical maladjustment and perceives that in such a case the struggle must take place in the realm of philosophy and theology. In Luther's case he gives accounts of the importance of Aristotelianism, Augustinianism and Occamism, and he sees that the resolution of the personal difficulty must then issue in a new theology. In Luther's case the outcome was a piety focused on the inward appropriation of the Passion of Christ. This work, then, calls attention to possible ways of understanding Luther which deserve to be considered.

Yet I find myself unable to subscribe to the conclusions. The difficulty is not primarily that the author's preoccupation with the earlier Luther and his relative unacquaintance with the later Luther lead him to misinterpret the earlier; the difficulty again is not primarily that his methods, candidly avowed, of arriving at the facts about the young Luther appear to me highly dubious. The central objection is to the presuppositions which he brings to bear upon the interpretation of the facts.

Luther's theological development is portrayed in terms of his struggle to achieve independence of his parents that he might be a person in his own right. His theology was sometimes a projection of this struggle upon the cosmos, sometimes a rationalization and sometimes a device for solving a personal problem.

Take the view of God. Luther is held to have created God in the image of his father, a choleric, impulsive, irascible *pater familias,* who looked upon himself as "the very conception of justice." One trouble with this assumption is that Luther did not need to create such a God for He had already been created by the scholastic theologians. Some of them, the Scotists, taught that God was absolute will—which meant sheer caprice—and that He would finally save or damn men not in accord with their merit but according to His whim. The predestinarians claimed, however, that God had long since made the decision with regard to every individual human destiny and again without any regard to merit. Luther testified that this theology drove him to the very abyss of desperation.

Next we are told that Luther had to surrender to his God in order to get out from under his father. Luther was "weighed down by an overweening superego, which would give him the leeway of a sense of identity only in the obedient employment of his superior gifts . . . and only as long as he was more follower than leader." In other words he wanted to be independent, yet he had to follow somebody. That somebody was God. The entry into the monastery was an emancipation from obedience to the father by substitution of obedience to God. The period in the monastery served also as a moratorium in which Luther was able to pull himself together before his emergence "with a sense of identity."

But then we are told that "the conversion was necessary so that Martin could give all his power of obedience to God, and turn all his venom of defiance against the pope." Why was it necessary to rebel also against the pope in order to gain the sense of identity? And incidentally why would not obedience to the pope have sufficed for emancipation from obedience to the father? We are actually being given the picture of such a congenital, overweening egoist that he must overthrow every obedience on earth in order to be a person, which is no new insight but is precisely what was said by Aleander when he composed against Luther the Edict of Worms.

If this was the motivation one wonders why the emancipation did not occasion relief instead of the most intense suffering. Luther said that no one knows how hard it is to stand alone against the judgment of all the churches and of one's most noble and respected friends. Luther compared himself to Noah suffering the jeers of all his neighbors for building an ark at a place remote from the sea coast. How much harder, said Luther, it must have been for Noah because he lived so many hundreds of years and must have had to endure the mockery of the godless even before he started the ark. "Had I been he I would have given up my ministry in desperation." Erikson would probably be unconvinced by this rejoinder. He himself insists that Luther's breach with his father was fraught with sadness.

But then take another point. Can one say that Luther was struggling simply for the satisfaction of his ego by taking a course which bade fair to end in speedy martyrdom? When he attacked indulgences his opponents predicted that he would be burned in two weeks. And he thought they were right. And they would have been right had it not been for the chicanery of papal politics and the peculiar involvement of the Church with the empire. But this rejoinder probably will not satisfy because Erikson tells us that Luther "somehow stood in need of martyrdom." And if the pope and the emperor would not confer it upon him, then he must be martyred by the devil. But how now does this picture comport with the one given earlier of the man with the overweening superego seeking to employ his superior gifts? Did he suppose that they could be exercised only in heaven?

One wonders whether the author is saying that at bottom every man is knave, and all his rebellions, all the risks he runs, and all the sufferings he endures are designed only to satisfy his ego? Perhaps Luther would have agreed, for he insisted that in the eyes of God no human act or motive is clean. But Luther never would have denied a distinction between a prince massacring defeated peasants and the first Protestant martyr in the Netherlands dying at the stake. To do so would be to take all meaning out of the concept of nobility. One wishes that the author would come to grips with this question. He has great respect for candor, which is an aspect of nobility. Yet he makes one feel that in Luther there was pathos but hardly heroism.

Another point to be observed is that Luther in the monastery, when he is assumed to have been gathering his forces in order to emerge "with a sense of identity," actually conceived of the Christian goal, not as self-fulfilment and self-realization, but as humility and humiliation. Erikson might reply that this only proves the point and that Luther made humility an ideal precisely because he was not humble. But to this one may say that Luther no more created the theology of humility than the picture of the angry God. The theology of humility was the theology of his confessor, Staupitz. And one who would understand Luther's early development must understand not only Aristotle, Augustine and Occam but also Staupitz.

We are given to understand that the repressions of Luther's youth affected his mature behavior. Because he was caned as a child for speaking German, he was later torrential in speaking German. Here we must recall that he was caned for speaking German only in school where he was required to speak Latin. Now, if in consequence he became all the more attached to German, one would suppose by the same token that he would have become very averse to Latin. But as a matter of fact in later life he was just as torrential in Latin as in German.

We are informed that Luther's hatred for his mother caused him to dethrone the Virgin Mary. But however he felt toward his mother, he did not dethrone the Virgin Mary. His sermons on the Nativity come today as a shock to modern Lutherans because of their reverence for the Virgin Mary.

At the end of the book we seem to have gotten away from the interpretation of theology in terms simply of personal adjustment because Luther's piety is seen to center upon an inward appropriation of the Passion of Christ. Yet the stress is on inwardness, and the inwardness again arises from the need for inward peace. But Luther never made inward peace the goal of religion. This consisted rather in the attainment and acceptance of objective truth. Of course the Crucifixion, said he, is nothing for me unless it is repeated in me. But it first took place in time, in history and it was an act of God to take away the sins of the world. Luther would have nothing of the theology of Sebastian Franck, who made the Crucifixion and indeed the whole life of Christ only an allegory of the inner experiences of the soul. For him the Nativity was simply the birth of Christ's spirit in me and all men. Such an inwardizing of religion was thoroughly alien to Luther, who on this point conducted a struggle with the radicals in his own camp with a passion and pain exceeding that of his controversy with Rome.

Apropos of these controversies one may note the author's statement that "in later life Luther displayed an extraordinary ability to hate quickly and persistently, justifiably or unjustifiably, with pungent dignity and utter vulgarity." This is simply not so. Not that Luther was not vulgar and vitriolic, but he was never vindictive. He was fighting error not men, and whenever he saw the least disposition on the part of an opponent to embrace what Luther deemed to be the truth, immediately the polemic was dropped. Under such circumstances Luther wrote most conciliatory letters to Henry VIII and Duke George. When Tetzel, the opponent in the indulgence controversy, was disgraced by his own church Luther sent him a note of sympathy. And when Carlstadt, who had been banished from Saxony at Luther's instigation on theological grounds, came as a refugee from the Peasants' War to Wittenberg, Luther took him as a guest into his own house.

The difficulty of psychoanalyzing the young Luther is almost insurmountable because of the sparsity of the evidence. What we know of the young Luther comes very largely from the old Luther at an interval of thirty years and then only at second hand in the table jottings of inaccurate student note-takers. Nevertheless, Erikson believes that we should take what we have and use legends and half-legends. "We are thus obliged to accept half legend as half history provided only that a reported episode does not contradict other well established facts; persists in having the ring of truth; and yields a meaning consistent with psychological theory." But how shall one determine what has the ring of truth? And should not consistency be demanded, not only with psychological theory, but also with everything that is definitely known about the man?

Erikson is ready to work not only with secondhand reminiscences of the old Luther but also with secondhand and equally late reminiscences of his detractors. Cochlaeus, his Catholic critic, writing in 1549, three years after Luther's death, recorded that when in the monastery Luther had once raved like one possessed and roared with the voice of a bull, "It's not me," referring to the demoniac cured by Christ. Now the story of itself is not incredible. Luther believed in the possibility of demoniacal possession and in a fit of depression may have been fighting against the suspicion that he himself was possessed. But one would be on sounder ground to appeal to Luther's indisputable sayings on the devil and to his indisputable depressions.

Yet although I dissent from so much in the methodology and more particularly the presuppositions of this book, for it seems to me that Luther's theological development might have been just the same if he had been left an orphan in infancy, at the same time there is much here of sound sense, notably in the treatment of Luther's view of sex and his use of scatology. And the view taken of Luther's attitude in the Peasants' War is thoroughly fair and sound.

III. Problems in Luther Biography

The greatest problem in writing a biography of Luther arises from the abundance of the material. The point is highlighted by a comparison with the life of the Apostle Paul. In his case a phrase must be inflated into a chapter, but when it comes to Luther a volume must be reduced to a paragraph. Something depends of course on the length of the biography. If one goes into detail after the manner of Scheel, who devoted nearly a thousand pages to Luther's pre-reformatory career, the total treatment might well exceed a dozen volumes. If the biography is kept within the compass of even a hefty single tome, the task becomes an exercise in omission and condensation.

Of all the inevitable omissions none is more regrettable than the exclusion of the reasons for judgments as to what Luther said or did. There are few points in his career devoid of pros or cons. The biographer can do no more than weigh the evidence, make up his mind, and arbitrarily announce his conclusion. The critical reader is left unsatisfied, and reviewers may level accusations of ignorance.

This paper was given as an address at the International Congress for Luther Research, meeting at Aarhus, Denmark, August 18-23, 1956. A German translation was published in *Lutherforschung Heute*, ed. Vilmos Vajta (Berlin, 1958). This is the first publication in English.

I venture to mention an instance in which this has happened to me because the point is itself of intrinsic importance. I had made the statement that Luther was actually placed under the ban of the empire before he was under the ban of the Church. Both an American and a German reviewer branded this assertion simply as error.[1] The American pointed out that the bull *Exsurge* gave Luther sixty days in which to recant. If he refused to comply at the expiration of the terminus he would be automatically under excommunication. For good measure, however, the pope composed the bull *Decet Romanum* on January 3, announcing that Luther was under excommunication. "The result of these bulls," said the American reviewer, "seems clear."

To contemporaries it did not seem clear. The bull *Exsurge* certainly said that if Luther did not submit at the end of the sixty days he would be excommunicated, but it did not say when the sentence would go automatically into effect, for who was to say when the sixty days had expired? The timeclock did not start ticking on the day when the bull was signed, but on the day when it was actually delivered to the person named. This, in Luther's case, had not taken place until October 10. His burning of the bull on December 10 was thus timed to coincide with the last day of grace according to his own reckoning. The general public, however, would not have been aware of the sequence. The bull *Decet Romanum* was not "added for good measure," but to announce that the terminus had been exceeded and that the penalty would now go into effect.[2]

But when in point of fact did this bull actually take effect? It was dated January 3 and was addressed to all the prelates and monks, divers and sundry, calling on them within three days after the receipt of the bull to execute it by the ringing of bells and the flinging of lighted tapers to the ground. The bull, then, had to be published before the penalty could go into operation. Nor did it suffice that the pope on January 18 informed the emperor that Lu-

---

[1] Sellery, in *The American Historical Review*, LVIII, 3 (January 1953). p. 345. Schottenloher, *ARG* XLVI, I (1955), p. 124.

[2] Section 3, German translation in the St. Louis edition of Luther's Works, XV, pp. 1704 f.

ther was under the ban of the Church.[3] He was not actually excommunicated until the clergy were notified to refuse him communion.

The publication of the bull was entrusted to Aleander, the papal representative at the Diet of Worms. On February 8 he wrote to Rome requesting that he be sent fifty copies of the bull against Luther in order that he might present it to the bishops and prelates.[4] On February 12 he wrote that he had received a copy and that he found in it many errors "inimical to our cause." These errors were not at the time specified, but we learn later in his correspondence that the chief offense lay in the inclusion of other names along with Luther's and, in particular, that of Ulrich von Hutten. Now at that very moment, Hutten was curdling the blood of Aleander with threats of violence. For that reason the bull was withheld from publication and sent back to Rome for a new version in which the name of Hutten should be expunged.

On April 5, Aleander wrote to Rome: "Highly needful is a bull in every respect like the preceding [*Decet Romanum*] but there is no need to mention anyone save Luther, making no reference to Hutten nor to the rest [Pirckheimer and Spengler], because there are some here who murmur that *they do not know whether Luther after the expiration of his period of grace has actually been declared a heretic, and they make this an excuse for favoring him.* Besides, this is not an expedient time for the publication of the former bull, since Hutten and all the German nobles will murder me even though I be in the bosom of the emperor. To be sure Hutten does not care a fig for excommunication on his soul's account, but because of the ignomy he would do something mad. Therefore, I beg you most immediately to send the requested bull that I may publish it at the Diet and the populace may thereby be terrified. I fully intend to publish this bull and the one against Hutten, and to print it after I am safely out of Germany, but God forbid that it should come out while we are at Worms, for it will do our cause no good, and cost us all our lives." (Italics mine.)

Again on April 29, Aleander wrote to Rome: "Please hurry the bull against Luther declaring him to be a contumacious here-

---

[3] Petrus Balan, *Monumenta Reformationis Lutheranae* (1884), Nr. 13.
[4] Theodor Brieger, *Aleander und Luther* (Gotha, 1888), p. 48.

tic, making no mention of Hutten nor the others save Luther. The bull already sent [*Decet Romanum*] would have been most excellent if the others had not been named. This bull is then to be revised and sent to me as speedily as possible, because the official of Trier tells me that some of the princes, no doubt at the instance of one of the Lutherans, *are commencing to say that the emperor should not issue a mandate against Luther before the pope has made such a declaration.*" (Italics mine.)

The letter concludes: "Finally I repeat that you send the bull against Luther printed immediately and disseminated everywhere. Give it the same date as the previous one, January 3d, and for the love of God, do it as quickly as possible, naming only Luther and his adherents in general. The other bull [*Decet Romanum*] I will publish when I leave Germany."

On May 8 he reported to Rome the arrival of the bull as follows: "The bull has come, naming only Luther and his adherents in general, yet I wish it had come earlier."

Yet even then Aleander did not publish the bull. He explained why in a letter of May 18: "Albert of Mainz objects to having the bull published because it names him as one of those commissioned to execute it. He says that he would be in a most invidious position if he alone of the German clergy were singled out for this role."

Not until October 1521 did Aleander inform a friend that he had actually published both bulls.[5]

---

[5] The above citations are translated from the following passages in Brieger: pp. 129-130, April 5, "Besogna necessariamente se facci una Bulla della condemnatione post lapsum termini in prima Bulla contenti, et in omnibus farla come sta quella, la quale ci fù mandata alli dì passati, ma non besogna nominar altri che Martin Luther, non facendo mention de Hutten, nè de altri. Poichè qui questoro mormorano, che non si sa, che Martino sii sta dichiarato post termini lapsum, et trovano excusatione per poter favoreggiarlo; et non è per niente tempo di publicar questa già mandata, perchè ne venirebbe ad ammazzarse etiam in gremio Cesaris, non solo Hutten, ma tutti questi nobili, perchè, ancorchè lui non facci stima de excommunicationi quantum ad animam, tamen per la infamia del mundo farebbe cose da pazzi. Però supplico che presto et omnino si mandi tal Bulla che demando, acciochè la si publichi in Dieta et il popolo habbi più terrore. Io ho ben determinato, nel partir di Germania far publicar questa Bulla et contra Hutten, et me ritirar al securo et farla imprimer; ma de farla mentre che qui stiama, non volii Dio, perchè non

One will observe from the above passages that contemporaries believed Luther not to be under the ban of the Church prior to the formal publication of the bull.

The point may appear to be of little import, but the consequences of Aleander's delay were far reaching. Because of his failure to produce the bull, he found himself driven to the most distasteful expedient of treating a diet consisting largely of laymen as a tribunal in cases of heresy. Instead of announcing simply that Luther, in accord with the pronouncement of the Holy Father, was a heretic and therefore to be placed under the ban of the empire, Aleander undertook to demonstrate Luther's heresy by copious citations from his writing and in so doing treated the diet as if it were a council of the Church. This is the reason why Hefele in his *History of the Councils,* between the Fifth Lateran, which ended in 1518 and the Council of Regensburg in 1541, included in his work accounts of the German diets.

The biographer the more regrets his inability to discuss moot points because so many points are moot and for so many reasons.

---

giovarebbe alla causa et privarebbe tutti noi della vita." Pp. 168-169, April 29, "... et li supplico si degni far, che più presto si pote si habii la Bulla, nella qual è dichiarato Luther del tutto heretico et contumace post elapsum terminum, senza far mention nè de Hutten, nè de altri che de Luther; questa, che fù mandata ultima, sarebbe bonissima, se no fussero nominati altri; per ho se pol subito reformar et mandarla, perchè l'official de Trever mi ha detto, che alcuno di questi Principi ad suggestionem utique alicuius causidici Lutherani, già comincia a dire, che Cesar non ha da far alcuno mandato contra Luther, finchè non costi, che Nostro Signore l'habii dichiarato come de sopra...." P. 175, "Repeto postremo, che se manda questa Bulla contra Luther, et sarebbe bono farla subito imprimer et spargerla per tutto. Si facci de data dell'altra: tertio nonas Januarii. Et per l'amor di Dio, che la se spacci per el più presto, nominando solum Luther et suoi adherenti in genere; quest'altra poi nel mio partir di Germania la publicarò." Pp. 191-192, May 8, "Poi scritta et chiusa l'altra mia sono arivate le di V.S. Rma et la Bulla, dove è solo nominato Luther et in genere li fautori, la qual veniva ben a proposito, atque utinam fusse stata mandata alquanto più presto, perchè l'harei publicata et quì et a Maguntia, como rechiede detta Bulla, et de essa ne haressemo fatta mention nelli mandati, quod nunc non potest fieri..." P. 217, May 18, "El Rmo et Illmo Moguntino non vole sentir parlar, che se divulghi de questa Bulla, dove è nominato Sua Signoria, il Nuncio, Messer Eccio et io de poter procedere contra li Lutherani et absolver li penitenti cum potestate substituendi, non già perchè lui Luthero faveat, ma perchè dice essergli per concitar immenso odio appresso tutti li Germani, se lui solo de Prelati Alemani è nominato in tal impresa."

The clarification of these points entails an application of the principles of historical criticism. First of all, obviously, we must have a correct text, which the Weimar editors are laboring valiantly to supply. Then we must have a text properly edited with all of the citations identified. Professor Rueckert has invited us to call attention to any deficiencies in the present edition. I have one case for which I have found the answer and one for which I have not.

The first is a correct citation on Luther's part which has commonly been incorrectly understood by the editors. Luther was fond of quoting a saying by Panormitanus that the word of a single private person is to be preferred to that of a pope if based on superior authorities from the Old and New Testaments. Luther cited this passage in his reply to Prierias,[6] in the interview with Cajetan,[7] again at the Leipzig debate,[8] and in the ensuing controversy with Eck.[9] Sometimes Luther gave neither the author nor the source, sometimes both, and sometimes only the source, namely the incipit *Significasti*. Modern editors have therefore assumed that the reference was to the Decretals of Gregory II, lib. i, tit. 6, c. 4 beginning *Significasti*. This passage is not, however, by Panormitanus, but is a letter of Pope Pascal II to Panormitanus telling him that to receive the pallium he must swear allegiance to the pope, without whose confirmation even the decrees of councils are invalid. The point is thus the very reverse of Luther's citation. Yet Luther's reference was correct. He was quoting another Panormitanus. This name means simply "from Palermo." Pope Pascal was writing to an archbishop of Palermo in the early twelfth century. Luther was citing another archbishop of Palermo in the early fourteenth century, and the name of this Panormitanus was Nicolo de Tudeschi. He attended the Council of Basel and was the author of a compendious commentary on the canon law, which inevitably follows the rubrics of the original text. Under the heading *De Electione, Significasti*, this Panormitanus takes issue with the letter of Pope Pascal to that other Panormitanus, and asserts that conciliar decrees are so far from dependence on papal confirmation that, on the

---

[6] *WA* I, p. 656.
[7] *WA* II, p. 10.
[8] *Ibid.*, p. 279.
[9] *Ibid.*, p. 649.

contrary, the judgment of a private person if supported by better
Scriptural authority is superior to that of a pope.[10] Luther, then,
was entirely correct in referring to *Panormitanus Significasti,* but
the only modern editors to give the right references were Enders
and Kawerau in their notes on Luther's letter to Cajetan.[11] These
editors cite both Tudeschi and the canon law, but without explaining the confusion. Unfortunately this letter was not reworked in
the Weimar *Briefwechsel* because it was already printed in the *Acta
Augustana* of 1518 but without the note of Enders and Kawerau.[12]

My second example has to do with a point which I have not
yet been able to clarify. In the tract on *The Babylonian Captivity,*
Luther refers to the "well known saying of Gregory that the mass
would have been equally valid whether performed by Judas or by
Peter."[13] The Weimar edition attempts no identification and the
Bonn edition simply refers to the article *Messe* in the *Realencyclo-
pedie,* where the views of Gregory I are explained, but nothing of
this sort is there reported. One would scarcely expect the question
to have been raised in Christian antiquity because during that period the validity of the sacraments, apart from the worthiness of
the priest, was considered only in respect to baptism and ordination, so, for example, in Gregory of Nazianza.[14] Gregory the Great
does discuss the mass but only to make the point that the priest
who celebrates unworthily brings to himself thereby greater condemnation.[15] One wonders, then whether the Gregory cited by
Luther may have been some other of that name of a later period.
One would scarcely look for such sentiments in Gregory VII, who
exhorted the laity to reject the mass at the hands of the married

---

[10] *Abbatis Panormitani Commentaria* (Venice, 1571), Tom. 1, p. 142.
"Nam in concernentibus fidem etiam dictum unius privati esset praeferendum
dicto Papae, si ille moveretur melioribus rationibus novi et veteris testamenti
quam papa."

[11] Enders and Kawerau, *BR* 252.

[12] *WA* II, p. 10.

[13] Bonn ed., I, p. 458 and *WA* VI, p. 525. "Ex isto nunc facile illud quivis
intelligit, quod usitatissimum ex Grego. dicitur, Missam mali sacerdotis non
minoris ducendam, quam boni cuiuscunque. Nec sancti Petri meliorem fuisse,
quam Iudae traditoris, si sacrificassent."

[14] *Orat. XL in Baptismo.*

[15] *Ep.* 1, XXV, Migne *PL,* LXXVII, p. 469.

clergy. Gregory IX might be the author of Luther's citation, but I do not find it in the Decretals. Perhaps Gregory of Rimini may be the source.

Assuming, however, that we have before us Luther's works adequately edited, then we are confronted with the necessity of differentiating between that which is directly and that which is indirectly reported. Some works Luther composed and himself saw through the press. Others consist of notes taken down by his students, as for example, the *Table Talk* and some sermons and lectures. This material is not to be indiscriminately rejected. Often it is highly piquant and has the veritable ring of Luther. Sometimes it is our only source for an aspect of his life or thought. It will have to be tested, of course, by comparison with uncontested material.

I cite an instance which has lately been used by Catholics in the United States for polemical purposes. Arnold Lunn, in his book entitled *The Revolt Against Reason,* maintained that Luther made a statement so dreadful that it could be cited only in the appendix and only in Latin (for the corruption of the learned). In the end, however, the English reader learns that Luther affirmed Christ to have been guilty three times of adultery: with the woman taken in adultery, with the woman at the well and with the woman who was a sinner. A reference was given by Lunn to the *Table Talk*.[16] The most charitable explanation which Lunn could conjecture was that Luther was drunk when he said it. But a prior question should be whether he said it in the form recorded in the *Table Talk*. The way to find out is to examine his sermons on these three women. The comments on the woman taken in adultery and the woman at the well afford no clue, but the enigma is resolved in the case of the woman who was a sinner who washed the Master's feet with her tears and wiped them with her hair. The incident is related in the seventh chapter of Luke immediately following the statement that "John the Baptist came neither eating bread nor

---

[16] *The Revolt Against Reason* (1951), pp. 43-61, note p. 257, citing *TR* 1472. "Christus adulter. Christus ist am ersten ein ebrecher worden, Joh. 4 bei dem brunnen cum muliere, quia illi dicebant, Nemo significat, quid facit cum ea? Item cum Magdalena, item cum adultera Joan. 8., die er so leicht davon liess. Also mus der from Christus auch am ersten en ebrecher werden, ehe er starb."

drinking wine, and ye say, 'He hath a devil.' The Son of Man is come eating and drinking, and ye say, 'Behold a gluttonous man, a wine bibber and a friend of publicans and sinners.' "[17] Luther comments on the two incidents as one. "Wherefore we see," says he, "that Jesus was a wine bibber, a glutton and an adulterer in the eyes of the world—*coram mundo*."[18] Plainly this is the expression which has fallen out in the cryptic version of the *Table Talk—coram mundo*. Christ had to endure the utter shame of the false accusation of adultery, just as his Mother suffered under the suspicion of her husband.[19]

The use of the *Table Talk* and the sermons at second hand is doubly complicated in case the reference is to events in Luther's life greatly anterior to the time when the comment was made. An excellent example is afforded by the successive accounts of his first mass. The event itself took place in 1507. Our first description of how Luther felt on that occasion appears in the *Table Talk* in the year 1532. Thereafter the accounts in the *Table Talk* are frequent. The most explicit comes, however, from the commentary on Genesis, which also is available only in student notes, dated 1545, the year before Luther's death. The note-taker obviously made a mistake because he treated the words *Offerimus tibi* as belonging to the canon of the mass.[20] Nevertheless, in this instance the accounts and even the very last account appear to me to be substantially correct. One can scarcely feel that Luther would have made such repeated and explicit references to his tremor during his first mass if there were no basis in fact. A still more crucial consideration is this: that one needs something of the sort to explain the recurrence of his *Anfechtungen* after the year of tranquility in the monastery.

[17] Luke 7:31-39.

[18] *WA* XLI, p. 647. "Joannes ass nicht, non hielt er zu leuten, quis eum audiret? et dicunt eum diabolum. Christus remissionem peccatorum: filius hominis ein seuffer, helt zu buben und huren, macht leute mutwillig. Das ist loblich regiment, quod nobis imponit, das wir coram deo lesterer, ketzer ut Johannes, coram mundo seuffer und huren, buben gesellen. Si ipse, ergo et nos. Ideo mussen wirs machen, quod nemini placeat, praesertim qui in officio."

[19] *WA* XXVII, pp. 482-483.

[20] Consult Otto Scheel, *Dokumente zur Luthers Entwicklung* (Tübingen, 1929). Use the index under *Primiz*. For a discussion, Otto Scheel, *Martin Luther*, II (1930), pp. 81 ff.

And as for the character of the experience, such horror of the holy is abundantly documented for other occasions of his career.

What this means for historical method is that accounts, remote by years from the events which they describe and reported only at second hand, may be credited if they serve to make the event more credible and meaningful, and provided they are not contradicted by evidence at first hand or evidence closer to the event, though even here a strictly contemporary account is not always to be preferred, because there is the possibility that a more mature reflection may be sounder than an immediate ejaculation.

The problem of the late versus the early confronts us again when we are dealing with material strictly from Luther's pen. Sometimes an idea is greatly expanded in a later treatment, and the question then is whether the fuller explication was already present in Luther's mind at the time when he penned only a laconic statement. No absolutely certain answer can ever be given, but it would seem to me that one may regard the later and fuller version as implicit in the earlier if the elaboration is necessary to explain how Luther behaved on the prior occasion. The particular instance here in mind is his exposition of the Twenty-second Psalm. In the lectures of 1513 to 1515, the treatment is brief.[21] It could scarcely have been otherwise because the lecture notes were in the form of *glossae*, elucidations on the meaning of particular words. From these jottings one would not suspect a spiritual upheaval. Yet we have reason to believe that during these lectures Luther experienced his evangelical awakening. This he could not have done without coming to grips with the meaning of the Passion of Christ, and he could not have avoided confrontation with the significance of that event when commenting on the Twenty-second Psalm, which contains the verse, "My God, my God why hast Thou forsaken me?"

The treatment in 1519 is not philosophical but theological. Luther begins by saying that to understand the verse, "My God, my God, why hast Thou forsaken me?" one must understand what God is and therefore what it is to be separated from Him.

---

[21] *WA* III, pp. 134-139.

God is life, light, wisdom, truth, justice, goodness, power, joy, glory, peace, beatitude and every good. To be forsaken by God is to be in death, darkness, folly, deceit, sin, malice, infirmities, sadness, confusion, disquiet, desperation, damnation and every evil. What then follows? Shall we make Christ foolish, lying, sinful, evil, desperate and damned? These are obscure and hard sayings. See for yourselves that they are true. All will concede that in Christ were to be found at the same time the greatest joy and the greatest sadness, the highest glory and and the deepest confusion, the supreme peace and the most profound disquiet, the loftiest life and the utmost death. In this verse he appears to contradict himself when he calls himself forsaken by God and at the same time exclaims 'My God.' But what could appear more absurd than to say of the same man that he enjoyed the highest life and suffered the deepest death? Shall we then say that Christ was both just and a sinner, a deceiver and true, glorifying and despairing, both blessed and damned? Unless we say this I do not see how we can call him forsaken by God.

This my mind discerns that Christ was and remains just because no guile was found in His mouth. For this reason He was conceived and born of a Virgin that He be without sin, for otherwise how could He have delivered us from our sins? Yet in the hour of His passion He took to Himself our sins as if they were really His own . . . for truly He has borne our griefs and carried our sorrows. For the sins of my people I have smitten Him because He hath done no wrong. Nor was any guile found in His mouth [quoting Isaiah 53]. And this smiting God means not simply the pain of death but also the fear and horror of the anguished conscience which feels eternal wrong, as if forever abandoned and rejected from before the face of God. . . .

Some may object that if this be true Christ did not love God with all His heart when He cried, 'Why has Thou forsaken me?' . . . but Christ did love the Father with all His heart. The torments beyond His strength compelled His innocent and weak nature to groan, cry, shudder and flee as when through the weakness of nature, though innocent, He sank beneath the weight of the Cross. . . .

We must not, however, deny that Christ was terrified and tormented . . . That cry was no jest or make-believe when He said 'forsaken me' . . . Let not human temerity extenuate or make void the multitude in the camp below and permit the disciples to ascend to Christ in the Mount. Not for all persons was this Psalm written, for all have not the same gifts and the same passions. Scripture has milk for babes and wine and solid food for adults.[22]

This passage I have ventured to cite thus fully in order to show that here we have the core of Luther's evangelical experience.

[22] *WA* V, pp. 602-606.

For that reason it does not appear to me to be too bold an assumption that the emotional response and profound insight into the meaning of the cross evident in the exposition of the Twenty-second Psalm in 1519 had already taken hold of Luther when he was confronted with this very Psalm in 1513. To posit less requires the assumption that his evangelical experience did not as a matter of fact come until much later, which some indeed have lately contended. Provided that the experience can be dated in 1513, then to read back the fullness of the later exposition is not unwarranted.

9. Interpretations of the Reformation

Ranke did a great service to Reformation history by discarding the philosophical presuppositions of the idealistic school and insisting that the history of the sixteenth century religious upheaval should be written only after a fresh and full confrontation with the sources. But his hope that history might be written with utter objectivity just as it happened proved to be illusory. In order to bring the record of the past into manageable compass, the historian must perforce select his sources, and that selection can be highly subjective. Witness for example Janssen's *History of the German People*, which by judicious inclusion and omission of sources contrived to present the Protestant Reformation in ugly colors. Or again Döllinger's *History of the Reformation*, which filled three volumes with direct quotations from the despondent utterances of the Protestant reformers, who lamented that their achievements fell short of their hopes.[1] Then Wilhelm Walther countered with a solid body of statistical evidence.[2] Here were sources fighting against sources.

The modern historian is aware of all this and seeks to fortify himself by declaring his prejudices in advance. Then he strains in the opposite direction as a corrective and ends by being non-objective in the very effort to be objective. But a deeper difficulty is that we are not even aware of our prejudices because frequently they are those which we share with our age. If we are to recognize that they are prejudices, we must engage in a comparison between the point of view of our time and those of previous times. Thus we invoke history to disclose to us our presuppositions in the approach to history. Hence today the vogue of historiography.

First published in *The American Historical Review*, LXVI, 1 (October 1960).

[1] J. J. Döllinger, *Die Reformation* (3 vols., Regensburg, 1848).
[2] Wilhelm Walther, *Für Luther wider Rom* (Halle, 1906).

In the field of the Renaissance it has produced the admirable work of Wallace K. Ferguson.[3] For the Reformation there is nothing comparable. We do, though, have studies of how individual leaders of the Reformation have been treated throughout the succeeding centuries: Erasmus, Zwingli, Luther and Castellio.[4] The historiography of the Reformation as a whole, however, still awaits treatment.

The main lines for such a study may be indicated. The age of the Reformation itself was polemical and documentary. The *Magdeburg Centuries* on the Protestant side and Baronius' *Annals* on the Catholic marshaled sources in support of confessional claims. The eighteenth century tried to achieve impartiality. This was done in either of two ways: by the historian's dissociating equally from all parties and movements or by projecting himself into them all with equal sympathy. The rationalists of the Enlightenment were inclined to the first. It is interesting that in this period we have the first effort at an objective account of Michael Servetus by Johann Lorenz von Mosheim.[5] Pietism took the other method and responded with equal warmth to every vital religious movement of the past whether orthodox or heretical, Catholic or Protestant. The great exponent of this viewpoint was Gottfried Arnold.[6] This is not to say of course that he was sympathetic toward everything. He commended piety and condemned institutionalism and arid speculation. But his line cut through all of the confessions, and it split Luther down the middle. The earlier Luther was regarded as a warm evangelical, the later as an encrusted institutionalist.

[3] Wallace K. Ferguson, *The Renaissance in Historical Thought: Five Centuries of Interpretation* (Boston, 1948).

[4] Andreas Flitner, *Erasmus im Urteil seiner Nachwelt* (Tübingen, 1952); Kurt Guggisberg, *Das Zwinglibild des Protestantismus* (Bern diss., 1934); Heinrich Bornkamm, *Luther im Spiegel der deutschen Geistesgeschichte* (Heidelberg 1955); Ernst Walter Zeeden, *Martin Luther und die Reformation im Urteil des deutschen Luthertums* (2 vols., Freiburg, 1950-52); Hans Rudolf Guggisberg, "Sebastian Castellio im Urteil seiner Nachwelt," *Basler Beiträge zur Geschichtswissenschaft* (Basel, 1957), LVII.

[5] Johann Lorenz von Mosheim, *Anderweitiger Versuch einer vollständigen und unpartheyischen Ketzergeschichte* (Helmstedt, 1748).

[6] Gottfried Arnold, *Gottfried Arnolds Unpartheyische Kirchen und Ketzerhistorie* (2 vols., Frankfurt, 1700-15).

Under the impact of idealistic philosophy the nineteenth century sought to surmount the disjointedness of all previous treatments and to discover connections, motifs and laws. Hegel saw in the Reformation a movement toward the emancipation of the *Weltgeist* to be valued in terms of its cultural effects, but none of the idealists produced a history of the Reformation. In the meantime, the romantics disparaged the Reformation for disrupting the medieval heritage.

Ranke swept away philosophical theorizing with his demand for a thorough and extensive examination of the sources. But he, too, had a philosophy—that of divine providence in history, evidenced in order, necessity and cohesion. The discontinuities of the Reformation were therefore minimized and the conservative side of Luther was exalted.

The liberal Protestants of the late nineteenth and early twentieth centuries associated the Renaissance and the Reformation as conjoint phases of a movement of emancipation away from the authority of the Church. The German nationalists saw in Luther's religion an expression of the profundity of the German *Geist* and in the Reformation a stirring toward the emancipation of the German people. Then in the early twentieth century Ernst Troeltsch approached the question from the point of view of the interconnection of religion and culture. Christianity, if it is to influence a culture, must to a large degree identify itself with that culture. Protestantism, he held, was that form of Christianity which corresponded to sixteenth century cultural needs. But these needs, he felt, were still largely those of the Middle Ages, and for that reason he stressed the medieval character of the Reformation alike in theology and ecclesiology. To his mind, the great dividing line between the medieval and the modern period was to be found not in the Reformation but in the Enlightenment, though to be sure the Reformation created a situation out of which the later emancipation could arise. The Reformation itself, however, was addicted to dogma, intolerance and constraint.[7]

---

[7] Ernst Troeltsch, *Die Bedeutung des Protestantismus für die Entstehung der modernen Welt* (Munich, 1911), translated with the misleading title *Protestantism and Progress* (New York, 1912; Boston, 1958).

The most radical break with all of these positions was inaugurated by the essay of Karl Holl in 1917, "What Did Luther Mean by Religion?"[8] Holl rediscovered the core of Luther's piety, his overpowering sense of moral obligation, his feeling of utter impotence before the demands of God, his terror of the divine wrath justly impending, his unshakable clinging to God's Word and promises. Luther was afflicted with the *malaise de l'univers* and found surcease only through a new view of God and the Scriptures. Neither philosophy, sociology, nationalism nor economics can explain Luther. Only religion can provide the explanation.

From this analysis, which inaugurated the Luther renaissance, we may take our departure. The question immediately arises, if this be a true picture of Luther, what then of the Reformation? Why did he gain a following? Did his disciples really understand him or did they rally for the wrong reasons? Were they convinced that indulgences were blasphemy because they are based on the contention that the saints have earned merits which can be presented as a claim upon God, or did the populace respond in order to rid themselves of financial exploitation?

There are those who say that this or some other extraneous consideration must have been determinative because, as a matter of fact, Luther's religious affirmations were in no sense novel and when previously made had had no such effect. Luther happened to emerge amid a set of circumstances peculiarly auspicious. Without such a stage, and without concomitants both economic and political, the Reformation would never have taken hold.[9]

As for the claim that Luther was in no sense original, there is no better reply than that to be found in the recent work of Erich Hassinger,[10] who finds Luther's contribution to have been his rediscovery of the historical core of Christianity. The claim of the Christian religion is that God did something unique in history. In the year that Caesar Augustus ordered all the world to be taxed,

---

[8] Karl Holl, "Was verstand Luther unter Religion?" (1917), reprinted in *Gesammelte Aufsätze zur Kirchengeschichte* (3 vols., Tübingen, 1928-32), I.

[9] Albert Hyma, *New Light on Martin Luther, with an Authentic Account of the Luther Film of 1953* (Grand Rapids, Mich., 1958).

[10] Erich Hassinger, *Das Werden des neuzeitlichen Europa, 1300-1600* (Braunschweig, 1959).

the Word became flesh. The Incarnation, the Crucifixion and the Resurrection constituted a unique self-disclosure of God in Christ. To Him the ages lead up, and from Him the centuries lead out. By faith in His redeeming work man is forgiven and remade. The assertion of the unique historical role of Christ is an offense because it assumes unevenness in the work of God, who, if this be true, declared Himself more manifestly to the men of the first century than to those in any other. There are various ways of escaping from the historical singularity of Christ. One is mysticism: God is accessible at all times equally to the waiting heart. Another is moralism: man is saved by his own good deeds done here and now. And still another is institutionalism: the Church is the custodian and continuator of the revelation once and for all given. Luther asserted unequivocally the historical uniqueness of the work of God in Christ. Its continuance in the present is mediated through Scripture, which is the record of the event. And though it must be interpreted by the Spirit, yet the Spirit can never be dissociated from the outward Word. This position divided Luther from Catholics on the one side and from Protestant sectaries on the other.

But if it be granted that Luther was original as to religion, the question still remains whether men were stirred by his religion or merely by his revolt. Some historians, here as elsewhere, offer an economic explanation. This of itself is by no means novel. The charge arose almost at once that the princes supported Luther in order to expropriate the goods of the Church, that the peasants at first rallied to him in the hope that the freedom of the Gospel would mean freedom from serfdom, that the masses espoused the Gospel in order to throw off tithes, fees and indulgences. To such an explanation there are several replies. The most decisive is that in short order the populace and the princes risked their goods and their lives by adherence to the new faith. At the Diet of the Empire in 1530, the German princes presented the Augsburg Confession, fully aware that the emperor might in consequence deprive them of their titles, lands and lives. In the 1540's the emperor came with Spanish troops to crush Protestantism, but neither princes nor people would yield. Had their concern been only economic, one cannot understand such intrepidity. One may note also that some simple laymen like Hans Sachs did grasp what Luther meant in the very core of his theology. Perhaps one reason why they did and could understand his message was that the way had been in some measure prepared by the German mystics who had stressed not outward good works but inward attitudes of humility and love.

The economic explanation for the movement's success in Germany is more plausible if it is compared with the failure in Italy. Some writers have suggested that the Protestant reform did not take hold there because the gold flowed from over the Alps into Italy. That may have been a partial factor, but there are other possibilities. One historian suggests that Protestantism failed because Catholicism is ingrained in the very fiber of the Italian people. But that simply is not true. No European land had seen so many revolts, not only against the Church but also against the faith, from the late twelfth to the sixteenth century as had Italy. The peninsula pullulated with sects. One by one they were plucked by the Inquisition. Italy was tired. Heresy was played out. That may be one explanation. Another is the adroitness of Rome in capturing and utilizing the movements of vitality. Had there been a great revolt against the papacy in Italy in the sixteenth century, it could probably have come only from the Capuchins, imbued as they were with the ideals of the Spiritual Franciscans. If the popes had rejected the first Capuchins, they might easily have become rebels and heretics. Discretion made of them apostles and saints. A still further explanation is the nature of the preparation. The preaching in Italy in the fifteenth and sixteenth centuries was highly moralistic, directed against specific sins: usury, prostitution, luxury, exhortion, tyranny, feuding and the wearing of vanities. Lyrical raptures over the wounds of Christ ended in appeals to imitate his sufferings. The inference was that penitence and amendment of life would win God's pardon.[11] But this was just the point that Luther denied. He could denounce sins with all the vehemence of a Savonarola, but his point was that divine forgiveness is a sheer act of God's grace and in no way contingent upon anything that man can do. Amendment of life flows from the assurance of pardon. The German mystics had come closer to this than ever did the

---

[11] Arsenio d'Ascoli, *La Predicazione dei Cappuccini nel Cinquecento in Italia* (Loreto, Ancona, 1956).

Italian friars, and the difference in the religious preparation may have had more to do with the outcome than had economics.

Other interpreters stress political factors, contending that the Reformation could have begun in no other country than Germany because of the political decentralization. The point is that in a great monarchical state an obscure professor would have had little chance to persuade a monarch like Francis, Henry or Charles to embrace his religious ideas. And if the monarch were not at least neutral, the advocate of new religious ideas would be promptly snuffed out. Saxony was small enough and the relations sufficiently personal that a teacher at the University of Wittenberg, supported by his colleagues, could gain the support of a little prince like Frederick the Wise, who was sufficiently independent to pursue a strategy of obstructionism over against the emperor. There is some point no doubt in this contention. Had Luther first appeared in the Netherlands he would have gone quickly to the stake, since here Charles ruled as a hereditary prince. But one cannot say that an academic reformer might not have converted a monarch. There is no inherent reason why John Colet in England or Jacques Lefèvre d'Etaples in France might not have converted the crown. As a matter of fact, Henry VIII did introduce the Reformation into England without provoking a serious revolt, though to be sure it was not Luther's variety. Perhaps one may safely say that the Reformation took hold and survived only where it coincided with some sort of political interest, but the identification must not be too precise.

Contemporary histories of the Reformation tend to be misleading because the religious understanding of the Reformation is subordinated to the exigencies of teaching. Political history predominates in the works of Paul Joachimsen, Harold J. Grimm, Hajo Holborn, E. Harris Harbison, Eric Hassinger and Gerhard Ritter.[12] This is certainly not because they have failed to grasp the

---

[12] Paul Joachimsen, *Die Reformation* (Munich, 1951); Harold J. Grimm, *The Reformation Era, 1500-1650* (New York, 1954); Hajo Holborn, *A History of Modern Germany*, I, *The Reformation* (New York, 1959); E. Harris Harbison, *The Age of the Reformation* (Ithaca, N. Y., 1955); Hassinger, *Werden des neuzeitlichen Europa*; Gerhard Ritter, *Die Neugestaltung Europas im 16. Jahrhundert* (Berlin, 1950).

nature of Luther's religion and the sources of his critique of the Church. Ritter in particular has written a most penetrating book on Luther.[13] The explanation may be that these works actually are not histories of the Reformation, but rather histories of Europe or of Germany during the period of the Reformation. The scope of the treatment is somewhat determined by the purpose for which the books are to be used, namely as texts in courses on European, German or world history. The titles indicate the scope: *The Reformation Era, The Age of the Reformation, Die Neugestaltung Europas.* In these works politics and sociology play as much or even a greater part than religion. One suspects that the demands of university courses have determined the allocation of space.

But if the Reformation was primarily religious, what then of its relation to the Renaissance? The answer of course depends in part on the interpretation of the Renaissance. The diversities in that area are well illustrated by three recent works on Erasmus. The first of these, by Siro Attilio Nulli,[14] depicts Erasmus as neither a Catholic nor a Christian. Nulli appreciates Erasmus' position because he holds the same beliefs. He is sorry only that Erasmus wasted so much time trying to prove that he was what he was not. Émile V. Telle[15] presents an Erasmus who may have been a Christian, but was certainly not a Catholic since his attack on monasticism was earlier, more virulent and persistent than that of Luther. But Louis Bouyer[16] claims Erasmus to have been both a good Christian and a good Catholic. Several questions are involved here: What is a Christian? What is a Catholic? And what was Erasmus? The answers to these questions have an obvious bearing on judgments with regard to the Reformation.

A cleavage between the Reformation and the Renaissance certainly existed, but the tendency of late has been to accentuate it. The Renaissance was, as a matter of fact, a complex phenomenon, but certainly persons like Colet, Pico, Ficino, More and Erasmus

---

[13] *Id., Luther, Gestalt und Tat* (Munich, 1943). An earlier edition was called *Luther, Gestalt und Symbol.*

[14] Siro Attilio Nulli, *Erasmo e il Rinascimento* (Turin, 1955).

[15] Émile V. Telle, *Érasme de Rotterdam et le septième sacrement* (Geneva, 1954).

[16] Louis Bouyer, *Autour d'Érasme* (Paris, 1955).

are not to be called frivolous or irreligious. Yet Renaissance religion was not Luther's religion. There was in it a strong ingredient of the Neoplatonic disparagement of the corporeal which, when not restrained by the authority of the Church, issued in iconoclasm, sacramentarianism, that is, the denial of the real presence, and even in a rejection of music. Tendencies in this direction were already present in Erasmus. At this point Luther was a good medieval Catholic. Another ingredient of Renaissance religion was tolerance toward other religions, a readiness to recognize that there is more than one way to God. And this was because the Renaissance minimized the historical uniqueness of Christianity. Luther, however, would have absolutely nothing to do with any such attenuation. Again the Renaissance shared with Catholicism a higher estimate of the capacity and worth of the natural man than Luther allowed. This was the core of his debate with Erasmus. Yet Luther enthusiastically appropriated and the Reformation adopted all of the philological tools and the historical critical method of the humanist.

During the last quarter of a century several new approaches to the Reformation have emerged. The first is the application of psychiatry to history. In his presidential address before the American Historical Association in 1957, William Langer held that the "next assignment" is to apply the insights of psychoanalysis to history.[17] He is perfectly right in asserting that whatever illumines the present should be brought to bear upon the past, provided sufficient material of the right sort is available to implement this technique. There are, however, grave difficulties in psychoanalyzing the dead. In the case of Luther, we know much, and for some thirty years of his life we know something that he did on twenty days out of every month. What we know, however, is not what, for this purpose, we need to know. The result is that the psychiatrist fastens on three or four remarks of the aged Luther about his boyhood, remarks transmitted to us only at second hand. Then on the basis of such sparse material the psychiatrist reconstructs all the turmoils of Luther's inner life. There is, however, a more serious difficulty

---

[17] William L. Langer, "The Next Assignment," *American Historical Review*, LXIII (Jan. 1958), 283-304.

in the case of all of the psychiatrists who have turned their hand to Luther thus far. They do not envisage the possibility that he could have been impelled by any motive except egocentricity.[18] In any case, if one should succeed in psychoanalyzing a man there would still be the more elusive task of psychoanalyzing a movement.

Catholic historiography of the Protestant Reformation has advanced notably in recent years. Research has become much more objective, and the tendency is to pity the misguided rather than to rail at rebels. In Luther's own day he was traduced by Johannes Cochläus. Recently a German Catholic, Adolf Herte, has exposed Cochläus' misrepresentations and their baneful effect upon all Catholic historiography to our own day.[19] Georges Tavard points out that in Luther's day medieval Catholicism resembled a vase already shattered but with the pieces still in place. Luther's unhappy historical destiny was to come at the moment when a touch sufficed to make them fall apart.[20] Joseph Lortz poses the question: How could Luther have persuaded his generation that Catholicism amounted to nothing more than purchasing heaven?[21] A generation after Luther this might be explained as a Protestant legend, but not in the first decades of the Reformation. The only possible conclusion is that the behavior of the majority of Catholics lent itself to this interpretation. As for Luther's own religion, his trembling before the majesty of God and his demand for utter self-emptying are not to be brushed off lightly as exaggerations. And in the portrayal of sin, what terrific earnestness! At a number of points, nevertheless, Luther did exaggerate and therefore distorted.

With all such treatments a Protestant historian can come to grips. One of the Catholic historians' greatest contributions is their placing of Luther in the setting of late medieval Catholicism.

Another school of interpretation is that of the neo-orthodox.

---

[18] Erik H. Erikson, *Young Man Luther* (New York, 1958). What he says about Luther on sex and on the Peasants' War is very sensible.

[19] Adolf Herte, *Das katholische Lutherbild im Bann der Lutherkommentare des Cochläus* (3 vols., 1943).

[20] Georges Henri Tavard, *Holy Writ or Holy Church* (New York, 1959).

[21] Joseph Lortz, *Die Reformation in Deutschland* (2d ed., 2 vols., Freiburg, 1941).

The rebels against Protestant liberalism affirmed the depravity of man, the salvation of man solely through the grace of God, the utter transcendence of God, and the possibility of knowing God only through His self-disclosure in Christ. These theologians claimed that they were reviving the theology of the sixteenth century reformers. In so doing they unquestionably called attention to points in Reformation theology entirely missed by the interpreters of the liberal school, who because of their presuppositions had not the eyes to see what was there. But by the same token the neo-orthodox were tempted to impose their own meanings upon their reputed progenitors.

Their attempt to derive everything from Christ, including religious knowledge, salvation and ethics, leads to exaggerations. First as to the knowledge of God: if knowledge is possible only through Christ then there is no room for natural theology. Peter Barth attempted to show that this was Calvin's view.[22] But for all that Calvin said about the depravity of man's will and intellect he was to the end too deeply steeped in Stoicism ever to eliminate all natural religion.

Again, if Christ be the only source of ethics, what place is left for natural law, unless perchance for the non-Christian? The neo-orthodox tend to exclude from Luther's thinking not only natural law but all law, claiming that his ethic was entirely spontaneous and unstructured. Incidentally, this view is not a particular discovery of the neo-orthodox. Before them it was advanced by Karl Holl, who anticipated more than one of their contentions not by approaching Luther with their assumptions but simply by steeping himself in Luther. At this point, however, one may suggest that they have all exaggerated. A Catholic author published a book on natural law in Luther in which he cited many passages that sound like Thomas Aquinas.[23] To be sure, the theological framework in which natural law thinking was set differed for Aquinas and Luther, but it was, nevertheless, decidedly present in Luther.

Finally, if for the Christian everything proceeds from Christ,

[22] Peter Barth, "Das Problem der natürlichen Theologie bei Calvin," *Theologische Existenz Heute,* XVIII (1935).

[23] Franz Xaver Arnold, *Zur Frage des Naturrechts bei Martin Luther* (Munich, 1937).

must not the Christian feel himself to be a stranger in the world, if not indeed an alien? No one would deny that Luther called upon the Christian to demean himself as a good citizen, but Heckel insists that this was not because the Christian belongs to the natural order but rather that out of love for his neighbor he should stoop himself to an alien yoke.[24] The Christian, then, in his interior becomes a unified being. This view very sharply contrasts to that of Troeltsch, who asserted that for Luther the Christian belongs to two realms and is governed by two codes, one might almost say two ethics, and must be torn by the duality of his role as a Christian and as a man in the world. Holl had already bridged the gap by insisting that in both areas the Christian is to be motivated by love. But Heckel makes the bridge unnecessary by eliminating the gap, and that I think is going rather too far.

The broader problems of the interpretation of any period depend for the verification and progress on documentary evidence. And progress in research means a constant quest for new materials and their dissemination in the original form or in modern critical editions. Here we must recognize that there are large bodies of documents which, because of their sheer extent or minor significance, will never be made available in critical editions. For that reason, the Foundation for Reformation Research has begun the microfilming of every sixteenth century book bearing on any aspect of the Reformation. The entire material will be housed in St. Louis where the reproductions from the Vatican Library are now stored. The foundation has already made a beginning with the works of Brenz, the reformer of Swabia. The next move will be to film one after another of the major libraries of Europe. The Biblioteca Nazionale at Florence, for example, has nearly everything pertaining to the Italian Reformation. The plans for this entire enterprise have been carefully laid, but most of the funds are yet to be subscribed. Critical editions of many of the reformers are under way. The Weimar edition of Luther's works will eventually be re-edited with additional critical annotations. At Yale a project has

[24] Johannes Heckel, "Lex Charitatis," *Abhandlungen der Bayerischen Akademie der Wissenschaften, phil.-hist. Klasse* (Munich, 1953), N.F. XXXVI, and "Im Irrgarten der Zwei-Reiche-Lehre," *Theologische Existenz Heute,* LV (1957).

been initiated on an entire corpus of the works of St. Thomas More; Strasbourg is at work on Martin Bucer; and Geneva is bringing out the correspondence on Theodore Beza. The publisher Sansoni at Florence announces the forthcoming publication of a whole series on the Italian reformers, and the Polish reformers are already appearing in their native tongue. The Anabaptist documents have now reached formidable proportions. For the Reformation in Spain, John E. Longhurst and Mrs. Angela Sanchez Barbudo are publishing new documents from the records of the Inquisition.

The most prominent omission is a critical edition of the works of Erasmus. Mr. and Mrs. P. S. Allen have done his letters, the Holborns have edited selected works, and Wallace Ferguson has done the works not included in the great Louvain edition.[25] But the great bulk has not been touched. For years Yale has been collecting first editions in order to lay the groundwork. Erasmus suffers from the misfortune of not having founded a church. The Lutherans take care of Luther, the Calvinists of Calvin and the Schwenckfeldians of Schwenckfeld. The Mennonites are chiefly responsible for the publication of the Anabaptist documents. Erasmus, however, kept *au-dessus de la melée* and there he stays.

Bibliographic surveys of the Reformation must start from the great work of Karl Schottenloher.[26] The literature as it appears is covered in the *Archiv für Reformationsgeschichte* as well as in frequent surveys in *Church History*. Anabaptist literature is treated in the *Mennonite Quarterly Review*. Two admirable recent surveys are those of Hassinger in the work already mentioned and that of the International Commission for Comparative Ecclesiastical History.[27] Much work remains to be done.

[25] *Desiderius Erasmus Roterodamus Ausgewählte Werke*, ed. Hajo and Annemarie Holborn (Munich, 1933); Wallace K. Ferguson, *Erasmi Opuscula* (The Hague, 1933).

[26] Karl Schottenloher, *Bibliographie zur deutschen Geschichte im Zeitalter der Glaubensspaltung* (6 vols., Leipzig, 1933-40).

[27] *Bibliographie de la réforme, 1450-1648: Ouvrages parus de 1940 à 1955* (2 vols., Leiden, 1958, 1960). Hans Joachim Hillerbrand, *A Bibliography of Anabaptism* (Elkhart, Ind., 1962).

II. The Left Wing of the
Reformation

10. The Left Wing of the Reformation

The title of this paper has been unduly credited with originality. John T. McNeill entitled a chapter in a book that appeared in 1940 "Left-Wing Religious Movements."[1] As a matter of fact, neither of us was original. The terminology is to be found in Luther's writings, where he said that he took a middle course between the Catholics on the left and the radicals on the right. One observes that the connotation of the directions was for him the reverse of our own. Similarly, Schwenckfeld said that he stood in the middle between the Lutherans and the Zwinglians, and Pilgram Marpeck took the *via media* between the Lutherans and Schwenckfeld.

The term *left wing* has lately been called into question as savoring too much of modern parliamentary alignment, and George Williams prefers to speak of the *radical Reformation.*[2] This usage has the merit of substituting one word for two but does not simplify or clarify the situation. A radical reformation implies a conservative reformation, and a reformation implies a body to be reformed so that one still has three groups: the Catholics, the Lutherans and related bodies, and the radicals.

But more important than the terminology is the recognition that the Reformation was too complex and too much in flux for any precise classification. Whether one speaks of the left wing or of the *radical Reformation*, the allocation of persons and movements will vary according to the point chosen through which to draw the

First published in the *Journal of Religion*, XXI, No. 2 (April 1941).

[1] *A Short History of Christianity,* ed. Archibald G. Baker (Chicago, 1940).

[2] George Williams, "Spiritual and Anabaptist Writers," *Library of Christian Classics,* XXV (Philadelphia, 1957) and *The Radical Reformation* (Philadelphia, 1962). Compare Robert Friedmann in *Church History,* XXIV (1955), pp. 132-151 and his article "Anabaptism" in the *Mennonite Encyclopedia.*

line of demarcation. If the relation of Church and state is the test, then on the right one has the Catholic Church with its theocratic pretensions, in the middle the Lutherans and the Anglicans with possible Erastian tendencies. The Zwinglians and the Calvinists are also in the middle but a little closer to the right because of their theocratic leanings. The Anabaptists and spiritual reformers are on the left. But if the norm is to be the teaching of the sacraments, then Zwingli moves to the left. If the theory of the Church is to be determinative, the Anabaptists move to the right as over against the Spiritualists who dissolve the visible Church. And if the doctrine of the Trinity is to be the point, then the Socinians are all by themselves on the left. And, of course, the movements themselves were not uniform. Anabaptism was inchoate and could include the *Schwertler,* who would use the sword, and the *Stäbler,* who would carry only the staff.

The entire Reformation movement was inchoate and in flux. To Luther at first rallied a number of groups who, when they understood him better, fell away: the humanists, who regarded indulgences as a silly superstition; the German nationalists, who saw in the traffic an example of Roman extortion; and the common folk, who recognized in themselves the sheep to be sheared. All united around the reformer for whom indulgences were a monstrous blasphemy. But in a few years the differences in their points of view became apparent. The humanists recoiled before Luther's religious intensity and violence. The military power of such nationalists as von Sickengen and von Hutten was broken on the field of battle. The peasants were alienated because Luther excoriated the means which they employed to redress their grievances. The outcome was that many among the humanists retreated to the Catholic camp and many of the lower classes formed radical sects. This generalization, of course, is somewhat too simple. Some humanists such as Melanchthon remained with Luther, and some like Grebel and Denck became Anabaptists. Not all peasants became Anabaptists, and not all Anabaptists were peasants. But, broadly speaking, the movement inaugurated by Luther was thinned out by 1525.

At the same time we must bear in mind that the Protestant movement never was an integrated whole because independent movements sprang up in various political territories. In fact, political division was a prime factor in enabling the reform to spread piecemeal and to maintain itself at one point when suppressed in another. Such a situation of necessity meant diversity. Zwingli was subject to no institutional control from Luther, and Calvin took orders from neither. Henry VIII paid slight attention to any of the rest; and Lutheran, Zwinglian, Calvinist and Anglican, which we today regard as the main varieties of early Protestantism, by no means exhausted the roster of the sixteenth century. Each principality in Germany, such as Hesse, Brandenburg, Württemberg; each of the imperial cities, like Augsburg and Strasbourg; and each canton and town of the Swiss Confederation, such as Berne and Basel, had a reform of a variant complexion. Any formula descriptive of initial Protestantism tends inevitably toward oversimplification.

Nevertheless, lines can be drawn and for this discussion the primary line is the relation of Church and state. The left wing is composed of those who separated Church and state and rejected the civil arm in matters of religion. These groups were commonly on the left also with regard to Church organization, sacraments and creeds. An attempt will be made to describe the main notes of this more radical reformation.

Specifically, the groups I have in mind in rough chronological order are: first, the Zwickau prophets who commenced a ferment of disintegration by introducing highly individualistic norms of authority; then, Thomas Müntzer, a weird combination of medieval mysticism, sectarianism and social revolution; next, the Swiss Anabaptists who, in their effort to restore especially the moral quality of primitive Christianity, ended by severing the connection of the Church with the community as a whole, and particularly with the state; thereafter, the Melchiorites who, under the pressure of persecution, turned to extravagant eschatology, as did the Münsterites to violent revolution; the Mennonites in the Netherlands who repudiated such aberrations and returned to the sobriety of their Swiss forerunners; the Hutterian Brethren in Moravia who adopted religious communism; the Schwenckfelders who, independently of other groups, sought to recapture the piety of the early Church; and the Socinians who were characterized alike by social, religious and intellectual radicalism. The following discussion seeks to delineate the main ideas which appear and re-appear in varying combinations among these groups.

The first note was ethical. The primary defect in the Lutheran Reformation according to the radicals was moral. The Reformation had not produced an adequate transformation of life. The Lutheran was not distinguishable from the Catholic at the point of conduct. Some of these critics laid the blame at the door of the doctrine of justification by faith with consequent disparagement of good works and of the doctrine of predestination with its severing of the nerve of moral effort. Others among the radicals perceived that these doctrines were not so much responsible, since justification, if genuine, would issue in sanctification, and a belief in predestination would stimulate the moral efforts of those who thought of themselves as the elect. The fault, according to these radicals, lay rather in the theory of the Church, as including all members of the community by virtue of infant baptism rather than on the basis of inner conviction and moral fruits.

These critics were resuscitating an ancient conflict by which the Church had long been tormented. Should the Church be thought of primarily in terms of leaven, or of light? Should it think of itself as a body commissioned to permeate all society even at the risk of losing its own purity, or rather as a light set upon a hill to influence the world by example rather than by participation? The one concept has been characterized by Troeltsch as that of the Church and the other as that of the sect. The one tends to be Augustinian and the other Pelagian. The one is commonly sacramental, the other moral. The one believes in the Church catholic and the other in the Church holy. In the early period Augustine represented the former and the Donatists the latter. In the fourth century, as in the sixteenth, this difference as to the composition and role of the Church in society led the one group to unite Church and state and to justify religious persecution, and the other to separate the two and to deny the competence of the magistrate in the sphere of religion. The very term "Anabaptist" was fastened upon persons, preferring to call themselves Baptists, by their opponents, who sought thus to identify them with the ancient Donatists, who also repeated baptism and likewise separated Church and state.

A second note of the left wing was Christian primitivism. The Church must be patterned after the primitive movement— back to Jesus, back even to Abraham. This is a note which commonly characterizes reformatory movements. The Montanists wished to return to the primitive prophesying of Agabas and the daughters of Philip. The Marcionites thought of themselves as restoring Paul after the corruptions of the intervening years. St. Francis was returning to the rule of the Gospel, and the Franciscans were constantly recurring to the rule of St. Francis. Such primitivism commonly marks the sect and leads its advocates into separation from any Church which claims to be so guided by the spirit as to be in a position to set aside ancient practices in the light of new conditions. The Catholic, Lutheran and Anglican churches have frankly taken this view. Zwinglianism and Calvinism have had much more of the primitive note, which explains why Anabaptism arose out of Zwinglianism and why Calvinism has had so many inner conflicts.

Primitivism admits of varying degrees and qualities. There is the chronological question of how far to go back. Luther was in favor of sloughing off the corruptions of the papacy. For him the fall of the Church commonly was assigned to the time of Boniface III in the seventh century, when supposedly the temporal power of the papacy had its rise. The Anglicans set the fall after the fourth ecumenical council. Everything previous for them could be regarded as normative. This view incidentally was the starting point for both Newman and Kingsley. The one endeavored to show that medieval Catholicism could be discovered in germ in the first four centuries, and Kingsley, on the other hand, in *Hypatia,* tried to prove that the fourth century itself was an age of corruption and the fall must be set still further back. The Reformation sectaries found the dividing line in the age of Constantine, because at that time the union of Church and state, to which they so strenuously objected, occurred. Others, still more radical, claimed that the Gospel was corrupted immediately after the days of the apostles and that the Bible alone could be regarded as the true pattern.

But how much of the Bible? Only the New Testament, or the

Old Testament as well? Some were New Testament literalists and endeavored to restore the Gospel pattern by reviving the discipline of Matthew, chapter 18, the religious communism of Acts, the non-resistance and no-swearing of the Sermon on the Mount, as well as foot-washing and immersion. Old Testament literalists revived the polygamy and other immoralities of the patriarchs, as well as the eccentricities of the prophets. In imitation of Isaiah (20:3), who "walked naked and barefoot for a sign," some of the Amsterdam Anabaptists went naked through the streets, and one of their leaders, mindful of Isa. 6:6, took a hot coal from off the hearth and touched his lips, with the result that he could scarcely talk for a fortnight. Such aberrations, however, were not characteristic of the movement.

Literalism was not the dominant note, but the recovery of the spirit of the apostles. The restoration of primitive Christianity and the spiritual new birth were practically synonymous for the Anabaptists. The gift of the spirit which they craved had a twofold function: to produce, on the one hand, moral transformation and, on the other, to give religious knowledge. Here lay the root of the distinction between the outer and the inner word. The letter of the Scripture, said the champions of the inner word, will convince only the convinced. To understand the apostles we must be in the spirit of the apostles. Otherwise Scripture is nothing more than paper and ink. The reformers, such as Luther, Zwingli and Calvin, who relied on the outer word, were stigmatized as *Schriftgelehrten*, which cannot be rendered with a single term in English. The word means literally "those who are versed in Scripture." It is also the translation of the Biblical "scribe." Hence the woes against the scribes could be hurled against the Biblical literalists, and Biblical scholarship was derided as human learning.

The disciples of the inner word sometimes turned to mysticism and sometimes to communications of the spirit in dreams and visions which in turn became so bizarre and contradictory that the norm of the outer word had to be revived as a check. The problem of the inner and outer word, however, did not rend Anabaptism as much as might have been expected, because such programs as non-resistance, no-swearing and religious communism could be justified on both grounds.

Another note characteristic of the left wing was a heightened sense of eschatology. This could easily be derived from the Bible. Those who pored over the Gospels and the Book of Revelation could hardly miss it. All the reformers were steeped in the Scriptures and all were affected by a sense of the imminence of the end. Yet there were degrees. Luther's justification by faith and Calvin's exemplification of the glory of God were timeless, and both men were too occupied with the erection of religious institutions within the framework of society to welcome a sharp eschatology which would cut the ground from under the work of their hands. The sects found eschatology more congenial.

The way was paved by movements in the late Middle Ages. Eschatology had slumbered from Augustine to Joachim of Fiore. This Calabrian prophet reintroduced the radical note with his proclamation of the third age of the spirit and of the ephemeral character of the papacy itself. The Spiritual Franciscans indulged in specific predictions of the end with frequent settings of the date by the device of adding 1,260 years (derived from the number of days spent in the wilderness by the woman in Revelation) to the year of some event in the history of the early Church, selected with a view to throwing the end slightly in advance of the prediction. Thus, reckoning from the birth of Christ gave the year 1260, and from his death the year 1293. In the Reformation period the date of the Council of Nicea in A.D. 325 as a point of departure yielded 1585 as the time of the cataclysm. The significance of this whole type of thinking was that it rendered all human institutions and churches ephemeral and divested Lutheranism and Calvinism, as much as Catholicism, of any abiding role in the divine plan.

Eschatology in some rare instances passed into a program of revolution. Strictly speaking, the two are incompatible. Eschatology believes in an imminent divine event to shatter the present scheme of history and to be inaugurated without the hand of man. Revolution depends upon human instruments. But the one idea can readily pass into the other. If the Lord tarries, man becomes impatient and begins to argue that the prelude to the divine catastrophe is the putting of the sickle to the harvest by the hand of the human reaper. A similar ideological incompatibility has characterized the Marxian dialectic.

The Protestant left wing, for that matter, found itself involved in more than one incongruity. Eschatology was not altogether at home with the mysticism which many drew from Tauler and the *Theologia Germanica*. If God is ever present in the seed of the soul and if the object of the religious life is to merge the personality in the abyss of the Godhead, why should God have to make himself manifest in a historical upheaval? New birth theology and mysticism also did not lie any too well together, for the new birth assumes that before conversion man is altogether alienated from God and requires a sudden seizure, whereas mysticism holds to the spark of the divine in all which can be gradually fanned into full flame. Revolution and the doctrine of suffering as the road to God, so common in the mystics, likewise present difficulties except in so far as revolution itself can be interpreted as a way of suffering for those who have small chance of success. But we must not expect a clarification or even an awareness of these incompatibilities among folk who were not trained to critical inquiry and were nervously distraught by persecution and wrought up to a temperature at which incompatibles fuse on an emotional rather than a logical level. A thermometer is more appropriate than a ruler for measuring such theologies.

This brings us to the note of anti-intellectualism. Even those of the left wing who had had a humanist training were indisposed to finespun theological speculations. In this respect they were in part the heirs of the *Devotio moderna* and Erasmus or of the Spiritual Franciscans. Likewise the cult of the inner word centered on the recovery of the radiance of the gospel and eschewed the speculations of Nicea. A favorite figure among the anti-intellectuals was the penitent thief who was saved without any knowledge of the substance and persons of the Godhead, paedo-baptism, consubstantiation, transubstantiation, predestination, election, reprobation, etc. The criticism of dogma as inimical to the life of the spirit passed very easily, however, into acute refutation of particular tenets and thus developed into a radical intellectualism.

Theological radicalism is discernible chiefly in one branch of anti-Trinitarianism, itself a diverse movement. Some anti-Trinitarianism was mystical and tended to obliterate all distinctions in the Godhead. If, then, Christ was regarded as God, the outcome was Sabellianism. The other variety of anti-Trinitarianism, conspicuous among the Italians, wrestled with all the logical difficulties which long before had troubled the Arians, and more recently the school of Occam, as to the reconciliation of being and becoming within the Trinity. The relationship of Father, Son and Holy Ghost appears in one aspect as a static condition of equality, but inasmuch as the Son is begotten by the Father, and the Spirit proceeds from the Father and the Son, a generative process is involved. How can one then recognize such a sequence without conceding subordination? The Socinians solved such problems by rejecting the doctrine of the Trinity altogether.

The left wing was united in its demand for the separation of Church and state. Government was ruled out of the sphere of religion. Heretics should not be constrained, for if they be brought into the Church against their will, the result will be as if water were poured into a barrel low in wine. The rise in quantity will be offset by the dilution of the quality. Constraint cannot engender the religion of the Spirit and may rather disintegrate the moral integrity of the man who saves his life by repudiating his convictions. Executions do not establish doctrines. "To burn a man is not to prove a doctrine, but to burn a man." Moreover, the doctrines for which the burning is done are the least certain because precisely the most controverted. Let us then leave judgment to God, remembering that the wolves may be distinguished from the sheep by this mark alone, that the one rends and the other is rent.

The exclusion of the magistrate from the sphere of religion, however, did not determine the extent of his right within his own domain. Here the problem was to reconcile the teaching that the "powers that be are ordained of God" (Rom. 13:1) and "resist not evil" (Matt. 5:39). Luther's solution was an initial dichotomy between a Christian society, in which no constraint is necessary, and the world from which force cannot be eliminated. Christ ruled only with a staff because he was only a shepherd of sheep, but the ruler of wolves and lions must be better armed. May a Christian, however, be a ruler of wolves and lions? Luther, at this point, demolished the dichotomy by the answer: "Yes, out of love for those who are not sufficiently advanced to relinquish force. The magistrate is ordained of God and the Christian may be a magistrate."

"Resist not evil" applies only to private ethics, or in the case of the magistrate to an inner disposition.

But the radicals, at this point, were more outward than Luther. They recognized that the ruler is ordained of God, but only among non-Christians. God has a concern for justice and order even in the world, but the world and the Church do not mix. The Christian must not participate in or avail himself of the aids of government. He has to be as a sheep for the slaughter.

With regard to the attitude toward society, the term "inner-worldly asceticism" applies in some measure to all Protestants. They differed in the degrees of their asceticism and of co-operation with secular institutions, but all stood with Luther in his repudiation of monasticism. The Catholic Church had found a resolution for the antinomy of the Church catholic and the Church holy by segregating a special group to keep intact the ideal of holiness— namely, the monks. In the late Middle Ages the quality of monasticism had declined. Luther repudiated the whole institution and invested secular occupations with religious significance as divine callings. The precepts of the Gospel had then to be worked out within the framework of society.

Protestants varied in the rigor of their interpretation of the Gospel and in the degree to which they were prepared to attempt a realization within the framework of the world. Luther endorsed such an attempt within the domestic and political areas but was shy of the economic. Calvin gave his approval to all three but was more ascetic with regard to the program to be realized. The Anabaptists accepted the domestic area, repudiated the political and went halfway with the economic. In all, they were as ascetic, if not more so, than Calvin. The communism of the Anabaptists draws our particular attention. It was Lutheran in its desire to avoid mendicancy and Franciscan in its determination to avoid luxury. It was practiced, in accord with Lutheranism, on a family rather than a celibate basis. Thus the Anabaptists while simplifying their problem through withdrawal from the political sphere, were involved in the domestic and economic areas in the common Protestant difficulty of standing ready to follow Jesus in selling all and forsaking wife and child, while at the same time marrying and rearing families on a property basis.

The left wing of the Reformation was for long neglected by the historians of the Reformation who were dominated by confessional interests and preferred to investigate the groups to which they themselves belonged rather than to delve into the records of a lost cause. In recent years, however, the historians of Lutheranism and Calvinism have become increasingly aware that an understanding of their own movements is impossible apart from a grasp of the currents to which they were opposed. A deeper reason for seeking to understand the left wing, in my judgment, is that here we can discover one clue among others to the spiritual cleavage between Germany and the "West." In Germany in the sixteenth century Anabaptism and related movements were thoroughly suppressed and never again raised their heads, whereas in England in the seventeenth century the spiritual descendants of the left wing gained a permanent foothold and did even more than the established Church to fashion the temper of England and America.

11. New Documents on Early Protestant Rationalism

We rejoice that the indefatigable Cantimori has assembled from the archives of Switzerland, England and Poland a body of documents illustrating the intellectual left wing of the Reformation as represented chiefly by the Italian refugees. On discovering that the editing of Castellio's *De Arte Dubitandi* had already been undertaken by Miss Elizabeth Feist (then of Berlin; now Mrs. Felix Hirsch of the New Jersey State Teachers College), he generously associated her with himself in the enterprise and thus made possible the publication of her work.[1]

However careful the editing, new materials of this sort always call for discussion. Cantimori frankly contended himself simply with the presentation of an accurate text. The significance of the materials, he has been discussing elsewhere in various articles to which I will call attention. Miss Feist has attempted to identify all references and has succeeded in the case of definite citations. In many instances, however, Castellio refers vaguely to the views of "certain ones." I will try to add something to the identification of sources and to the elucidation of the documents.

Castellio's work is concerned with the problem of religious liberty in relation to religious truth. The fate of the manuscript of the *De Arte Dubitandi* is indicative of the interests of different epochs. In the early seventeenth century a section was published dealing with justification by faith, and in the middle of the eighteenth century another section bearing on Biblical criticism. Not until now has the body of the work on religious epistemology seen

First published in *Church History*, VII, 2 (June 1938), 179-187. In its original form, this paper began with a lament that so many documentary series for Reformation history had suffered serious setbacks. This situation has changed so greatly that this paragraph has been omitted.

[1] *Per la Storia degli Eretici Italiani del Secolo XVI in Europa*, Testi raccolti da D. Cantimori e E. Feist (Roma, Reale Academia d'Italia Studi e Documenti, VII, 1937, 432 pages).

the light. The age of the Reformation was altogether too sure of its affirmations to feel the need of systematic investigation of the problem of knowledge. Castellio, of course, was interested in the question from the religious point of view quite as much as his contemporaries. His concern was to reduce religious persecution by eliminating many of the subjects of controversy on the score of uncertainty. He had no mind whatever to demolish the whole structure of Christian belief, but merely to pare down to the minimal and assured fundamentals.

His initial attack was on Calvin's identification of faith and knowledge. And back of this lies a long history. In the late Middle Ages the so-called "Augustinians" took a position close to that of Calvin, for they believed that faith and knowledge are not mutually exclusive.[2] The Occamists were at the other extreme, for they not only separated faith and knowledge but also faith and reason.[3] Aquinas was in between. Faith and knowledge are to be distinguished, but reason leads up to and illustrates faith. In the Protestant camp Luther's view was Occamism grown religiously vital. Faith was pitted even more violently against "the harlot reason," but faith was mightily sure of itself.[4] Melanchthon and Zwingli, while toning down Luther, still held to the essential irrationality of faith.[5] Calvin with this background arrived at an accentuated "Augustinianism." Faith and knowledge are no longer different modes of apprehending the same object at the same time, but

[2] Hugo Lang, *Die Lehre des Hl. Thomas von Aquin von der Gewissheit des übernatürlichen Glaubens* (Augsburg, 1929), 5-9. Karl Heim, *Das Gewissheitsproblem in der systematischen Theologie bis zu Schleiermacher* (Leipzig, 1911), 25. Martin Grabmann, "Die philosophische und theologische Erkenntnislehre des Matthäus von Aquasparta" (Wien, 1906), 159ff. *Theol. Studien der Leo-Gesellschaft* XIV.

[3] Nicola Abbagnano, *Guglielmo di Ockham* (Lanciano, 1931), 239. Heinrich Denifle, *Luther und Luthertum* (Mainz, 1906), I, 609-611. Carl Prantl, *Geschichte der Logik im Abendlande,* III und IV (Leipzig, 1867). Karl Heim, "Zur Geschichte der Satz von der doppelte Wahrheit," aus *Studien zur systematischen Theologie, Theodor v. Haering zum 70 Geburtstag* (22 April 1918) *von Fachgenossen dargebracht* (Tübingen, 1918), 14.

[4] Denifle, *op. cit.,* 639. Jacques Maritain, *Three Reformers* (New York, 1928), 31-34.

[5] On Melanchthon, see Ernst Troeltsch, *Vernunft und Offenbarung bei Johann Gerhard and Melanchthon* (Göttingen, 1891) and *Corpus Reformatorum,* XIII, 650. Cf. 151. On Zwingli, see Wilhelm Thomas, *Das Erkenntnis-*

rather faith can be described as *agnitio, cognitio and scientia*,[6] and all the more impregnable because bestowed by God and not achieved by man. The role of the "Augustinian" *illuminatio* is performed by the *testimonium spiritus sancti*. The rational natural theology of Aquinas is avoided, because the reason of man has been depraved by the fall, and likewise the inspired theology of the Anabaptists is eschewed as imperiling the revelation once and for all delivered in the Scriptures. The function of the Spirit is merely to illumine the Word.

Castellio desired to demolish Calvin's assurance on such points as predestination and the Trinity. The first attack was directed against the equation of faith and knowledge. There was a return here to the position of Aquinas. Next Castellio rejected the view that faith is a gift of God. Here he was exaggerating the position of Aquinas that *accipere fidem est voluntatis*,[7] and thereby unwittingly relinquishing a common basis for religious liberty. The radicals argued from the premise which runs from Augustine through Calvin that *fides* is a *donum Dei* to the conclusion that it must be beyond the jurisdiction of the sword of the magistrate. The declaration of liberty in Hungary in 1568 was based on just that ground.[8] Castellio retrieved himself, however, by substituting for a determinism of faith a determinism of intellect. Reason is a gift of God and the mind can be convinced only by evidence and not by the sword of the magistrate.[9]

Calvin's whole picture of man was subject to attack. Castellio admitted that morally Adam fell down, but intellectually he fell up, for he ate of the tree of knowledge and his eyes were opened. The fall in no sense impaired the intellectual capacities of man.[10]

With regard to Scripture, Castellio demanded a rigorous

---

prinzip bei Zwingli (Diss. Leipzig, 1902) and *Huldrici Zwinglii opera*, Schuler und Schulthess (Zürich, 1832), III, 491.

[6] *Calvini opera*, II, 399-410, *Instit.* III, ii, 2-14. Peter Brunner, *Vom Glauben bei Calvin* (Tübingen, 1925). Chapter VI is devoted to *Erkenntnis*. Edward A. Dowey, Jr., *The Knowledge of God in Calvin's Theology* (New York, 1952).

[7] *S. Th.* II, 2, Q.X, a.viii, *Opera Omnia* VIII, 89.

[8] Friedrich Teutsch, *Geschichte der evangelischen Kirchen im Siebenbürgen*, 2 vols. (Hermannstadt, 1921-22), I, 284.

[9] *De Arte Dubitandi*, 380 and 350.

[10] *Ibid.*, 367.

Biblical criticism and the recognition that the sacred writers sometimes recorded their own opinions rather than the mind of God.
Some might feel that such an assumption would destroy the authority of Scripture. *Ad quod ego respondeo etiam, si ita esset, non
idcirco non esse vera quae dixi.*[11]

Nevertheless, Castellio and Calvin were not so far apart in
their view of Scripture. Calvin was no verbal literalist and was
quite prepared to recognize error in Acts 7: 16 and Matthew 27: 9.[12]
For that reason I suspect that Castellio had someone else in mind
when he referred to those who think *Sacras enim literas esse
divino afflatu conscriptas neque hominum, sed dei arbitrio aeditas,
quarum si vel unum verbum in dubium vocetur, periculum sit, ne
cadat earum authoritas.*[13] Now Calvin, as the editors note, would
say that the Word of God must not be increased or diminished,
but that is not to say that *unum verbum* must not be called in question. One thinks rather of a passage like this from Matthias Flacius
Illyricus: *Singula ergo eius uerba tanti momenti esse apud nos
debent, ut nobis coelo ac terra maiora esse uideantur.*[14] But here
again one is on controverted ground. Otto Ritschl hailed Flacius
as the father of verbal inspiration.[15] But Moldaenke has just stoutly contested this view,[16] and opposes to a passage like the above the
following statement of Flacius to Schwenckfeld: *das sey jm yetzt
geantwort das vns nicht vmb die schrifft oder silben zuthun sey
auch nicht vmb die stimm schal laut vnnd buchstaben oder auch
vmb die weyse zu reden sondern vmb die lehre meynung oder
sentenz.* Can Flacius be harmonized with himself? I do not know.
But Castellio might easily have had in mind a passage like the one
given above.

---

[11] *Ibid.*, 340.

[12] *Calvini opera*, XLVIII, 138 and XLV, 749. Cf. Émile Doumergue, *Jean
Calvin*, IV, 76-78. Dunlop Moore, "Calvin's Doctrine of Holy Scripture," *Pres.
and Ref. Review*, IV (1893). Benjamin Warfield, "Calvin's Doctrine of the
Knowledge of God," *Princeton Theol. Rev.*, VII (1909) reprinted in *Calvin and
Calvinism* (Oxford Press, 1931).

[13] *De Arte Dubitandi*, 337.

[14] *Fidelis Admonitio*, first ed., 1562, in the *Omnes Libelli Matthiae Fl.
Illyrici* (Antwerp (?) 1567), 98.

[15] *Dogmengeschichte des Protestantismus* (Leipzig, 1908), I, Kap. XI.

[16] Günter Moldaenke, "Schriftverständnis und Schriftdeutung im Zeitalter
der Reformation," Teil I, *Matthias Flacius Illyricus* (Stuttgart, 1936), *Forschungen z. Kirchen- und Geistesgeschichte*, IX.

The editors are at a loss to identify those who say *Fides est actio intellectus* (p. 387). One thinks of Abelard who associated *intelligere* and *credere*. Again, who are those who reduce the atonement to the influence of the precept and example of Christ (p. 397)? Abelard does not quite fit. For him the atonement was the divine love awakening a response in human love. One thinks rather of the general tone of Erasmus. He would never have denied the propitiatory death of Christ, but he laid the whole emphasis on precept and example. Under those who think that not God but man was reconciled the editors see a reference to Ochino and rightly, save that behind him lies a long development. He fuses the Scotist view that the propitiation must not be interpreted to conflict with the absolute independence of the divine will, and the Valdesian view that propitiation must not detract from the divine love, and the Neoplatonic view that anger in God conflicts with the divine impassibility.[17]

Castellio's own theory of knowledge is based on sense experience and reason. The testimony of the senses, after due correction for optical and other illusions, may be accepted as valid. Here Castellio is doing little more than elaborating the view of Cicero,[18] and the whole picture of reason is a combination of the early patristic logos doctrine with Ciceronian strains.[19] The succession in which Castellio stands runs from Cicero to Locke with reliance on the data of sense experience, save for those truths which can be disclosed only by revelation. This is not the line which runs from Augustine to Descartes, which takes the rational consciousness as the point of departure.

Now let us turn to the larger body of documents edited by Cantimori. His plan has been to give an accurate rendering of the

---

[17] The standard work on the history of the atonement is Albrecht Ritschl, *Die christliche Lehre von der Rechtfertigung und Versöhnung*, 2 vols. (Bonn, 1903). On Juan Valdés, see J. Heep, "Juan de Valdés" (Leipzig, 1909), *Quellen und Darstellungen aus der Geschichte des Reformationsjahrhunderts, XI.*

[18] Cf. Castellio, *op. cit.*, 371 with *Ciceronis Academicorum Priorum liber secundus, qui inscribitur Lucullus*, cap. VII. See Ludwig Stein, "Die Erkenntnislehre der Stoa." (Berlin, 1888), *Berliner Studien für classische Philologie und Archeologie*, VII, 1.

[19] Justin Martyr, Migne, *PG*, VI, 397, 465. Cicero *De Legibus*, II, iv, 9-10; *De Finibus*, II, xii, 37; *De Natura Deorum*, II, xii.

text with only a slight measure of critical apparatus. I will run through the collection indicating the content and importance of each document and the problems connected with it.

The first text is that of the *Dialogo Religioso,* anonymous and undated. The discussion of the benefit of Christ's death, indulgences, monastic vows and purgatory suggest the early days of the reform. Citations from the scholastics are frequent. One of the interlocutors, for some curious reason, consistently uses an Italian dialect different from the speech of the others. Criticism independent of Valla is directed against the historicity of the *Donatio Constantini.*

The tract by Camillo Renato is an attack on infant baptism. Strictly speaking the position is not Anabaptist since there is no plea for re-baptism. But, for that matter, the Anabaptists did not admit that the baptism of those previously baptized in infancy constituted a repetition since the dipping of infants was no baptism at all. The rationalist character of Italian "Anabaptism" appears in that the ground for adult baptism is not the new birth but an assured faith.

Two works of Lelio Socinus are published, his "Theses on the Trinity" and his comments on the Johannine Prologue. Both call for lengthy discussion as to their authenticity as works of Lelio. The introduction is able to treat the subject only with extreme brevity, but the lack is made up in an article by Cantimori, "Gli ultimi anni e gli ultimi scritti di Lelio Sozzini" (*Religio*, XII, No. 6, 1936). The article contains also a discussion of Lelio's share in the composition of the *De Haereticis Coercendis* (1554), commonly attributed to Castellio. Bruno Becker's discovery of Castellio's last reply to Beza, not yet published, definitely excludes Lelio. More plausible was the attribution to Lelio on grounds of handwriting of the *Apologia Alfonsi Lingurii Tarraconensis hispani pro Serveto.* But in the meantime Stanislas Kot has indisputably proved that Alphonsus Lyncurius Tarraconensis was Celio Secundo Curione.[20]

---

[20] *Calvini opera*, XV, 239 f. Stanislas Kot offers the proof in *Autour de Michel Servet et de Sebastien Castellion,* ed. B. Becker (Haarlem, 1953), pp. 86-94.

The next documents are connected with the flight of Matteo Gribaldi Mofa from Tübingen, a subject already treated by Cantimori in the article "Matteo Gribaldi Mofa Chierese e l'Università di Tubinga" (*Bollentino Storico-Bibliografico Subalpino,* XXXV, No. 5-6, 1933). Celio Secondo Curione of Basel was involved in difficulties because of his relations with Gribaldi. A review is given in the book of a document bearing on his expurgation at Basel.

Giorgio Blandrata comes next. The accompanying article in his case is Cantimori's "Profilo di Giorgio Biandrata Saluzzese" (*Bollettino Storico-Bibliografico Subalpino,* XXXVIII, No. 3-4, 1936). None of the texts published in the book illustrates better than this tract of Blandrata the importance of the embedded sources and the desirability of identifying them. On page 107 there is a reference to the book of Joachim of Fiore accusing the Lombard of making the Trinity into a quaternity. The ideas of Joachim can be studied in a work by his disciples recently recovered and published by Carmelo Ottaviano, "Joachimi Abbatis Liber contra Lombardum" (Scuola di Giacchino da Fiore), *Studi e Documenti,* 3, Reale Accademia d'Italia (Roma, 1934). Next in Blandrata's work we have mention of the condemnation of Joachim's book in *capite Damnamus.* The reference is to the decretal of Innocent III in *Corpus Juris Canonici* Lib. 1, tit. i, *De Summa Trinitate, cap. ii, Damnamus.* On the next page Blandrata cites, among others, *Robertus Olchot in primo Sententiarum distinctione* 5. The passage intended is Robert Holcot, *Super quatuor libros Sententiarum,* 1, *quaest.* 5. Next we read *Vide quoque et Ioannem maioris in primo Sententiarum, distinctione,* 4. The reference is to *Joannes Major Scotus in primum Sententiarum, Dist.* 4 et 5, q. 6. Next comes *Vide et Petrum de Aliaco libro* 1, *quaestione* 5. This is Pierre D'Ailly, *Quaestiones magistri Petri de Alliaco . . . super primum tertium et quartum Sententiarum* Lib. 1, *Quaest.* 5.

The location of these passages has something more than academic interest, because they are all to be found in the *De Trinitatis Erroribus* of Michael Servetus, from whom I suspect Blandrata derived them, for he speaks on the next page of *Michael Servetus vir eruditus.*

The presence of these passages both in Servetus and Blandrata throws significant light on a controverted point with regard to the continuity of anti-Trinitarian thought. Adolph Harnack[21] contended that the Nominalist school directed against the doctrine of the Trinity a subversive criticism which was prevented from full fruition by the authority of the Church always in reserve, but when that authority was extinguished by humanism the critique came into its own. And the man who exemplified this outcome was Michael Servetus. Dunin Borkowski attacked this view,[22] contending in the first place that the Nominalists had no mind to be subversive and in the second that the anti-Trinitarians of the sixteenth century had no direct acquaintance with the scholastics. *Um eine Abhängigkeit wissenschaftlich zu erweisen, genügt es nicht, ideengeschichtliche Zusammenhänge in einer möglichen and wahrscheinlichen Ordnung zu entdecken, man müsste sie im Schrifttum der Unitarier genau nachweisen, man müsste die scotistischen and terministischen Werke einzeln anführen, aus denen sichtbar geschöptft wurde.* I do not see how the learned Jesuit could have written this, if he had taken the trouble to look in the very place to which Harnack pointed, namely Michael Servetus. This is not to say that Harnack's picture of Servetus is adequate, nor did he identify the passages demanded by Dunin Borkowski. But they are there and have been located by E. Morse Wilbur in his excellent translation and edition, *The Two Treatises of Servetus on the Trinity,* (Harvard Theological Studies, XVI, Cambridge, Mass., 1932). The presence of the citations from the Nominalists at first hand by Servetus and probably though not necessarily, at second hand by Blandrata, is a sufficient witness of the continuity of thought from the *Moderni* to the anti-Trinitarians.

There is more evidence too. Servetus has a further citation

---

[21] *Lehrbuch der Dogmengeschichte* (Freiburg i.B., 1890), III, 659. This is the second edition. The statement is fuller than in the sixth with which alone I have been able to compare it.

[22] Stanislas Dunin Borkowski, 75 *Jahre Stella Matutina Festschrift* (Feldkirch, 1931), Bd. 1, "Quellenstudien zur vorgeschichte der Unitarier des 16. Jahrhunderts," 91-138. Bd. II, "Untersuchungen zum Schrifttum der Unitarier vor Faustus Socino," pp. 103-147. On the particular point Bd. 1, pp. 135-37. The Library of Congress enters this work under Feldkirch, Austria.

which eluded Wilbur and Blandrata,[23] a reference to another of the *Moderni,* namely Gregory of Rimini, *Lectura Sententiarum* 1 *Sent., Dist.* XIII.[24] Servetus also used Occam, *Quaestiones et Decisiones, Dist.* 26.[25] Dunin Borkowski's attempt to exonerate late scholasticism from a share in the responsibility for Protestant anti-Trinitarianism does not stand examination.

Blandrata is followed in the collection by Francesco Pucci, who came over to the Reform through revulsion against the massacre of St. Bartholomew, but was disillusioned by the intolerance of the reformers and returned to Rome. Cantimori has given an account of him in the *Enciclopedia Italiana.*

The next document, entitled *Forma d'una Republica Catholica,* is anonymous. The general plan is that advocated by Acontius of reducing Christianity to those minimal and common terms on which agreement would be possible between Greek and Latin, Papist and Protestant, Armenian, Ethiopian and Indian.

The final documents are connected with Faustus Socinus in Poland and are of interest for social as well as religious history. Cantimori was indebted for the discovery of this material to the outstanding scholar of the Polish Reformation, Stanislas Kot. For the understanding of the documents one should consult Kot's *Idealogja Politycznai i Spoteczna Braci Polskich zwanych Arjanami* (Warsaw, 1932). The substance of this work in condensed form was incorporated in his *Le Mouvement Antitrinitaire au XVIe et au XVIIe siècle* (Paris, 1937). The whole has since appeared under the title *Socinianism in Poland* (Boston, 1957).

---

[23] *Trin. Err.,* 39b. Wilbur, *op. cit.,* 61, thought it a mistake for Augustine. The reference to Gregory is blind, but the clue to the solution appears in Servetus' *Restitutio,* 41.

[24] Edition of Paris, 1482, sig. S4. Copy in the John Carter Brown library, Providence, R. I.

[25] *Trin. Err.,* 42a. Wilbur, *op. cit.,* 66.

12. Sebastian Castellio, Champion of Religious Liberty

Sebastian Castellio is one of the few fortunates who have been rescued from oblivion without distortion. Not infrequently the forgotten are resuscitated only in order to serve the purpose of some party after the order of Melchisedek which has come to feel the need of a genealogy and pitches upon a likely personage of the past in order to make of him a symbol and an instrument of propaganda. Thus the German Socialists fastened upon Thomas Müntzer only to ascribe to him a concern for economic change essentially alien to his religious spirit. Somewhat similarly the Baptists, desiring a progenitor in the age of the Reformation, selected Balthasar Hubmaier. He was not so much distorted as allowed again to fall into oblivion after the discovery that he was not a felicitous choice. But Sebastian Castellio has not been warped to serve a party and has increased in prestige and influence precisely on account of what he actually was trying to say. The reason may be that his revival was due almost to accident. It was the by-product of another con-

First published in *Castellioniana, Quatre Études sur Sébastien Castellion et L'Idée de la Tolérance* par Roland H. Bainton, Bruno Becker, Marius Valkhoff et Sape Van Der Woude (Leiden, E. J. Brill, 1951). This paper is the third which I have written on Castellio and incorporates very largely the contents of the two preceding, namely: "Sebastian Castellio and the Toleration Controversy of the Sixteenth Century," from *Persecution and Liberty, Essays in Honor of George Lincoln Burr* (New York, 1931), and a chapter in *The Travail of Religious Liberty* (Philadelphia, 1951). Into the present study has been carried over the text of an unpublished fragment from the first paper and inserted here in fn. 69. The literature especially in English is covered at the end of this article up to the date of its appearance. In 1953 an important work appeared with a number of essays edited by Bruno Becker under the title *Autour de Michel Servet et de Sebastien Castellion* (Haarlem, 1953). The influence of Castellio is traced by Hans Rudolf Guggisberg, "Sebastian Castellio im Urteil seiner Nachwelt vom Späthumanismus bis zur Aufklärung," *Basler Beiträge zur Geschichtswissenschaft* LVII (Basel, 1956). The recent editions and translations as well as the secondary literature are surveyed admirably by Marius Valkoff, "Chronique Castellionienne," *Neophilologus* (Groningen, 1958).

cern, for Ferdinand Buisson, to whom we owe the magisterial biography of Castellio, approached him first as an educator and only in the course of his studies and with growing breathlessness of enthusiasm, unearthed the gallant champion of freedom.

If today we do honor to Castellio it is not simply that we may build the tombs of the prophets but that we may again heed their message. Liberty in our time in many quarters is in eclipse. We need once more to re-examine the presuppositions of freedom and we can do so no better than by reviewing the struggle of a former time. And yet this very effort on our part is fraught with the possibility of renewed intolerance, for Castellio's championing of liberty was itself a spirited attack upon intolerance, particularly as manifested by John Calvin and his associate Theodore Beza. If we recount the story in a manner sympathetic toward Castellio we shall hardly escape from portraying Calvin and Beza in an unfavorable light and we may appear to be indulging in covert attack upon Calvinism itself.

This would be not only unfortunate but historically unfair since one of the anomalies of history is that Calvinism, though intolerant in the sixteenth century, proved in the end to be one of the great forces contributing to modern religious liberty. The reason was simply that Calvinism at the outset demanded liberty only for the truth. Error was conceded no rights and truth would tolerate no infractions. Calvinists would die and fight rather than suffer any dishonor to truth and God. The Catholics were thus given no alternative other than either to exterminate or to recognize the Calvinists. Both ways were tried, sometimes alternately in the same land or exclusively in different lands. Eventually recognition was to triumph. The whole struggle tended to harden Calvinism against any defection from within. Notably was this true in France and Holland.

But England was different. Here Calvinism itself came to manifest varieties. In theology many Anglicans, some Baptists and all Presbyterians and Congregationalists were Calvinists. Thus Calvinism was confronted with the prospect of devouring itself unless some wider latitude were accorded. This could be done without abandoning the earlier presuppositions by widening the area of the adiaphora, by mitigating penalties and by giving up the theocratic role of the Church within society. At other points the pretensions of the founders were mellowed and modified, by an appropriation of elements from the mysticism and the humanism which persisted, particularly in England from the late Middle Ages and the Renaissance. Thus in the England of the seventeenth century Calvinists came to employ some of the ideas and arguments which in the previous century had been characteristic rather of Sebastian Castellio.

In such a paper as this, one might seek to do proportionate justice to the traditions alike of Calvin and Castellio as they affected liberty. But a commemoration is an occasion for doing honor by recounting the achievements and explaining the ideas of the one commemorated. This is Castellio's turn. Neither ought one in the interests of tolerance to hold back from a faithful delineation of the errors, nay even of the crimes, committed in a former age in the name of religion, nor diminish the meed of honor due to one who had alike the insight and the courage to speak a valid word against persecution.

Castellio's plea for liberty was naturally directed against religious coercion and a particular instance elicited his protest against the intolerance of Calvin and Beza. The case was the execution of Michael Servetus. He was a Spaniard who denied the orthodox doctrine of the Trinity although by no means denying the divinity of Christ. Likewise he rejected the practice of infant baptism. He was thus guilty of anti-Trinitarianism and anti-paedo-baptism, the two offenses subject to the death penalty not only in the canon law of the Catholic Church but even in the civil law of the Christian Roman Empire, the Code of Justinian. Calvin looked upon Servetus as a traitor to the kingdom of God and did not scruple to supply evidence against him to the Inquisition in France. Servetus, having escaped from its toils, sought to pass secretly through Geneva on his way to Zürich whence he planned to take refuge in Italy. But he was recognized and brought to trial at the instance of Calvin on a capital charge. The outcome was burning at the stake.

Some today feel that this episode has been magnified out of all proportion to its historic significance. Why, they ask, should the burning of this one man be deemed so much worse than the thousands of burnings instituted by the Catholics or the drownings perpetrated by the Protestants in the sixteenth century? The answer is simply that the stake of Servetus is more crucial because it became the *cause cèlèbre* of the toleration controversy, and Sebastian Castellio is responsible for making it that by his spirited protest which continued to reverberate even after oblivion had engulfed the author.

For the understanding of the toleration controversy the Servetus case does not afford an adequate beginning. Back of it lay an entire view of God, man and society, apart from which Calvin would never have denounced Servetus and the Council of Geneva would never have sentenced him to the flames. They did so because of a body of beliefs which in part they held in common with their age and in part in an even more intensified form. Well nigh everyone in the sixteenth century, whether Catholic, Lutheran, Zwinglian or Anglican, considered salvation to be contingent upon a right belief in God. A false belief was deemed an affront to the divine majesty and an offense against society because God would visit His displeasure not only upon the culprit but also upon the community. Futhermore, to seduce others by error into the way of eternal damnation was more grievous than any sin against the body to the degree that the spirit excels the flesh and the life to come is more dimensional than the brief earthly pilgrimage. By the same token, burning at the stake for half an hour was deemed but a slight foretaste of the everlasting fires of hell, nor did the stake appear cruel on the part of man when unending torment was blithely credited to God. This entire heritage of belief was appropriated by the reformers from the late Middle Ages.

But Calvin exceeded his generation in the strenuousness of his activity because the intensity of his zeal and the fury of his endeavor were derived from a heightening of current beliefs. His point of departure was the sovereignty of God. No man in that age was so profoundly moved as was John Calvin by the contemplation of God as the Lord of all the universe. The favorite expressions for God were *le Seigneur, l'Eternel.* He was the ancient of days sitting throned in glory, the sovereign ruler of all lands and times. All of the language derived from the relationship of the subject to the ruler became applicable, and heresy as an offense against God was conceived as the most heightened form of treason—lese majesty. Hence, all of the frightful penalties visited in that day upon these

Fig. 1. Dürer as a Man of Sorrows, "Self-Portrait." (Bremen, Kunsthalle)

Fig. 2. Fritz Kuntz, "St. Francis and Christ." (From Vittorino Facchinetti, *San Francesco d'Assisi,* Milan, 1921)

Fig. 3. Liebschera, "Hus at the Stake."

Fig. 4. Lucas Cranach, "Woodcut with Self-Portrait as Simon of Cyrene."
(From Luther's *Passional Christi und Antichristi* of 1521)

Fig. 5. Woodcut of 1545, "Luther Declaring the Word of God, with John Frederick Bearing the Cross." (From Max Geisberg, *Die Reformation in den Kampfbildern der Einblattholtzschnitte,* Munich, 1929)

Damit man aber
sehe/ wer der münch
sey/ so stehet er da yn
seiner klaydung/vnd
hat sein zeychen/ die
Rosen yn der handt/
Ich mayn ja es sey
der Luther. Die weil
aber Esaias spricht
am .xl. Alles flaysch
ist wie grass. Stehet
er da mit eyner sich-
eln/ vnnd schneydets
ab/ nicht grass/ son-
der flaysch/ vnd alles
was flayschlich ist/
Denn da wider pre-
digt er/ vnd wenn es
außgereutet ist/wirdt
er mit dem fewer ey-
sen/das fewer d' Chri-
stlichen lieb/das er lö-
schen ist/ wider auff
schlagen vnd anzün-
den.

Das thet der heldt Martinus Luther
Der macht das Euangeli lauther
All menschen leer er gantz ab hauth
Vnd selig spricht/der/ Gott vertrawth.

Fig. 6. Martin Luther represented as an Augustinian monk. (From *Eyn wunderliche Weyssagung . . .* , 1527)

Ide iterū alicnū exiſtentis modum falcem magnam et roſam manuꝗ ſe/
rentem:tertiū autem duplicatū:in primo elemento diuiſa ſunt.Item cō/
iūcta falciſeri quattuor meſſiū ſcribo erit.ſ.Principatus aūt omnis quē ꝑſum/
pſiſti cū gladio in Templis dolorum poſt paululum reſuſcitabis:tres annos in
mūdo uiues:ſenex ualde in inſimum duabus. tribulationibus in medio cor/
rues.

Fig. 7. Baldasare Cossa (Pope John XXIII) represented as an Augustinian monk. (From *Joachimi Abbatis Vaticinia . . .*, 1515)

VATICINIO XX

^a *Elatione* ^b *della pouertà, obedientia, caſtità, deſtruttione della cupidigia sfrenata di mangiare, & de gl'Hipocriti.*

a al. ſi legge in alcuni libri ſolamente la uoce Elatione, per titolo, & niente altro. *b* al. pouerta.

Fig. 8. A later representation of Figure 7, modified by the Church of Rome. (From *Joachimi Abbatis Vaticinia . . .*)

offenses were considered all the more appropriate when the king affronted was none other than the Lord God omnipotent.

The vindication of the glory of God for Calvin transcended all other considerations. "For if we consider what His glory really is we shall see that it deserves to be more precious than all the world. What does one see in heaven and on earth but little sparks of His virtue, justice, goodness and wisdom which are infinite in God? There is no measure. But we have only a few little signs and marks in heaven and on earth. It were better, then, that the world should perish a million times than that the glory of God should be obscured."[1]

Every human consideration must be subordinated to God's glory, which means not only that friendships must be canceled and alliances dissolved if a difference of faith intervenes, but that one should not recoil from inflicting the severest penalties on the very nearest if they be recreant to the divine honor. Commenting on Deuteronomy 13 Calvin said, "God now expressed himself more clearly in that we ought to trample under foot every affection of nature when it is a question of His honor. The father should not spare his son, the brother the brother, nor the husband his own wife. If there is a friend dearer than life put him to death."[2] In defending the execution of Servetus, Calvin further asserted, "Not in vain does God remove all affections by which the heart is accustomed to be softened. He almost denudes men of their nature lest there be any obstacle to holy zeal. Why is His severity so implacable unless that we should know that God is not properly honored unless the devotion due Him is preferred to every human office and whenever his glory is concerned we erase at once from memory our mutual humanity."[3] "The most tender affections with which nature has endowed us and in which the best of men may otherwise indulge, these when they impede the vindication of God's glory He pronounces vicious."[4]

Such curdling words could come from the lips of Calvin not because he was devoid of human feeling, for he was devoted in his

---

[1] *Calvini opera*, XXVII, 266.
[2] *Ibid.*, 251 f.
[3] *Ibid.*, VII, 476, cf. XLIV, 346.
[4] *Ibid.*, XXIV, 360.

friendships and tender in his emotions. He struggled to denude himself of natural affections because he believed that God Himself could not be regarded as tender toward all mankind. God is a Father only to the members of Christ. "It is audacious to infer because God made the animals love their young that He therefore loves His offspring. When beasts will fight to the death for their young, how is it that God suffers little children to be mangled and devoured by tigers, bears, lions and wolves? Is His hand too short that He cannot protect them? . . . He allows men to be born blind, deaf and deformed. They alone experience His fatherly favor and the hope of eternal salvation who have been freely redeemed through His only begotten Son. . . . Why does He create dullards, simpletons and idiots? . . . Whenever I see an idiot I am reminded of what God might have made me. . . . They alone experience His fatherly favor in the hope of eternal salvation who have been freely redeemed in His only begotten Son."[5] The doctrine of predestination could thus be utilized to justify religious persecution and make plausible the failure to recoil from any extremities. Had not God through Moses commanded that the cities of the Canaanites be razed and every living thing utterly destroyed? "But we may rest assured that God would suffer only those infants to be killed whom He had already damned and destined to eternal death."[6] So argued Calvin.

Thus far one might assume that for him the only offense to be visited with such implacable rigor was a denial of some cardinal tenet of revealed religion, that the offense lay in the insult of refusing to take God at His Word. But more was involved than this. Calvin believed that God had a plan for the ages. No more magnificent dream of man's unfolding destiny was ever conceived than that which John Calvin found implicit in the word of God. In this respect he differed from all of the reformers of his age. Luther and the Anabaptists conceived of the time to come on earth as about to be cut short by the speedy return of the Lord to judgment. In the interim Luther believed the elect to be indistinguishable from the non-elect and obviously therefore the elect could not undertake

[5] *Ibid.*, IX, 289-290.
[6] *Ibid.*, XXIV, 363.

to set up the kingdom of Christ on earth. Rather, the fervent believers should dwell together with the formal Christians in an effort to restrain outrageous villainy until the coming of the Lord. The Anabaptists, on the contrary, considered that the elect could be discerned by the quality of their lives and by the experience of the new birth. But the saints should not aspire to rule. Rather should they withdraw into holy communities, seeking in the meantime to convert individuals and despairing of any transformation of society. The audacity of John Calvin consisted in this, that he assigned to the saints a directive role in the leadership of society at large. He did so, in part, because he envisaged not the speedy coming of the Lord but a considerable time span in which *le Seigneur* could unroll the drama of the ages and set up *le royaume de Dieu*. Calvin's view of man was just as gloomy as that of Luther or the Anabaptists, but his view of history was almost roseate because the Lord has a plan which cannot fail, not because men are good but because God is great and none can withstand His outstretched arm or abide the breath of His mouth. Through the elect as God's instrument the plan is to be achieved. They may form selective communities as at Geneva or may exercise leadership through convinced and militant minorities in unwinnowed lands.

This grandiose enterprise rested of course on the assumption that God can be known, that His plan can be known, and that the elect can be recognized. On all these counts Calvin was utterly confident. No one else in Christian thought had ever gone quite so far as he in claims with regard to religious knowledge. The prevailing opinion hitherto had been that of Thomas Aquinas who distinguished faith and knowledge as mutually exclusive. What is believed is not known and what is known is no longer believed. The mystics of the late Middle Ages such as Bonaventura, however, had held to the possibility of the vision of God in this life and therefore refused so sharply to distinguish faith and knowledge which are rather two modes of apprehending the same object at the same time. Calvin went even further in his declarations. "Faith," said he, "is lodged not in ignorance but in knowledge (*cognitio*). . . . Faith lies not in reverence for the Church but in the knowledge (*cognitio*) of God and Christ. . . . We hold faith to be acquaintance (*notitia*) with God's will for us as given in his Word. . . . We shall have a just definition of faith if we say that it is a firm and certain knowledge (*cognitio*) of the divine benevolence toward us. . . . Scripture rightly declares that faith is 'the full assurance (*agnitio*) of understanding.' By the Apostle John it is called knowledge (*scientia*) since he testifies that the faithful know themselves to be sons of God. . . . To be sure faith is not apprehension, but it is certitude."[7]

Neither could there be any doubt for Calvin with regard to the plan of God which is clearly revealed in the Scriptures. One of Calvin's favorite books was that of Deuteronomy which announces the purpose of God to usher his chosen people into a land where they should inherit vines which they had not planted and wells which they had not dug, provided only they should keep the covenant and remember His precepts to do them. This, however, they had failed to do and from the Apostle Paul one learned that the old Israel had been superseded by the new Israel of God, namely the Christian Church. To this Church had been transferred the role of the chosen people and their mission was to erect the holy commonwealth. For them Scripture is the warrant and Scripture provides the pattern. Finally, the elect may be recognized by certain tangible tests. For all practical intent the chosen of the Lord are those who believe in the doctrine, walk uprightly and partake in the sacraments. The creed, the deed and the rite thus distinguish the elect. Any persons capable of meeting these requirements should assume their election, stop worrying and set themselves to strenuous endeavor. The Church to be sure is not a company of saints. It is not a field completely weeded of tares. Nevertheless, the Church is God's instrument. Here was a faith big with hope and confident of success. By this sublime conviction heroes were forged, martyrs were nerved, kingdoms were subdued, the wilderness tamed and some semblance of a holy community approximated upon earth. But woe to him who should stand in the way of the divine plan. He was not merely a reviler of God but an impeder of the grand design.

Repellent as many elements in this picture must appear to a generation nauseated by religious strife, to the men of that age Calvin's program was a word of ringing hope. Even the appeals to

[7] *Ibid.*, II, 399-410. *Instit.*, III, ii, 2-14.

renunciation and discipline exercised an austere seduction. One of the young men enlisted for the grand endeavor was Sebastian Castellio. He was a Frenchman from Savoy who, leaving the circle of his peasant forebears, went up to Lyons and avidly pursued the new humanist learning. In accord with the current fad, he gave his name the Hellenized form Castalio from the nymph whose spring arose at the base of Parnassus. He exercised himself in literary feats in Latin and in Greek, for all of which in after years he reproached himself as having toyed with vanities. Shamefacedly he gave up the name Castalio but did not disdain to use the Latinized form, Castellio. In French his name was Chateillon.

But not for long did he indulge in dalliances with the Attic muse because the Gospel fell upon his ear. There was a day when this need not have meant a radical alteration in his ways, but the time was swiftly passing when an Evangelical could be either a Catholic or a Lutheran and not altogether sure of which, and yet remain secure in France. This was the hour of the God of Deuteronomy who said, "Choose ye this day whom ye will serve." How Castellio was recruited for the reform we do not know, whether by poring over the Scriptures among some clandestine student groups, whether by the sight of a martyr at the stake, whether through the singing of the Marseillaise of the reform, the Psalms of David. At any rate, the decision was made and the young scholar went into exile.

The place selected was Strasbourg. Why Strasbourg we do not know. Possibly because of geographical convenience. Quite possibly too because John Calvin happened to be there. This was for him an unsought interlude in his Genevan career. He had made an initial attempt to erect *le royaume de Dieu* in a city particularly apt for the plan because recently emancipated from the control alike of the Bishop and the Duke of Savoy through the assistance of the Protestant city of Berne. Protestant preaching had accompanied the political overthrow. To the Bishop succeeded the Reform. When Calvin assumed the wheel he was speedily to discover, however, that the Republicans who had fought to expel the overlords were of no mind to submit to the yoke of the Gospel. The attempt to impose on them the regime of the saints precipitated exile. Calvin was for that reason in Strasbourg. There Castellio joined him

and was thus on hand when the invitation came to Calvin to return
and resume his interrupted endeavor. He needed for his purpose
someone to train the young both in the tools of Protestant scholarship and in the teaching of the divine founder of the holy commonwealth. Some one distinguished in the field of education was preferred but none was at the moment available. Castellio though
young was well trained, gifted and devoted. He was invited to become the schoolmaster of Geneva and with zest entered upon the
task.

A classic work in the field of education resulted from this activity. Castellio wanted his boys to know Latin, since it was the
universal language of learned men throughout Europe, and he
wanted them to know classical Latin and not the jargon of the
Scholastics. But he feared to educate the lads on the bawdy passages
of Plautus, Terence and Ovid. The plan took shape to render the
piquant Biblical stories into lively dialogues in Ciceronian diction
and accompanied by a rendering in French. The work was to enjoy
an immense vogue, less perhaps in France than in other lands such
as Germany, England and the American colonies, where of course
French was replaced by the corresponding vernacular or the Latin
was used by itself. These sprightly dialogues have an interest also
for the theme of tolerance. The manner is strikingly different between the ways in which Calvin and Castellio handled, for example, the exposure of Moses in the bulrushes and the selling of Joseph by his brethren. In both instances Calvin pointed out that
the evil of men might nevertheless serve to accomplish the providence of God. Castellio rather was moved to indignation by the
cruelty of Pharaoh and with admiration for his daughter who
dared to disobey and circumvent her father's wicked design. And
Joseph's brethren were portrayed as monsters for selling a callow
lad, their own brother, for no other crime than dreams. Besides, if
his dreams were bound to come true, why try to foil them, and if
not why be concerned? Here predestination was turned into an
argument for liberty.

But these implicit differences led to no breach between Castellio and Calvin and probably would not have been sensed had
not subsequent controversy given them significance. The rift came
over quite another matter. Castellio got married. Shortly thereafter

he requested an increase in salary but was denied. He sought then to take a church which would have an adequate stipend. For that purpose he needed to be ordained and applied to the Genevan consistory but was rejected on two counts. The first was that he denied the inspiration of the Song of Songs, which he considered to be a lascivious love poem; and secondly that he could not accept Calvin's interpretation of the descent of Christ into hell as stated in the Apostles' Creed. Castellio thereupon resigned as the master of the school and asked for a testimonial of good character. This was gladly given by Calvin and the ministers who declared that he was a man of upright life in every respect worthy of the ministry save for these two counts. But they could not suffer any one in the ranks of the reformed clergy who repudiated a book in the sacred canon. If this book could be called into question, why might not some other also be rejected, and what a disintegration would then ensue!

Castellio arranged to remove to Basel where the atmosphere was less rigorous. Here the great Erasmus had breathed his last and left behind him a circle of admirers of a similarly moderate temper, Boniface Amerbach for example. But Castellio did not succeed in completing the transfer for several months and in the interim indulged at Geneva in some very caustic criticism of the regime. His complaint was that a man who was deemed altogether acceptable in his life should be rejected on what was considered a minor point of doctrine, whereas other men whose characters were far from being above reproach were already in the ministry and were retained. The strictures received an acrimonious barb because of the circumstance that sometime previously, when the Town Council had requested the ministers to send one of their number other than Calvin as a chaplain to the Plague Hospital, they had acknowledged this to be their duty but confessed a lack of courage, whereas the schoolmaster Castellio had offered to go. He was not accepted because needed at the school. Then, too, there were ministers who were far from impeccable at the points of drink, sex and the payment of debts. Calvin and his colleagues were of course confronted with a formidable task in creating overnight a worthy ministry, but this is only a greater cause for wonder that they should reject a man so eminently qualified save at two points of doctrine.

The reason was plainly that although in the eyes of Calvin

and his associates both the discipline and the doctrine were important, and none strove so strenuously to effect a combination of the
two, yet if a choice had to be made, a rejection of the presuppositions was more serious than a defection in behavior. A man who
was not in accord with the great plan, no matter how upright he
might be, could not qualify as an associate, whereas a man who
subscribed, if he then proved unworthy, might for a time at least
be treated with leniency in the hope that he would mend his ways.
Plainly this meant that a foe might be nobler than a friend, yet a
foe he must remain so long as he was on the wrong side. But Castellio's concept of Christianity was much more in terms of behavior
than of belief. The cleavage between the discipline and the doctrine was involved and one could predict that these two men would
come again to grips on deadlier issues.

Once in Basel, Castellio for some years lived a Spartan existence supporting himself, his wife and growing family. By his first
and his second wife he had in the end eight children. The income
was derived from varied and largely menial tasks, carrying water
for the gardeners, harpooning driftwood from the Rhine, correct-
ing proof for the printers. All spare time was devoted assiduously
to literary pursuits. Minor productions began to appear—a translation of the Pentateuch into Latin called *Moses Latinus,* with a
preface lauding Moses as a master of all literary forms and of all
the arts. Then a poem in Greek and in Latin recounting the story
of the prophet Jonah in dactylic hexameters. Humanist conceits
had not yet been abandoned. The waxing of the gourd was described after the manner of Virgil's Bucolics, and Jonah was made
to quote Cicero in the belly of the whale. Apart from these excres-
cences, the exposition of the prophet afforded Castellio an opportunity for developing his favorite themes. At this point it is very in-
structive to make a comparison of the manners in which Luther,
Calvin and Castellio commented on this same book. To Luther the
central figure was Jonah and the central theme his utter desolation
of spirit when convicted of sin and swept by the billows into the
belly of darkness where all of the physical discomfort was as nothing compared to the sense of alienation from God. For Calvin the
central figure was God, His providence and His justice. The sailors
were commended indeed for their humanity toward Jonah but

even more because they did not reproach God for having involved them innocently in the chastisement of the prophet. Again God was vindicated from any suspicion of mutability in threatening disaster and then sparing Nineveh, for this mercy was in accord all along with His nature and purpose. For Castellio the principal figures were the heathen sailors who exhibited such natural humanity in that they were willing to risk perishing rather than throw overboard the prophet. And again, his favorites were the heathen Ninevites who simply because of contrition became the recipients of the divine mercy. Castellio's fancy turned to the cattle, who according to the Biblical account also donned sackcloth. The poem relates that the ox foregoes his fodder and the goat his bush, the ass will have no straw and the lamb declines the udder. This penitence of the dumb creatures was the sole condition of forgiveness on the part of the heavenly Father.[8]

More extensive work was under way—complete translations of the Bible into classical Latin and vernacular French. In the Latin, Castellio sought to eliminate all Greek roots and at first went to extremes in substituting for the Greek *baptizare* the Latin *lavare.* In French similarly he would coin words from native roots to avoid expressions of foreign derivation. Instead of *holocauste* he would use *brulage.* Calvin and Beza rediculed his extravagances and in subsequent editions he toned them down, but despite minor blemishes the effort was sound and the result distinguished. Some of the changes were designed not merely to achieve purity of language but to convey also the stab of the original meaning. "Tell any one," said Castellio, "that he should take up his cross and he will readily agree because the cross is no longer in use as an instrument of execution, but tell him to carry the rope for his own lynching and he will not so readily accede."[9]

The Latin appeared in 1551, the French in 1555. Each was preceded by a dedication and both were pleas for religious liberty. The particular point was that Scripture is fraught with uncertainty and if there is to be constraint it were better to wait until one

---

[8] Luther's commentary in *WA*, XIX, pp. 185-251; Calvin's commentary in *Calvini opera*, XLIII, pp. 210-280.

[9] *Def. Trans.*, p. 31. For a fuller explanation of the sources used in this chapter, see the Selected Bibliography at the end of the chapter.

knows for what. God has declared His will with regard to crimes
and in this area there is no controversy. "But the case of religion
and of the knowledge of Sacred Scripture is altogether different,
for the things contained in it are given obscurely and often in enigmas and inscrutable questions, which have been in dispute for
more than a thousand years without any agreement, nor can there
be agreement without love, which breaks and appeases all controversies and drives away ignorance. Yet for this cause the earth is
filled with innocent blood. We ought certainly, however much we
may think we know everything, we ought, I say, to fear lest in cruci-
fying thieves justly, we crucify also Christ unjustly."[10]

The French dedication to Henry II, the great persecutor,
made the same point in other terms:

"When night falls upon the battlefield the combatants wait
for the day lest by chance friends be killed instead of enemies, for
it is better to spare one's enemies than to kill some of one's friends.
Likewise also in the daytime, when the hand to hand combat begins the artillery ceases for fear of the aforesaid mischance. Here I
should like to point a moral if your Majesty will deign to listen.
The world today is embroiled in great disturbance principally
touching the question of religion. There never were so many calamities and evils, from which we may well perceive the night of ignorance. If not all are enveloped, at least many are. If it were day
there would never be such diverse and even contrary judgments
about the same color. Or if it is day, at least the good and the evil
are so confused in the matter of religion that if one wishes to dis-
entangle those who are at variance as to the truth there is danger
lest the wheat be rooted out with the tares. That would be an irreparable loss. Hitherto the world has always made this mistake. The
prophets, the apostles, so many thousands of martyrs, and even the
Son of God were put to death under color of religion. An account
must be given for all this blood by those who have been striking at
random in the night of ignorance.... Believe me, your Majesty,

---

[10] *La Bible nouvellement translateé* (Basel, 1555). This Preface circulated
in manuscript as early as 1553. *Calvini opera*, XIV, p. 586, n. 7, *Ep.* 1769 (Aug. 6,
1553). The first section of the following translation is from a photostat of signature 2 from the copy in the British Museum. The second paragraph is from
the portion reprinted in *Calvini opera*, XIV, p. 737, No. 1889.

the world today is neither better nor wiser nor more enlightened than formerly. It were better, therefore, in view of so much doubt and confusion to wait before shooting until the dawn, or until things are better disentangled, lest in the darkness and confusion we do that of which afterwards we shall have to say, "I did not intend to.'"

The Latin Bible did not fail of its reward. When the chair of Greek in the University of Basel became vacant Castellio was elected to the post. This was in the fall of 1553 in the 38th year of his age. The problem of maintenance for his family was thus solved and he could now look forward to a tranquil career of literary labor.

So might it have been save for the execution on October 27 of that year in Geneva of Michael Servetus on the charge of heresy. Castellio's earlier publications had already made plain that he could scarcely look upon such measures with equanimity. His concern for humanity and his spirit of critical inquiry with regard to the Scripture itself disposed him to reject alike the cause and the method. No one in his day doubted that his hand was the chief in an anonymous publication which appeared with the title in French *Traité des Hérétiques. A savoir si on les doit persecuter, et comment on se doit conduire avec eux, selon l'avis, opinion, et sentence de plusieurs auteurs, tant anciens, que modernes.* And likewise in the Latin as *De Haereticis, an sint persequendi.* The work was a compilation of opinions, ancient and modern, against persecution. In several instances contemporaries were embarrassed by the publication of liberal utterances from which their present practice was remote. Calvin received such a reminder. Luther, though dead, was similarly treated. The liberal statements of St. Augustine were revived, for although he had formulated a theory of persecution he had never condoned the death penalty. The Fathers of the early Church were placed side by side with sixteenth century figures such as Erasmus and Sebastian Franck. Since the latter was in ill odor in orthodox circles, in some editions of Castellio's work he was given the pseudonym Augustine Eleutherius. All of these passages were readily recognizable. The only question could be as to who had compiled them and who was the author of three additional passages ascribed to the pseudonyms: Martin Bellius, George

Kleinberg and Basil Montfort. The reader was given to infer that they were not Castellio because a passage from his dedication of the Latin Bible to Edward VI was included under his own name. The book was published ostensibly at Magdeburg.

Beza quickly surmised that this Magdeburg was on the Rhine. He was quite right. A list of the works brought out by Oporinus of Basel and discovered after his death included *De Haereticis*. As to the compiler and the author of the anonymous passages suspicion quickly fastened upon Castellio, but from that day until quite recently the possibility remained open that he might have been assisted by certain collaborators including such liberals as Lelio Sozzini, Coelio Curione, and David Joris. The question was not laid to rest until the discovery by Professor Becker of Castellio's final reply to Beza which makes plain that the author of the whole was none other than Castellio himself, however much he may have been aided by collaborators in the collection of the material.

The opening section by Martin Bellius addressed to the Duke of Wurttemberg commenced with the parable of the white robe and reads as follows:

Most Illustrious Prince, suppose you had told your subjects that you would come to them at some uncertain time and had commanded them to make ready to go forth clad in white garments to meet you whenever you might appear. What would you do if, on your return, you discovered that they had taken no thought for the white robes but instead were disputing among themselves concerning your person? Some were saying that you were in France, others that you were in Spain; some that you would come on a horse, others in a chariot; some were asserting that you would appear with a great equipage, others that you would be unattended. Would this please you?

Suppose further that the controversy was being conducted not merely by words but by blows and swords, and that one group wounded and killed the others who did not agree with them. "He will come on a horse," one would say.

"No, in a chariot," another would retort.

"You lie."

"You're the liar. Take that." He punches him.

"And take that in the belly." The other stabs.

Would you, O Prince, commend such citizens? Suppose, however, that some did their duty and followed your command to prepare the white robes, but the others oppressed them on that account and put them to death. Would you not rigorously destroy such scoundrels?

But what if these homicides claimed to have done all this in your name and in accord with your command, even though you had previously expressly forbidden it? Would you not consider that such outrageous conduct deserved to be punished without mercy? Now I beg you, most Illustrious Prince, to be kind enough to hear why I say these things.

Christ is the Prince of this world who on His departure from the earth foretold to men that He would return some day at an uncertain hour, and He commanded them to prepare white robes for His coming, that is to say, that they should live together in a Christian manner, amicably, without controversy and contention, loving one another. But consider now, I beg you, how well we discharge our duty.

How many are there who show the slightest concern to prepare the white robe? Who is there who bends every effort to live in this world in a saintly, just, and religious manner in the expectation of the coming of the Lord? For nothing is there so little concern. The true fear of God and charity are fallen and grown cold. Our life is spent in contention and in every manner of sin. We dispute, not as to the way by which we may come to Christ, which is to correct our lives, but rather as to the state and office of Christ, where He now is and what He is doing, how He is seated at the right hand of the Father, and how He is one with the Father; likewise with regard to the Trinity, predestination, free will; so, also, of God, the angels, the state of souls after this life and other like things, which do not need to be known for salvation by faith (for the publicans and sinners were saved without this knowledge), nor indeed can they be known before the heart is pure (for to see these things is to see God Himself, who cannot be seen save by the pure in heart, as the text says, "Blessed are the pure in heart for they shall see God"). Nor if these are known do they make a man better, as Paul says, "Though I understand all mysteries and have not love it profiteth me nothing." This perverse curiosity engenders worse evils. Men are puffed up with knowledge or with a false opinion of knowledge and look down upon others. Pride is followed by cruelty and persecution so that now scarcely anyone is able to endure another who differs at all from him. Although opinions are almost as numerous as men, nevertheless there is hardly any sect which does not condemn all others and desires to reign alone. Hence arise banishments, chains, imprisonments, stakes, and gallows and this miserable rage to visit daily penalties upon those who differ from the mighty about matters hitherto unknown, for so many centuries disputed, and not yet cleared up.

If, however, there is someone who strives to prepare the white robe, that is, to live justly and innocently, then all others with one accord cry out against him if he differ from them in anything, and they confidently pronounce him a heretic on the ground that he seeks to be justified by works. Horrible crimes of which he never dreamed are attributed to him and the common people are prejudiced by slander until they consider it a crime merely to hear him speak. Hence arises such cruel rage that some are so incensed by calumny as to be infuriated when the victim is first strangled instead of being burned alive at a slow fire.

This is cruel enough, but a more capital offense is added when this conduct is justified under the robe of Christ and is defended as being in accord with his will, when Satan could not devise anything more repugnant to the nature and will of Christ! Yet these very people, who are so furious against the heretics, as they call them, are so far from hating moral offenders that no scruple is felt against living in luxury with the avaricious, currying flatterers, abetting the envious and calumniators, making merry with drunkards, gluttons, and adulterers, banqueting daily with the scurrilous, impostors, and those who are hated of God. Who then can doubt that they hate not vices but virtues? To hate the good is the same as to love the evil. If, then, the bad are dear to a man there is no doubt but that the good are hateful to him.

I ask you, then, most Illustrious Prince, what do you think Christ will do when he comes? Will he commend such things? Will he approve of them?

After the publication of this spirited protest, Castellio found himself not a little curtailed in his freedom of publication. Censorship was taken for granted in that century and every town had a sense of solidarity and responsibility for pronouncements made by any of its members. A theological tract might easily have political repercussions and might embroil the community actually in war with Catholic neighbors or at least in rifts and ruptures with Protestant allies. Basel was less rigorous than Geneva and breathed still the spirit of Erasmus, but the tolerance of Basel should not be exaggerated. Boniface Amerbach, the literary executor of Erasmus, was the very one who prodded the ministers and magistrates to take action when heresy was discovered in the person and household of the deceased David Joris. A full twenty years before, Basel had not been willing to harbor Servetus, and Castellio, though he might be tolerated for himself, would not be permitted to affront the leaders of the Genevan reform.

He had no difficulty of course with editions of the classics, Homer, Diodorus Siculus, Xenophon, the Sybilline oracles or Thucydides. All these were innocuous. And translations of mystical writings, such as the *Imitatio Christi* and the *Theologia Germanica* passed muster. Somewhat more dubious was an appeal at the outbreak of the wars of religion in France alike to the Evangelicals and to the Catholics to lay down their arms and compose their differences. Perhaps this work evaded censorship, for it appeared without author, date or place. But theological works did not fare so well. The Latin translation of the Bible was accompanied by annotations and those on the 9th chapter of Romans were suppressed because they denied the doctrine of predestination. A defense of Castellio's translations was suffered only after certain expurgations, and the theological treatises which came directly to grips with the problem of predestination saw the light only in late editions, first of all by Faustus Sozzini in 1578. A work dealing with the problem of religious knowledge remained in manuscript until it was edited by Miss Elizabeth Feist (now Mrs. Felix Hirsch) in 1937. The controversial tracts over religious liberty exchanged with Calvin and Beza naturally fared no better. Calvin even before the appearance of Castellio's *De Haereticis* had issued a defense of the execution of Servetus calling it a *Defensio Orthodoxae Fidei contra Errores Michaelis Serveti*. Castellio responded in his *Contra Libellum Calvini* which did not appear until 1612 in Holland. Then Beza answered in a book also entitled *De Haereticis*. This appeared in 1554. Castellio replied both in French and in Latin but his manuscript was lost to view until accidentally discovered by Professor Becker in the Library of the Remonstrant Church in Rotterdam. A few fragments only have been released by Etienne Giran in *L'Esprit et la Vie*. The manuscript in its entirety still awaits publication.

Since Castellio was prevented from speaking on controversial issues one might have supposed that personally he could have been left alone. There were those who hoped so. Simon Sulzer, one of the pastors of Basel, and friendly with Calvin and Beza, begged them not to stir up Castellio who was innocuously engaged in editing the classics.[11] But Beza notably would not desist, and partly because he could not be persuaded that Castellio was quiescent and was not in fact the author of other anonymous works attacking the position of Geneva. Anonymity may prove a protection but again it may lay a fog of suspicion. Investigated in Basel as to his views

[11] Simon Sulzer to Theodore Beza, Basel, May 2, 1560, Musée de la Réformation, Geneva.

on predestination, Castellio fully agreed that the saved owe every-thing to God, but denied roundly that the damned were hated by the Lord before ever they had committed any sin. For this position he was not molested. The situation, however, grew more tense when David Joris, with whom he had been friendly, was discovered two years after his death to have been an exile from the Netherlands not for Lutheranism but for a most virulent form of Anabaptism. After a trial of his remains his corpse was burned in the public square at Basel. Castellio was among the throng of witnesses. What his feelings were on that occasion may be judged from the report of a visitor to Basel who said that while there he had seen Castellio but at first scarcely recognized him since he was as pale as if he had just come up from the grave. His friends were concerned for him and one of them sought to arrange a haven in Poland. It was an Italian, the Marquis of Oria, who had come to know Castellio dur-ing a period of residence in Basel before his own migration to Poland. This country at that time had close relations with Italy because the queen, Bona Sforza, was herself Italian; but even more intimate were the relations with Basel where many Polish students frequented the university, and among them were a number deeply devoted to Castellio. This Italian nobleman issued the following invitation:

"I know not whether your Attic letter brought me more joy or grief. For although I do not deny that, on account of its novelty, it gave me great pleasure, I must confess that what I read between the lines grieved me vastly. To come at once to the point, then, I will speak of what seems to me most essential to you. I see them laying aside the mask and wishing to wage open war on you. And if you put any faith in my opinion (that is, in the opinion of one who greatly loves you), you ought by all means to think of seeking a new country. This region would not be uncongenial, if you could put up with the beer. I do not mean that there is no wine here; but that, since it is not native-grown, it cannot be brought in from else-where for a low price. In other respects, in my judgment, it is not inferior to Germany; and in some respects it surpasses her. To make this clear, I will attempt without concealment to show as briefly as I can. You would have here great liberty—nay the very greatest—as regards thought and opinion, living, writing, publishing. There would be nobody to censure. You would have men who would love and defend you and (what ought to be pleasanter to you) those having a common cause with you. Think it over; you will finally make the decision. Corn is not very dear in this place; I judge that there is little difference between ours and yours. The cold is frightful, and the rivers freeze every year; but Germany is not one whit better."

Information is then given as to the preferable route to Poland. The letter concludes: "It does not seem to me out of place that you talk the whole matter over with Sozzini, either going to Zürich yourself, or having him come to Basel or sending him letters by trusty messengers. He is a man who loves you and knows thoroughly all Poland. Perhaps he would be your companion or guide on the future journey. May God bring you to decide that which He knows will be for your good."[12]

Castellio did not avail himself of this opportunity. He may have regretted it, for the very next year a new difficulty arose by reason of the fact that he had translated from the Italian into Latin the *Thirty Dialogues of Bernardino Ochino,* a very distinguished figure, formerly the general of the Capuchins, the Savonarola of his generation in Italy. In 1562 he was an exile for the reform faith, pastor of a refugee Italian congregation in Zürich. The relations between these exiles and their rescuers were strained. Ochino had not helped matters by irresponsible polemic against the Church of Rome which endangered the position of Zürich. He was instructed that he must henceforth comply with censorship, but he evaded the order by publishing outside of Zürich at Basel. The *Thirty Dialogues* which Castellio translated contained much to trouble Israel. There was one on polygamy in which Ochino, without acknowledging the source, incorporated in his Italian a German tract written in defense of the bigamy of the Landgrave Philip of Hesse. Ochino himself undertook to refute the arguments and did well enough until he came to the end when he said that if anyone had a special inspiration from the Holy Spirit to practice polygamy, he might act accordingly. This may have been only the innocuous formula commonly employed to explain the immorali-

[12] Frederic C. Church, *The Italian Reformers* (New York, 1932), Pp. 340-341.

ties of the patriarchs, but one could not be quite sure because Ochino himself was no stranger to inspiration and, moreover, the tract was addressed to the King of Poland, who at that moment was in the position once occupied by Henry VIII. Ochino appeared to be suggesting that the solution of the problem might be bigamy. Then there were other chapters dealing with the Trinity, the atonement, religious liberty, pacifism instead of wars of religion, and all of them espousing unpopular points of view.

This work in the Italian manuscript had been submitted to the censor at Basel. He was a friend of Castellio, the Italian Curio, who examined the work cursorily and reported nothing amiss. Castellio then went ahead with the translation but the Latin version was not again submitted to censorship, and this was considered to have been a violation. The upshot was that Ochino, banished from Zürich, was not permitted to winter in Basel, but in his 76th year and accompanied by three children was forced to make his way into Poland. The printer of the book, Perna, was given a term in prison.[13] An indictment was lodged against the translator, Castellio, and in all probability he would have suffered either imprisonment or exile had not death delivered him from the proceedings.

Now remains the task of analyzing more systematically his pronouncements on religious liberty. The sayings already cited are sufficient to show that Castellio was deeply tinctured by those two movements which, in the Catholicism of the late Middle Ages, had made for tolerance. The first was humanism and the second mysticism. Humanism, notably in the hands of an Erasmus, was marked by a spirit of critical inquiry with regard to the sources of the Christian revelation and at the same time by a moralistic view of religion with more stress upon a right life than upon a correct opinion. God was pictured as moral and merciful and man as capable of fulfilling God's demands. Christ was the great example and his whole spirit breathed compassion. This was required of man, not that he should know or believe much but that he should obey the few clear and simple precepts of which the greatest is this that he should love his neighbor as himself and be kind to the

[13] See my *Bernardino Ochino* (Florence, 1940).

erring. And mysticism re-enforced this picture in that the way to God lay not through dogma but through the annihilation of all self-will and the endurance rather than the infliction of suffering. Castellio's humanist training at Lyons may presumably have intro-duced him to the Erasmian tradition, and his translations of the *Theologia Germanica* and the *Imitatio Christi* brought him in touch with mystical currents.

His view of God differed as did that of Erasmus from the view of the great reformers. Castellio drew a healthy-minded pic-ture and made no valiant effort to include the uglier facts of life in a theodicy. He did not wrestle with Calvin's problem of why God suffers children to be devoured by tigers, or even worse to be born morons. Castellio's view of God was derived from the lovelier facts of life, of human justice, of the love of parent for child,[14] as well as from the character of Christ.[15] God, who created these, must be at least as good as they. He is a God of mercy and forgiveness.[16] If before the sacrifice of Christ he had compassion on guilty Nineveh, how much more afterwards would He pity innocent babes.[17] The doctrine of election and reprobation was rejected by Castellio on the ground that reprobation in advance of any misconduct is thor-oughly unjust and the damned in that case would have a perfect right to reproach God.[18] Still worse, if the damned cannot refrain from sinning, God will become responsible for their sin. To avoid this conclusion Castellio would limit God's power to the point that God can do what He wants only because He does not want to do that which He cannot.[19] He has no disposition to commit the un-worthy. To leave men free is a greater glory to God because in that case if they sin their punishment is just.[20] And God is such a God that He esteems in man an unconstrained response, a willing obe-dience. For that reason God draws, attracts, urges, invites and per-

---

[14] IV, pp. 7, 31, 33, 40, 50, 60, 92-93, 128, 180, 199.

[15] *Ibid.*, p. 34. *De Praedestinatione*, p. 273.

[16] IV, pp. 66, 93. Buisson, II, p. 443.

[17] *De Praedestinatione*, pp. 331-32.

[18] IV, 52.

[19] *Ibid.*, p. 28.

[20] *Ibid.*, pp. 44, 191.

suades but does not compel.[21] The imitation of this God leads men
to love their enemies, [22] and to err on the side of mercy.[23]

The picture of man is likewise different. Castellio believed
at least theoretically in perfection. He did not pretend to have
attained but he insisted that attainment is not impossible. The
natural man has great capacity for fulfilling the law of nature, and
the redeemed man is not in a position in which he cannot sin (*non
posse peccare*) but in which he can not sin (*posse non peccare*),[24]
provided he make even as much effort as he would to learn German or French, music, dancing or cards.[25] When critics scornfully
demanded "Show us a perfect man," Castellio retorted, "Such men
are generally obscure and unknown, but if I knew one I would not
point him out to them, for I fear that they are of the same mind as
Herod, who wished to be shown the newborn King of the Jews
that he also might worship him."[26] Castellio's view of man's capacities prompted him to assign to man a higher worth, and when
Calvin and Beza compared the burning of a man to the killing of a
wolf,[27] Castellio denied the comparison on the ground that man
never so degenerated as to become a beast.[28]

The different view of God and the different view of man entailed also a different view of salvation. To the question, "What
doth the Lord require of thee", the answer was that He requires
very little by way of belief. Here Castellio was the heir of Erasmus
who in turn was a disciple of the undogmatic piety of the Brethren
of the Common Life with its anti-speculative emphasis. *The Imitation of Christ* affirms that the Trinity is better pleased by adora-
tion than by speculation and in all such circles the penitent thief
was a patron saint because saved by so little theology. Castellio
made the point abundantly plain in the preface already cited of
Martin Bellius where it is said that to wear the white robe is to live

---

[21] *Ibid.*, pp. 151-52.

[22] *Conseil*, p. 54. *Def. Trans.*, p. 161.

[23] *Contra Libellum Calvini*, Fvb, Cal. 96, p. 102; Hviijb-1, Cal. 25, pp.
140-41.

[24] *De Justificatione*, pp. 41, 49.

[25] V, pp. 19-20. Cf. IV, pp. 204 ff.

[26] *De Obedientia*, pp. 234-35.

[27] *Calvini opera*, XXVII, p. 244. Beza, *De Haereticis*, p. 38.

[28] IV, 172.

in a Christian manner without contention, and it is not to dispute "about the state and office of Christ, where He now is, what He is doing, how He is seated at the right hand of the Father [a reference to Calvin's doctrine of the Lord's Supper], and how He is one with the Father, and so on about the Trinity, predestination, free will, God, the angels, the state of souls after this life and other like things which do not need to be known for salvation by faith."

Implicit in this whole passage is the distinction between the fundamentals and the non-essentials. Fundamentalism originated in the sixteenth century in the interest of liberty. The attempt was made to enlarge as widely as possible the area of the adiaphora in order to remove them from the arena of controversy and constraint. The distinction was one recognized by all parties, but naturally opinions differed violently as to where the line should be drawn. Beza was outraged by Castellio's list of non-essentials. "The publicans and sinners were saved without a knowledge of the state and office of Christ, O unheard-of impudence! Saved by Him on whom they had not called. Did they call on Him in whom they had not believed? Did they believe in Him whom they had not known? You do not want to know where Christ is and how He is seated at the right hand of God the Father. In vain then it is written that we have a high priest who will enter the heavens. You number the Trinity among matters which need not be known, and if known make a man no better. What can we call you but new devils who would drive God from the throne?"[29]

Castellio had certain tests by which he relegated to the adiaphora many of the points about which persecution was raging. His conditions were those which became familiar enough in the Age of the Enlightenment, namely that to be essential a doctrine must be knowable, clear and reasonable. He was thus at once led into the problem of religious knowledge. He commenced by rejecting any equation of faith with knowledge. "To believe is to give credence to what is told, whether true or false. Sometimes the false is believed no less than the true. But the same cannot be said of knowing. The false cannot be known though it may be believed. To be brief, where knowledge begins faith ends."[30] To know what

[29] *De Haereticis,* pp. 48-53.
[30] *De Arte Dubitandi,* p. 349.

may be known is plainly of the greatest importance, but equally important is it to recognize the limits of knowledge, for quite as great mischief may arise from failing to doubt what should be doubted as from not believing what should be believed.

The sources of knowledge are sense experience and divine revelation, and these are not sharply distinguished because there is a general divine revelation through the created world experienced by the senses as well as through the specific revelation recorded in Holy Scriptures. The data given from both sources are not inerrant and must be corrected and explicated by human reason. First come the data from sense experience. These are basically sound, for the powers of man at the point of perception were not vitiated by the fall. Castellio was amazed that the result of Adam's eating of the fruit of the tree of knowledge of good and evil should have been interpreted as an incapacity for knowledge. "I am positively astounded that men should make out of the tree of knowledge a tree of ignorance. What sense was corrupted, of the mind or of the body? Our first parents saw that they were naked, they heard the word of God, and they judged of their nakedness."[31] The testimony of the senses, however, needs correction, for a stick immersed in water appears bent. A prism will make one man appear to be several. Swiftly moving stars at far remove appear stationary, and so on. The mind of man is quite able to make these corrections.

Castellio appears at this point to posit innate ideas in the form of those universal and simple concepts discoverable among all peoples. "We must begin," he said, "with those things which are clear to all peoples and cannot be denied by those who are ignorant of the Sacred Scriptures. These things being so, we may confirm the Scriptures by their testimony and the Christian religion will be confirmed, being united with nature and reason."[32]

The highest source of religious knowledge is the Scripture. The question then comes to be one of interpretation. Calvin was sure that Scripture is clear, even though God has left some little obscurity to exercise our modesty. But nothing useful for our salvation is obscure. Castellio could agree only because he affirmed that nothing obscure is useful for our salvation. "The questions

[31] *Ibid.*, p. 367.
[32] Buisson, II, 494.

commonly controverted are obscure. This point can be readily established. No one doubts whether there is a God, whether He is good and just, whether He should be loved and worshipped, whether vice should be avoided and virtue followed. Why? Because these points are clear. But concerning baptism, the Lord's Supper, justification, predestination, and many other questions there are capital dissensions. Why? Because these points are not cleared up in Scripture. I could cite a thousand examples to show that God has desired to leave some obscurity in the Bible. If anyone asks why, I will answer that I do not know. There is nothing absurd in this reply. Why did not God put food in birds' nests as He put food in the ground for trees? Why did He give birds wings to go and get their food? Because He did not wish them to be lazy in exercising the resources of their intelligence. Now if this is plain in the works of nature, all who have not degenerated from nature, will confess that the same principle holds in Sacred Scriptures and doctrine. God desired to leave obscurity as an exercise to human industry that the mind, like the body, might gain its bread with the sweat of its brow."[33]

Not only is Scripture obscure according to Castellio but at points it is in error. The citation by Matthew in chapter 27, verse 9 of Jeremiah for Zachariah is simply a lapse of memory. "The Biblical writers did not take down everything through revelation of the Holy Spirit, but some things they recorded from memory and some from imagination, as their writings show. Some one may say then that if these statements be true, the authority of Scripture will be undermined and confidence in it will be destroyed. To which I reply, 'Even if the inference be correct the statements are not therefore false.' But I do not admit the inference."[34]

Nevertheless Castellio certainly did subject Biblical authority to critical and even subjective judgments. Doubly so when he ventured to reject a book from the canon. Well might Calvin ask him where the process would end, and what would become of the authority of Scripture if by some higher criterion books might be excluded and passages pronounced erroneous.

[33] *De Arte Dubitandi,* pp. 355-56.
[34] *Ibid.,* pp. 339-40.

The answer of Castellio was that reason would determine the limits. The tract on "Doubting and Believing" has an eloquent passage in praise of reason which makes of Castellio a veritable precursor of the Enlightenment. "Reason," he said, "is the daughter of God. She was before letters and ceremonies, before the world was made and she is after letters and ceremonies, and after the world is changed and renewed she will endure and can no more be abolished than God himself. Reason I say is a sort of eternal word of God, much older and surer than letters and ceremonies according to which God taught His people before there were letters and ceremonies and after these have passed away He will still so teach that men may be truly taught of God. According to reason Abel, Enoch, Noah and Abraham and many others lived before the letters of Moses and after these many have and will so live. According to reason Jesus Christ himself, the Son of the living God, lived and taught. In the Greek he is called logos, which means reason or word. They are the same, for reason is a sort of interior and eternal word of truth always speaking. By reason Jesus refuted the Jews who placed greater trust in letters and ceremonies. Reason worked upon the Sabbath day and taught the Jews that they might remove a sheep from the ditch on the Sabbath without offense."[35]

This passage for all its eloquence is not very clear. One does not quite know whether reason is deductive logic or the light which lighteth every man that cometh into the world. It is certainly some inward principle which others might define as the inner word or the inner light, but its characteristics are not too difficult to define and they are those which came to prevail in the Age of the Enlightenment. This reason in one sense may be regarded as anti-rational. It is emphatically not the kind of close reasoning which produces an integrated theological system of the sort which John Calvin had so magnificently achieved. It is rather anti-speculative. One of its tests is universality. "We must," said Castellio, "begin with those things which are clear to all peoples."[36] "The world which is the work of God, is unknown to no man and the precepts of love on which hang all the law and the prophets and which are fulfilled in Christ, these are so plain, so

[35] *Ibid.*, p. 363.
[36] Buisson, II, 494.

natural and so known to man that even the wicked know them whether they will or not, and cannot withhold their assent. . . . These rules are inscribed, as it were, by the finger of God in the hearts of all, and can no more be erased than the other common notions of men."[37] "The existence of God may be discerned by reason, for all nations following reason—unless they were savage and akin to the brute—have agreed on this."[38]

Further characteristics of reason are clarity and simplicity. The effects of these presuppositions upon theology are abundantly manifest in a dialogue composed by Castellio between Athanasius and an Anonymous with regard to the doctrine of the Trinity. The following excerpt may serve by way of illustration.

"Athanasius: Whosoever will be saved: before all things it is necessary that he hold the Catholic Faith. Which faith except every one do keep whole and undefiled: without doubt he shall perish everlastingly.

Anonymous: Yes, but the Catholic faith must be such that every one can hold it, the publicans and the sinners and the thief upon the cross believed and were saved. Otherwise they would have perished.

Athanasius: And the Catholic Faith is this: that we worship one God in Trinity, and Trinity in Unity.

Anonymous: I do not think the publicans and the sinners knew this faith. If you think so, prove it. There is not a word about it in Scripture. If you are right they are undoubtedly damned unless perhaps you are speaking of the future instead of the past, but it is not in your power, Athanasius, to change the times and to make necessary for faith what was formerly not necessary. . . . If you hold that there is one substance in three persons and three persons in one substance you are certainly speaking in a most obscure and enigmatic fashion which is not appropriate for a creed which is to be held by all. What every one must know must be expressed in a way which every one can understand. . . .

Athanasius: And yet they are not three eternals: but one eternal. . . . The Father is Almighty: the Son Almighty: and the Holy Ghost Almighty. And yet they are not three Almighties: but

[37] *De Arte Dubitandi*, p. 352.
[38] *Ibid.*, p. 383.

one Almighty. So the Father is God: the Son is God: and the Holy
Ghost is God. And yet they are not three Gods, but one God. . . .

Anonymous: This is as if you should say, 'Abraham is an old
man: Isaac is an old man and Jacob is an old man: yet they are not
three old men, but one old man.' If I were to believe this, Athanasius, I should have to say farewell to reason, the noblest gift of
God, by which man most markedly differs from the beasts, and I
should have to return to the nature and sense of the brute and
should lack the capacity for belief. One cannot believe without
reason. Those who are devoid of reason cannot believe anything.

For myself [it is Castellio speaking] I believe in 'God the
Father Almighty, Maker of heaven and earth, and in Jesus Christ
His only Son our Lord and in the Holy Ghost.' In this faith I will
live and die, God willing, and I think that this simple faith, given
to us by the Apostles, is sufficient for salvation, even if one neither
knows or believes inexplicable enigmas introduced by the curious
after the days of apostolic simplicity. If some are acute enough to
understand what I and those like me cannot grasp, well and good,
but to demand the same of everybody as a condition of salvation
means that the majority will be excluded."[39]

Finally, reason for Castellio meant Biblical criticism and all
its consequences. His great debate with Calvin was as to the clarity
and consistency of Scripture. Calvin insisted that Scripture is clear.
To be sure God has left some obscurity to exercise our modesty.
But if we are humble and suffer ourselves to be instructed by God,
nothing that is useful for our salvation will be obscure to us. Castellio would have said that too. But he would have added that anything which is obscure is not useful for our salvation.

The practical consequence for religious liberty to be drawn
from this type of rationalism was obviously the inappropriateness
of persecution in the interests of dogmas which cannot be positively known. Castellio held that we simply do not know enough
to persecute. "All sects hold their religion according to the Word
of God and say that it is certain. . . . Calvin says that his is certain
and they theirs. He says they are wrong and wishes to be the judge
and so do they. Who shall be judge? Who made Calvin the judge
of all the sects, that he alone should kill? . . . He has the Word of

[39] *Ibid.,* pp. 383-87.

God and so have they. If the matter is certain, to whom is it certain? to Calvin? . . . But why does Calvin write so many books about manifest truth?"[40] "There is nothing unknown to Calvin."[41] He talks "as if he might be in paradise."[42] "And yet he writes huge tomes to explain what he says is absolutely clear."[43]

The very fact of controversy proves that the matter in dispute is not clear. "Nobody ever defended homicide and murder, but the affair of religion and of the knowledge of the Sacred Scripture is altogether different, for the things contained in it are given obscurely and often in enigmas and inscrutable questions, which have been in dispute for more than a thousand years without any agreement, nor can there be agreement without love which breaks and appeases all controversies and drives away ignorance."[44]

In view of all this uncertainty, we must define the heretic simply as one with whom we disagree.[45] And if then we are going to kill heretics, the logical outcome will be a war of extermination, for each is sure of himself.[46] "Calvin would have to invade France and other nations . . . wipe out cities, put all the men to the sword, sparing neither sex nor age, not even the babes and the beasts."[47] "All who bear the Christian name would have to be burned except the Calvinists, that is, those who accept Calvin's *Institutes*."[48] "There would be left on earth only Calvinists, Turks, and Jews, whom he excepts."[49] Or if this is too large an undertaking, Calvin "ought at least to have apprehended the Cardinal Tournon, when, shortly before the death of Servetus, he went through Geneva on his way, as all knew, to burn the godly men who lay in chains at Lyons, and whom shortly after he did burn."[50]

---

[40] *Contra Libellum Calvini* H, Cal. 118, p. 125.
[41] *Ibid.*, D, Cal. 49, p. 61.
[42] *Ibid.*, A4, Cal. 4, p. 19.
[43] *Ibid.*, Bvi, Cal. 26, p. 39.
[44] *Traité*, p. 140.
[45] *Ibid.*, p. 24; *Def. Trans.*, p. 209.
[46] *Contra Libellum Calvini* Cvij, Cal. 42, p. 58; Fvjb, Cal. 96, p. 104; Ivjb, Cal. 129, p. 152; *Traité*, p. 14.
[47] *Contra Libellum Calvini*, Hiij, Cal. 122, p. 129; Kb, Cal. 129, p. 158; V, p. 25; *Traité*, p. 161; *Conseil*, p. 88.
[48] *Contra Libellum Calvini*, Aiij, Cal. 1, p. 17.
[49] *Ibid.*, Biijb, Cal. 20, p. 34.
[50] *Ibid.*, Hij, Cal. 121, p. 127.

This part of Castellio's attack on Calvin has been characterized as unjust, because Calvin did not contemplate a crusade, but merely intended that the magistrate should purify his own territory. To some extent this comment is justified. Calvin did recognize that other churches might have their own opinions. It was only in Geneva that there should be no dissent. Nevertheless he did feel grave responsibility for Christianity at large, and suffered himself to be persuaded to send evidence against Servetus to the Roman Catholic Inquisition in France. The distinction was not so much between Geneva and the rest of the world, as between the fundamentals and the points of comparative indifference. "A slight superstition may be corrected with patience." It is only "when religion is shaken from the foundations that one must have recourse to the extreme remedy."[51] Calvin did not propose to be led by Castellio into a war of extermination.

But of course Castellio's point was that there should not be any war at all. In the two prefaces to his translations of the Bible he had entered a plea to wait until the breaking of the day. In the unpublished manuscript of his reply to Beza, he points again to the same moral by an example of the disastrous consequences in legal matters of undue haste. "In a certain village that I know it so happened that a man and his wife left town together after a violent quarrel. Shortly thereafter he returned alone. Asked as to his wife, he replied that he had left her at a certain place. Since the circumstances were suspicious, he was cast into prison and examined under torture. He then confessed that he had thrown her to the bottom of a river. At the same time the drowned body of a woman was found a little below the place where he confessed to have thrown his wife. Now, Beza, how would you have decided this case? The circumstances were very incriminating. I think you would have condemned him. The judges did so, and he was executed. A day or so later his wife came back."

As the emphasis upon dogma was diminished, the stress upon morality was increased. This was already implicit in the view of God conceived less in terms of power than of justice and mercy, and implicit also in the view of man as a free agent capable of per-

[51] *Calvini opera*, VIII, 477.

fection. Particularly in the matter of persecution Castellio was indignant to find such severity employed against wrong opinions and such leniency exercised toward moral lapses.

"Now I know well that my detractors are accustomed to say that one must look not at the life, but at the doctrine, and that my life is hypocrisy. There are even some who say that to live well is the peculiarity of heretics. . . . I answer that it is a great shame for those who wish to condemn others to so live that their life is worse than that of those whom they condemn. . . . Shall it be said that the spirit of the heretics has more power than that of the Christians?"[52]

"This man you say is a heretic, a putrid member to be cut off from the body of the Church lest he infect others. But what has he done? O, horrible things! Yes, but what? Is he a murderer? an adulterer? a thief? No. What then? Does he not believe in Christ and the Scriptures? Certainly he does and would rather die than not continue in his belief. But he does not understand them correctly, that is, he interprets them differently from our teachers. . . This is a capital offense to be expiated in the flames."[53]

Castellio would say not merely that deeds are more important than creeds, but that deeds must be the test of creeds. The layman cannot pass judgment on the arguments of the medical sects, but he can tell which one cures the most. So he can evaluate the theological sects by observing which one best cures vices, and changes the greatest number from drunk to sober, from intemperate to continent, from greedy to generous, making them patient instead of impatient, kind instead of cruel, instead of impure, chaste.[54] Sound doctrine is that which makes men sound.[55] The doctrine of the persecutors must be bad because their lives are bad.[56]

Good deeds moreover are the condition of right creeds. These obscure religious matters can be known only by the pure in heart.[57] The Scriptures can be rightly understood only by Christ's

[52] Buisson 11, pp. 432-33.
[53] *De Calumnia*, p. 425. Cf. *Contra Libellum Calvini*, Fiijb, Cal. 93, p. 98; Gvb, Cal. 113, p. 118, and V, 23.
[54] *Contra Libellum Calvini*, Ivjb-K, Cal. 129, pp. 156-57.
[55] *Ibid.*, Cal. 129, p. 148.
[56] *De Calumnia*, p. 436.
[57] *Traité*, p. 13.

disciples, and they are his disciples who obey him and have love.[58]
Learning may be a positive hindrance because it engenders pride.
"They love to be called Rabbi and arrogate to themselves the
power of teaching. But if Christ himself came, they would not condescend to take a suggestion from him, unless he were called by
their order, and knew the languages by which he was crucified,
namely Latin, Greek and Hebrew."[59] To be sure Christ received
the Wise Men, and he would receive the Calvinists if they would
condescend to enter the stable.

This impassioned upbraiding of Geneva on the score of
moral indifference will doubtless occasion surprise. But Castellio
did not deny the earnestness of that moral discipline which we
commonly associate with the regime of the consistory. His criticism
was that the Reform was external and trivial, that it strained out
the gnat and swallowed the camel. In other words he differed from
Calvin not only as to the importance, but even more as to the content of his ethic. The Genevan consistory declared that a minister
should be deposed for heresy, card playing and dancing, but a fra-
ternal admonition would suffice were he guilty of scurrility, ob-
scenity and avarice.[60] To this scale of vices Castellio applied the
test of inwardness. "Why," he asked, "does Calvin not bring about
the death of hypocrites and the avaricious? Or does he think that
hypocrites are better than heretics?"[61] He claims that heretics destroy souls. "So do the envious, avaricious, and proud."[62] "But if
Calvin wished all the proud to be punished by the magistrate none
would be left to punish the magistrate himself."[63] "They consider

[58] *Contra Libellum Calvini,* Bvlj, Cal. 29, p. 41.

[59] *De Calumnia,* p. 420. Cf. *Contra Libellum Calvini,* Dvijb, Cal. 72, p. 74.

[60] *De Calumnia,* pp. 415-6, and *Contra Libellum Calvini,* Evi, Cal. 82, p.
87. The reference is to the *Ordonnances Ecclésiastiques* of 1541, *Calvini opera*
X, 17-19. Castellio's translation is loose unless he had some other document before him which I have not located. For "Jeux deffendus par les loix et scanda-
leux," he has "illiberalis Judus, ut aleae, chartae & id genus alia." (*De Calumnia,* p. 415). In the other reference the translation is "Lusiones legibus vetitas &
choreas."

[61] *Contra Libellum Calvini,* Evj verso-Evii, Cal. 82, pp. 88-89.

[62] *Ibid.,* Fiijb, Cal. 93, p. 98.

[63] *Ibid.,* Gv, Cal. 112, p. 117. Cf. *Conseil,* p. 81.

rebaptism much more heinous than adultery,"[64] which for Castellio was one of the cardinal sins because an offense against personality.[65] Calvin says indeed that adulterers and drunkards are impure, "but he does not realize that none are more impure than hypocrites."[66] Calvin burned the books of Servetus lest they corrupt men. Why then does he not suppress Ovid and Clement Marot? A French refugee, a few years ago, wrote back from Geneva, "I have left Babylon. Please send me all the works of Ovid with commentaries." And what shall be said of the works of Beza, his *Zoographia* and *Passavant?* [67] Castellio had privately remonstrated with him over the first, which described Cochlaeus as a *Cochlea,* that is, a snail, and pictured his unsavory functions.[68] Beza's response to the admonition was the publication of the *Passavant,* which contains more dirt than wit.[69]

[64] *Contra Libellum Calvini,* Eviij, Cal. 82, p. 91.

[65] *Moses Latinus,* p. 488.

[66] *Contra Libellum Calvini,* A 4, Cal. 5, p. 19.

[67] *Ibid.,* Dijb, Cal. 55, p. 64.

[68] Reprinted in Baum, J. H., *Theodore Beza* (Leipzig, 1843), I, pp. 357-363.

[69] The *Passavant* was reprinted by Isidore Liseux, Paris, 1875. Castellio tells of his remonstrance in *Defensio,* p. 358, and more fully in the suppressed portions of the *Def. Trans.,* which survive in two manuscript copies, at Cornell and in the British Museum. The passage in question is as follows: "Neque solum ipse me non admonuit, verum etiam hoc ipsum amicae admonitionis officium, quod verbis in praefatione sua, ab aliis postulat, reipsa a me praestitum jam pridem repudiavit. Cum *enim* ante septem annos famosum libellum (en novus e coelo in Ecclesiam Dei illapsus Doctor!) edidisset, zoographiam inscripsit in theologum quendam nomine Cocleum, quem cochleam appellans, tanquam deformissimam bestiam, per omnes corporis partes depingebat. Ego qui scirem hujuscemodi scurrilibus libris, et maledictis Ecclesiam Christi non magis aedificari quam moenia bombardis, eum admonere statui. Et cum non multo post per id oppidum in quo ipse degebat eo tempore, iter faciens, cum ibi, sicuti speraveram, non offendissem, quod potui, praestiti. Ejus amicum quendam, ut illi referret, ea de re *et* monui, et amice monui, sicuti ut ipse aliquando ab amicis monitus fui, et me moneri volo. Scit Deus an mentiar. At ille postea, tantum abfuit ut se correxerit, ut insuper ejusdem generis libellum ediderit, nomine Passavantium, ut quidem sciunt omnes, et postea de me omnia maledicta seminare nunquam destitit. Quae cum mihi a multis narrarentur, efficit suis adversum me scriptis ut non possem, non credere.

Atque scripsit mihi amicus quidam, totius illius in me odii causam fuisse, et esse admonitionem illam de Cochleo, quam modo posui. Nec sane aliam causam videre possum, quum mihi nihil unquam aliud negotii fuerit. Ita sum expertus in eo admonendo, quid sit Solomonis illud, Admone stultum, is te

Since righteousness for Castellio is inward, the criterion of morality becomes subjective. That is why so large a place is given to conscience, which is loyalty to what one thinks to be right.[70] This is better than a thousand witnesses,[71] better even than correctness. If a boy follows a man, supposing him to be his father, one need not correct the lad's intention, but merely his opinion.[72] If one says what one believes, one is telling the truth, even though mistaken. Servetus was put to death for telling the truth.[73] Calvin, charged Castellio, takes cover under the example of Peter, who killed Ananias. But for what? For lying. Servetus was executed because he would not lie. Had he been willing to recant and speak against his conscience, he might have escaped. He perished because he said what he thought.[74] "To force conscience is worse than cruelly to kill a man,"[75] because "I must be saved by my own faith and not by that of another."[76] If a man recant, his soul is destroyed,[77] and his moral integrity undermined. Castellio could cite examples enough of men who lived blamelessly so long as they were loyal to their convictions, but who, after recantation, suffered a complete moral disintegration.[78]

This whole position is one of the most radical elements in Castellio's thinking. Today it all sounds commonplace enough but that is only because his views came later to be axiomatic in the West. For Castellio's generation the erroneous conscience was denied any rights. Only the correct conscience was to be respected because what matters is not the inner feeling of man but the objective law of God. The relativizing of conscience was largely the work

---

oderit. Hunc hominem admonui de Cochleo, et ipse in me postea multo acrius debacchatus est, et debacchatur, quam in ipsum Cochleum." Manuscript, Cornell, pp. 14-15. I have followed the punctuation of the Cornell copy which is fuller. The two words in italics appear only in the British Museum copy.

[70] *De Calumnia*, p. 417.
[71] *Conseil*, p. 25; *Def. Trans.*, p. 4.
[72] IV, pp. 187-8.
[73] *Contra Libellum Calvini*, Eijb, Cal. 80, p. 80.
[74] *Ibid.*, Fiij, Cal. 91, p. 97. Cf. *Traité*, p. 166.
[75] *Conseil*, p. 15.
[76] *Traité*, p. 17. Cf. *Conseil*, p. 93.
[77] *Conseil*, p. 42.
[78] *Contra Libellum Calvini*, Evijb, Cal. 82, p. 90; Iv, Cal. 129, p. 149; *De Calumnia*, p. 423; Buisson, II, p. 466.

of the seventeenth century, especially in England where the welter of sects broke down the confidence in any obvious inerrancy. The question still remains of course as to what the state may feel obliged to do toward one who is at once conscientious and subversive. This was a problem which Castellio did not confront.

There was another question implicit in Castellio's position and equally, if not indeed even more important but by him only dimly envisaged, namely the theory of the Church. Quite plainly he had undercut the sublime Calvinist dream of a Christian society under the dominance of the elect. Castellio denied the very existence of the elect. This is probably the point at which his repudiation of the doctrine of predestination meant the most for liberty. In and of itself predestinarianism may be used to cut both ways. One may argue in favor of persecution on the ground that God has no tenderness for the damned. On the other hand one may say that persecution has no point if its object be the saving of souls, since the souls are already saved or damned by the immutable decree. Really more pertinent is the undermining of the holy commonwealth by destroying the very distinction on which it was based. Castellio believed in the saints, that is, in earnest Christians striving for perfection, but not in any body of the elect chosen by God from the foundation of the world.

What form then should be taken by the community of the saints? At times Castellio leaned to the Anabaptist view that they should be little cells despised and rejected of men, small and persecuted, as lambs before wolves. That whole theme runs through his Biblical dialogues and recurs over and over again throughout his works. "The just have always been killed."[79] "From the foundation of the world the truth has always been persecuted by the great and renowned."[80] "He who is according to the flesh persecuted him who is according to the Spirit."[81] Christ, the apostles and the martyrs were persecuted and such has always been in the fate of simple and true Christians.[82]

---

[79] *Traité*, p. 158.
[80] Buisson, II, p. 432.
[81] *Traité*, p. 191, from the tract *Des enfants de la chair*, etc.
[82] *Conseil*, p. 86, Cf. *De Calumnia*, p. 442; *Contra Libellum Calvini*, A, p. 13.

Associated with this picture is a renewed belief in the speedy return of the Lord. The Calvinist view of a religious theory of progress to be accomplished through the reign of the saints gives way again to the more primitive concept of the denouement when the Son of Man shall appear upon the clouds of heaven.[83]

But then again Castellio came very close to dissolving the Church altogether as an outward community with visible marks. Instead it became for him only the inward fellowship of those bound in faith and love and the Spirit. When Calvin inquired "by what marks the true Church could be recognized if the doctrine of piety were uncertain and in suspense," Castellio answered: "By an assured faith concerning things which are hoped for, not known, by love which is better than faith and may be clearly discerned, by the doctrine of piety which is to love your enemies, bless those who curse you, to hunger and thirst after righteousness and endure persecution for righteousness sake."[84]

Again, in a passage of the unpublished manuscript in reply to Beza, he reverted to the theme. "They are the true church who truly hear the voice of the shepherd, that is to say, those who obey him and who observe the true usage of the sacraments; that is, they are washed in the laver of regeneration; they are new creatures, baptized by fire and by the Spirit, who truly have eaten of the flesh of Christ and truly have drunk of His blood; that is, they have put off the old man of sin and have put on the new and they yield their members as instruments of righteousness unto God and no longer as instruments of unrighteousness unto sin (Rom. 6:13). This church is unknown to the Calvinists, as Calvin himself writes, because, being impeded by the visible and carnal and arrested by the visible tokens, they are not able to see or consider this church, for they follow the example of their forefathers the Jews, who were impeded and arrested by the shadows and ceremonies of the law so that they were not able to see the clarity and the end thereof, which is Christ. But those who are children of this celestial church know it as children know their mother and recognize their brothers no less than the carnal recognize their own. Not only do the spiritual recognize each other, but strangers know them as disciples of Christ

[83] In the *Jonas Propheta*.
[84] *Contra Libellum Calvini*, Bvj-vjb, Cal. 28, pp. 39-40.

by the fruits of love and of the Spirit, which are proper to those who love God, and not by exterior sermons and sacraments, which are common to the good and the bad. 'By this,' said the Master, 'shall all men know that ye are my disciples, if ye have love one to another' (John 13:35). To those who carp it seems strange that you do not run with them to dissoluteness. The difference is that those who are of this church know it as a musician knows music and sings accordingly, but the strangers know it only as one ignorant of music, who perceives music in another but cannot sing himself."

After reading such a passage one may wonder whether the price paid by Castellio for liberty was not the disintegration of the Church. And the problem for us today is to know whether we are able to forge an organization which will present a united front to a hostile world and at the same time preserve liberty within our own ranks.

A part of Castellio's plea was a rebuttal and demonstration of what persecution cannot do. It cannot beget a man in Christ.[85] It cannot generate a new creature.[86] "Religion resides not in the body but in the heart which cannot be reached by the sword of kings and princes."[87] By persecution and violence "one can no more build the Church than one can construct a wall with cannon blasts."[88] "To kill a man is not to defend a doctrine. It is to kill a man. . . . Doctrine is not the affair of the magistrate, but of the doctor. What has the sword to do with doctrine?"[89]

All that the magistrate can do is to constrain some to recant and thus turn heretics into hypocrites. The number in the Church is thus increased, but the quality is not improved. "I say that those who have regard to numbers and on that account constrain men, gain nothing, but rather lose, and resemble a fool who, having a great barrel and a little wine in it, fills it up with water to get more, but instead of increasing the wine, he spoils what he had."[90]

---

[85] V, p. 8.
[86] *Contra Libellum Calvini*, Divb, Cal. 63, p. 68.
[87] *Traité*, p. 4.
[88] Buisson, II, p. 445.
[89] *Contra Libellum Calvini*, Eb, Cal. 77, p. 78.
[90] *Conseil*, p. 47.

The Gospel was forced on England under Edward VI, but the accession of Mary revealed how few were genuinely persuaded."[91] "The Jews in Spain, who have been baptized by force, are no more Christians than before."[92]

Again, coercion may completely defeat its own end by simply advertizing heresy. Calvin complains that the views of Servetus are spreading. "He has only himself to blame. There was no mention of the first book of Servetus and the later could be sold like the others without disturbance, but now that the man has been burned with his books, everybody is burning with a desire to read them."[93] Castellio knew a man who had been converted to the views of Servetus by the extracts from his works which Calvin included in the refutation.[94] The Protestants flourished "like drops of dew at break of day,"[95] when they suffered persecution, which serves merely to make seven for one.[96]

Another and still more serious consequence of persecution is that it may provoke sedition. The common claim was that heresy would disturb the body politic. On the contrary, answered Castellio, "seditions come rather from the fact that they want to force and kill heretics rather than to let them live without constraint, for tyranny engenders sedition."[97]

Finally comes the problem of how one is to deal with error. Castellio, though he had done his best to make the concept of heresy unworkable, certainly did not deny the actuality of error. Indeed he was seeking constantly to convince his opponents that they were mistaken. But what then is the technique for dealing with the erring? The first step is to deal with oneself, in order that no anger, acrimony or ambition may impede soundness of judgment and effectiveness of persuasion. In a dialogue Castellio has Frederick ask Ludwig what he would do if he hated a man. Ludwig answers, "I would wish him all evil and envy him all good. I should grieve at

---

[91] *Traité*, p. 183.
[92] *Conseil*, p. 40.
[93] *Contra Libellum Calvini*, Biij, Cal. 18, p. 33.
[94] *Ibid.*, Bijb, Cal. 17, p. 32.
[95] *Conseil*, p. 50. Cf. p. 90.
[96] *Ibid.*, p. 86.
[97] *Ibid.*, p. 84.

his prosperity and rejoice at his adversity. If any one told me evil of him I should be glad and reward the messenger. I should love his enemies and hate his friends. I should watch his words and deeds to carp at them. I should wish him the cruelest death and would wipe out his memory." Frederick answers, "Transfer all this to yourself."[98]

The tract on "Doubting and Knowing" contends that the greatest obstacle to the appeasing of controversy is that both sides are deterred from arriving at the truth by an obstinate and closed mind. They are like the doting mother, so infatuated with her children as to refuse to believe the universal testimony of her neighbors as to their shortcomings. "Thus in all contentions and wars there is always an element of blindness and obstinacy derived from self-love." "Man must learn to hate himself, otherwise he is incurable."[99]

A further theme constant in Castellio is the appeal to the meekness and mercy of Christ. Nowhere is it better evidenced than in the passionate apostrophe to Christ which concludes the plea of Martin Bellius.

O Creator and King of the world, dost Thou see these things? Art Thou become so changed, so cruel, so contrary to Thyself? When Thou wast on earth none was more mild, more clement, more patient of injury. As a sheep before the shearer Thou wast dumb.[100] When scourged, spat upon, mocked, crowned with thorns, and crucified shamefully among thieves, Thou didst pray for them who did Thee this wrong.[101] Art Thou now so changed? I beg Thee in the name of Thy Father, dost Thou now command that those who do not understand Thy precepts as the mighty demand, be drowned in water, cut with lashes to the entrails, sprinkled with salt, dismembered by the sword, burned at a slow fire, and otherwise tortured in every manner as long as possible? Dost Thou, O Christ, command and approve of these things? Are they Thy vicars who make these sacrifices? Art Thou present when they summon Thee and dost Thou eat human flesh? If Thou, Christ, dost these things or if Thou commandest that they be done, what hast Thou left for the devil? Dost Thou the very same things as Satan? O blasphemies and shameful audacity of men, who

[98] IV, 221.
[99] *De Arte Dubitandi*, pp. 380-381.
[100] Isaiah 53:7
[101] Luke 23:34

dare to attribute to Christ that which they do by the command and at the
instigation of Satan!

Selected Bibliography

For his life see the monumental biography by Ferdinand Buisson, *Sébastien Castellion* (2 vols., Paris, 1892). The work of Etienne Giran, *Sébastien
Castellion* (Haarlem, 1914) is useful for the extensive translations. The trib-
utes paid to Castellio on the occasion of the erection of the monument at his
birthplace, Saint-Martin-du-Fresne (Ain), France, on Sept. 19, 1926, are printed
in a little pamphlet entitled, *Inauguration du Monument . . . à Sébastien Castellion* (Paris, Fischbacher, 1927). The treatments in English are very slight.
There is a brief notice in Lecky, *History of the Rise and Influence of the Spirit
of Rationalism in Europe,* II, pp. 53-56 (ed. of 1870. The latest edition is 1910),
and in Ruffini, *Religious Liberty* (London, 1912), pp. 73-78, which is a translation of *La Libertà Religiosa* (Turin, 1901), pp. 81-86. The passage which Lecky
cites on p. 77 of the English edition is not from the preface to the French Bible,
but from the *De Haereticis.* A chapter is devoted to Castellio by Rufus Jones in
his *Spiritual Reformers in the Sixteenth and Seventeenth Centuries* (London,
1914). A brief treatment is found in W. K. Jordan, *The Development of Religious Toleration in England* (Cambridge, Mass., 1932), I, 310-315. A discussion of Castellio's position will be found in my article "Sebastian Castellio
and the Toleration Controversy of the Sixteenth Century" in *Persecution and
Liberty, Essays in Honor of George Lincoln Burr* (New York, 1931), largely reproduced in this article with the consent of the publishers. The *De Haereticis*
is translated into English with introduction and notes by me in the work "Castellio Concerning Heretics," *Records of Civilization,* XXII (Columbia Univ.,
New York, 1935). An illuminating discussion may be found in Johannes Kühn,
Toleranz und Offenbarung (Leipzig, 1923).

There is a complete bibliography of Castellio's works in the appendix of
the second volume of Buisson's biography. For this article I have used:

Dialogorum sacrorum . . . libri quattuor. Buisson, Nos. 1-4. Abbr. *Dial. Sacr.*
Moses Latinus, Buisson, No. 5.
La Bible nouvellement translatée. Buisson, No. 9. Referred to as *Preface to the
French Bible.* There is no copy in the U.S. I used the one at the British
Museum.
Sebastiani Castellionis defensio suarum translationum Bibliorum. Buisson, No.
12. Abbr. *Def. Trans.*
Traité des hérétiques. Buisson No. 14. Reprinted by A. Olivet (Geneva, Jullien,
1913). Abbr. *Traité.*
Conseil à la France désolée. Buisson, No. 15. The only copy in the U.S. is at
Cornell. Abbr. *Conseil.*
Contra Libellum Calvini. Buisson, No. 16. The book is without pagination but
has signatures, and the excerpts from Calvin are numbered. In the Cornell
copy the pages are numbered in pencil beginning after the flyleaf. I have given
three notations, the signature, the excerpt from Calvin and the page. Yale
has a copy.

Sebastiani Castellionis Dialogi IIII *(De Praedestinatione, De Electione, De Libero Arbitrio, De Fide).* Buisson, No. 31. Abbr. IV.

The Gouda edition of 1613 has the following tracts bound with and numbered consecutively after the above:

An Possit Homo per Spiritum Sanctum Perfectè obedire legi Dei, pp. 227-253. Abbr. *De Obedientia.*

De Praedestinatione Scriptum Sebastiani Castellionis ad D. Mart. Borrhaum, pp. 254-339. Abbr. *De Praedestinatione.*

Sebastiani Castellionis Defensio ad Authorem Libri, cui titulus est, Calumniae Nebulonis, pp. 341-382. Abbr. *Defensio.*

Sebastiani Castellionis De Calumnia Liber, pp. 383-443. Abbr. *De Calumnia.* The printer, by mistake, has carried the headings of the preceding tract, *Defensio,* on to p. 431.

After these tracts there are three more, paged individually. Of these there will be references to:

Quinque Impedimentorum, quae mentes hominum & oculos a veri in divinis cognitione abducunt, succincta enumeratio, pp. 1-30. Abbr. V.

Tractatus De Justificatione, pp. 1-89. Abbr. *De Justificatione.*

De arte dubitandi. Buisson, No. 40. Edited by Elizabeth Feist (Mrs. Felix Hirsch) in *Reale Accademia d'Italia,* Studi e Documenti VII (Rome, 1937).

The letters are given in Buisson's appendix to vol. II.

13. Sebastian Castellio and the British-American Tradition

The ideas of Sebastian Castellio on religious liberty are commonly supposed to have exercised no direct influence whatever on the Anglo-Saxon world. He was known, to be sure, for his translation of the Bible and was widely used in schools for the learning of Latin through his *Sacred Dialogues*. But the treatise *Concerning Heretics* was an unknown book. John Knox indeed referred to it merely by way of condemnation and thereafter it was lost to view. In so far as Castellio may be said to have had any influence at all it was only indirectly through his following in the Low Countries or through successors like Acontius, who though familiar with his writings made no acknowledgment. Not until Rufus Jones treated of Castellio in his *Spiritual Reformers of the Sixteenth and Seventeenth Centuries* did he come to the attention of the British and American public.

In view of this prevailing opinion the discovery is not without interest that one of the most influential among the philosophers of liberty in England and the United States was familiar with the works of Castellio. John Locke, highly esteemed in Britain and the most revered and followed of all philosophers in America, during his exile in Holland, became acquainted with the works of his precursor. In the year 1693 a correspondence took place between John Locke then in England and Philip Limborch the Remonstrant and the author of a history of the Inquisition, relative to an edition of the works of Castellio. On November 10 of that year Limborch wrote from Amsterdam to Locke in these words: "Praesertim cum responsum tuum ad duo flagitaverim: de editione Bibliorum Castellionis quam hic elegantem et plenam meditantur bibliopolae quidam."[1]

First published in *Het Boek*, XXX, 4 (1952).
[1] Lord King, *The Life of John Locke* (London, 1830), II, 336.

Evidently there had been a previous inquiry because Locke replied on the very same day from London as follows:

"Bibliorum Castellionis editionem, qualem tu narras, apud vos designari valde laetor, et viris literatis apud nos gratum acceptumque fore opus, non dubito: Post diuturnam rusticationem, nuperus meus in urbem reditus nondum mihi concessit plurimorum doctorum colloquia; prout datur occasio, alios consulam, quamvis vix credi potest elegantem editionem, tam elegantis versionis, notis etiam aliisque scriptis eo spectantibus tam docti viri ornatam, non omnibus placituram."

A second reference in the letters of Locke is to be found on January 13, 1694 in which he said: "Editionem illam Castellionis, quam meditantur elegantem, libens viderem, et nostratibus gratam fore, nullus dubito."[2]

Thus we see that the very project which is now contemplated for the anniversary of the *De Haereticis in* 1954 was envisaged in 1694 and, unhappily and for what reason we do not know, was abandoned. And John Locke knew all about it and entered his hearty approval which he could scarcely have done had he not read the books.

This is highly interesting because so far as I know Castellio and Locke are the only two persons in the history of the struggle for religious liberty who wrote treatises both on the problem of liberty and on the problem of knowledge and brought the two into relation with each other. One is tempted to wonder whether by any chance Locke may have been acquainted not only with the printed works of Castellio but with the manuscript *De Arte Dubitandi et Sciendi.* Fragments of this work were published in Holland in 1751 by J. J. Wettstein, but in the year of the correspondence of Locke and Limborch in 1693 this Wettstein was only just born at Basel. However, he had an older second cousin, John Henry Wettstein, who migrated to Amsterdam in 1668 and there became a publisher. It was he who brought out Limborch's *History of the Inquisition*[3] and he may very well have been one of those bibliopolae to whom Limborch referred as desirous of bringing out the works of Castellio. Now, Locke knew well this Wettstein and in fact for a

[2] John Locke, *Works* (10th ed., London, 1801) III, 34-35.
[3] C. L. Hulbert-Powell, *John James Wettstein, 1693-1754* (London, 1937).

period called every day at his house to collect his letters.[4] John Henry Wettstein may already have brought the manuscript from Basel. In any case he was in touch with his relatives in the Swiss city. And that Locke through him may already have known the manuscript is by no means incredible.

Still one cannot press the point, and he did know the other works of Castellio. Of that we can be sure. Their influence upon him cannot have been decisive because he had already worked out the main lines of his position both on religious liberty and on the problem of knowledge before ever coming to Holland. He must have received reinforcement from the discovery of a kindred spirit and certain emphases in his thinking may well have received a sharper turn through the study of Castellio. A comparison of their ideas is interesting. In the area of epistemology they are both essentially Stoic, positing as the source of knowledge sense experience and revelation corrected by reason. A pure empiricism this could never be, otherwise reason could never surmount the data of sense. Castellio on this point was less sophisticated than Locke but more coherent, for Locke denied innate ideas and then posited intuitive moods of apprehension which amount well nigh to the same thing. Castellio more than Locke related the problem of knowledge to the problem of liberty. For this there was a very good reason, because persecution in Castellio's day was on behalf of truth, but in Locke's day in England only on behalf of good order. For the Anglican Church made no pretense of being the custodian of infallibility.

Among the arguments for liberty employed by Locke all had come to be so much common coin by this day that to discover in them any specific influence of Castellio would be precarious. Perhaps the most significant, though the most elusive, is a tone never absent from Castellio but only occasionally breaking through in Locke, of impassioned indignation against persecution. We cannot go so far as to make Castellio a direct progenitor of the English declarations of indulgence or acts of toleration. All we can say is this: that across the years one spirit may kindle another, and Locke certainly warmed his hands before the fire of Castellio.[5]

---

[4] H. R. Fox-Bourne, *The Life of John Locke* (London, 1876), II, 63.
[5] For a recent work on the influence of Castellio see supra p. 105 note 4.

14. William Postell and the Netherlands

Professor Kvacala in his admirable article on Postell,[1] was compelled for lack of evidence to leave unanswered a number of questions having to do chiefly with Postell's relations to the Netherlands. In his later years Postell was in correspondence with Plantin at Antwerp, and like him was an adherent of Hendrik Niclaes, the founder of the Family of Love. When did this connection with the Netherlands commence? The suggestion is made that Postell's works were widely disseminated by Anabaptists whom he came to know at Venice.[2] A more specific suggestion is that the letter to Schwenkfeld may have created sympathy in separatist circles

First published in the *Nederlands Archief voor Kerkgeschiedenis*, XXIV, 2 (1931), 161-172. Since the publication of this paper an admirable book on Postell has appeared by William J. Bouwsma, *Concordia Mundi, the Career and Thought of Guillaume Postel* (Cambridge, Mass., 1957), with a full bibliography. There is also an essay by Sigrid Stahlmann, "Die Stellung Guillaume Postels in der religiösen Propaganda," in *Aspects de la Propaganda Religieuse*, (Librarie E. Droz, Geneva, 1957), pp. 294-307. He quite agrees that the Davidists esteemed Postell, but takes issue with me in my supposing that Postell was ever at any time drawn to Joris. This I inferred from the statement that Joris "had had exceeding great knowledge of the secrets of God, the which he abused." This can be taken to mean that Joris degenerated. Plainly, Postell unequivocably repudiated the later Joris as Stahlmann abundantly demonstrates from the Ortelius correspondence which I had overlooked. Francois Secret is publishing "Notes sur Guillaume Postel" in successive numbers of *Bibliothèque d'Humanisme et Renaissance*, XXI, 2 (1959), pp. 453-467, XXII, 2 (1960), pp. 377-392; XXII, 3 (1960), pp. 552-567, XXV, 1 (1963), pp. 212-221.

[1] Kvacala, Ja., *Wilhelm Postell, Seine Geistesart u. seine Reformgedanken; ARG*, IX (1911/12), p. 285-330; XI (1914), p. 200-227; XV (1918), p. 157-203. The documents, because of the war, had to be published elsewhere and appeared under the title: "Postelliana, urkundliche Beiträge zur Geschichte der Mystik im Reformationszeilalter," in *Acta et Commentationes Imp. Universitatis Jurievensis (olim Dorpatensis)*, Tartu, Esthonia, 1915, p. XIX [I] + 88.

[2] *ARG,* XI (1914), p. 204.

even as far as Holland.[3] But this letter itself raises questions. How
was it sent and how received?[4] Kvacala believes also to have identified a second letter to Schwenkfeld, but is at a loss to explain when,
where and by whom it was sent.[5]

A partial answer, at least, to these questions is afforded by a
study of Postell's relations to the sect of David Joris of Delft, the
Anabaptist leader, who, from 1544 to his death in 1556, lived under the assumed name of Johann von Brügge in Basel. Plantin
asked Postell about his relation to this sect, "car je n'entends pas
bien vostre intention quand vous y melés je ne sçay quoy des Davidistes."[6] Postell's answer may be taken to imply that he had once
highly esteemed Joris for his religious illumination, but now
blamed him for having lived at ease. Here is the passage.[7]

L'autre question est, que j'entends in *consortii charitatis usum*,
parlant des Davidistes. Je vous asseure, et ce en la charité qui dure
éthernelement, voire et depuys que la foy et espérance cesseront, que je
n'entends de Georges David, ou David Jorgis, come lhom le disoit, aultre,
sauf que ce aye esté un meschant, et quant à ses actes, du tout tyran, et
plain d'amour propre, qui ha eu cognoissance du tout très grande des
secretz de Dieu, desquels il ha abusé, parcequ'il ha abusé tant de l'église
come de la *charité* qui en est la finale marke, en tournant à son profict
particulier et filautie ce que ayant receu du povre et moins intelligent
peuple qui le conduysoit par son povoir et richesse, estoit obligé, come
un bon chef à ses membres, à l'employer pour eulx et davantage à mettre
pour eulx, si il en eust eu de propres, mettre les biens, la vie et l'honeur,
et pour les siens, s'il est besoing, mourir en povreté, mespris et douleur.

The charge that Postell was a Davidist struck close enough
home to elicit a reply the title of which alone has been preserved.
It read:

"Retractationum liber, in sua de restitutione omnium scripta
institutus. Ms. A. 1560, ubi de Davidis Georgii Batavi Haeresi-
archae erroribus et exustione post mortem agitur. . . ."[8]

[3] *ARG*, XV (1918), p. 184.
[4] *ARG*, XI (1914), p. 224.
[5] *ARG*, XV (1918), p. 162.
[6] Max. Rooses, *Correspondance de Christophe Plantin* (Antwerp, 1883), I,
p. 80.
[7] *Ibid*, p. 82-83.
[8] *ARG*, XV (1918), p. 184.

But in spite of this repudiation Postell's relations with the Davidists had been more intimate than he cared later to admit. In working through the Jorist papers, confiscated at the time of the trial in 1559,[9] I was surprised at the frequent occurrence of the name of Postell or of his pseudonym, Elias Pandocheus.

These papers reveal the intimacy of Postell with the French doctor, Jean Bauhin, and also demonstrate that the *medicus gallus* was himself a Davidist.[10] He had come to Basel in 1541 three years before Joris' arrival. When Bauhin became an adherent of the sect we do not know, but he must have been quite outspoken as to his discipleship, while concealing the presence of his master in Basel. Our information on this score is derived from two letters of William Farel which are astonishing both for what they know and for what they do not know. On June 4, 1555, a year before Joris' death, Farel wrote to Ambrose Blaurer[11] that Bauhin was utterly devoted to Joris, "whose equal in impiety, the world today does not contain." Again on April 25, 1558,[12] nearly a year before the disclosure of the sect, Farel wrote again to Blaurer about that abominable heretic, Jean Bauhin, *qui medicus habetur Davidis Georgii*. It is surprising that Farel should know that Bauhin was a disciple and the physician of Joris, without knowing that Joris was in Basel. The disclosure of the sect in 1559 brought Bauhin into unpleasant prominence and even a brief imprisonment. Perhaps that is why he left Basel and went to Lyons.[13] On the other hand he was able to show that he had been associated with Bles-

---

[9] I had the pleasure in the summer of 1926 of going through this collection preserved in the Universitätsbibliothek at Basel. Krüger (*Handbuch der Kirchengeschichte*, Dritter Teil, *Reformation u. Gegenreformation* 2 ed. Maurer u. Hermelink 1931, p. 214), credits me with a study of David Joris published in New Haven, 1927. I am sorry that this is a mistake.

[10] This fact was conjectured by Ferdinand Buisson with rare divination on the basis of the Acronius letter; *Sébastian Castellion* (1892), II, p. 147, note I. Compare the whole chapter and p. 94-96. Paul Burckhardt was the first to furnish the proof in his David Joris, *Basler Biographien* (1900), p. 104.

[11] Traugott Schiess, *Briefwechsel der Brüder Ambrosius und Thomas Blaurer*, Bd. III, 1912, No. 1993. cf. *Calvini opera*, XVI, 549.

[12] *Ibid.*, No. 2139.

[13] For his history at Lyons and his subsequent return to Basel see Jean Barnaud, *Pierre Viret*, 1911, pp. 626 f.

dyck in a revolt against Joris dating from 1553.[14] Postell's letter to Bauhin was written the following year, and cannot, therefore, prove any leanings toward Joris. We can say merely that Postell was intimate with one whose adherence to the sect was no secret.

The letter to Bauhin introduces us at once to Schwenkfeld, for this is the very document which Kvacala has identified and published as the second letter to Schwenkfeld. Mosheim had already printed it without address at the end of Postell's *Apologia pro Serveto* and the British Museum manuscript which Kvacala used is also evidently without any address. Kvacala inferred that the letter was intended for Schwenkfeld because of the similarity of the content to that of the first letter, and because of the statement in the second, "Servate Epistolam 1553 scriptam, etc." The Basel manuscript is not addressed to Schwenkfeld, but to Bauhin. Nevertheless I think Kvacala's conjecture is correct, since the letter to Bauhin commences twice. First there is an address in French, "La souveraine misericorde du Seigneur face son effect en vous et en tout le monde,"[15] and then the French shifts to Latin and a new start is made with "Charissime frater." Bauhin was merely an intermediary. This is not a conjecture, but is established by a statement of Schwenkfeld, kindly communicated to me by the editors of the *Corpus Schwenkfeldianorum*. On April 7, 1554 Schwenkfeld wrote as follows to El.'Hecklin:[16]

"Hiemit schick ich euch ein Büntlen Brieff, die ich dem gelerten Manne, Postello, gehn Venedig, geschicht, seind mir erst, da er nicht zu Venedig funden, wider geschicht, ob ir sie wöllet dem Doctor Johan Buin mit meinem Grusse schicken. Jst Postellus

---

[14] MS Universitätsbibliothek, Basel, Joriskiste E. Heinrich von Schor Bericht über David Georg und die Niederländer 15 Dec. 1558, p. 10: „Dise Artikel alle hatt Nicolaus (Blesdyck) und der Artzet [Bauhin] vngefarlich by dryen Jaren von des Dauid Jorien des alten herrē ze Binningē absterben [1556] zu mehr malen widerfochten".

[15] Burckhart, *op. cit.*, p. 113 says that the Joriskiste contains a French letter from Postell to the younger Joris beginning: "La souveraine miséricorde du Seigneur fasse son effort en vous et en tout le monde." I could not find this letter and wonder whether he could have meant the one to Bauhin.

[16] Ms. B. 343.1.1. Schwenkfeld's opinion of Postell is given in Gottfried Arnold, *Kirchen und Ketzerhistorie* (1715), tom. 11, p. 1208a.

nicht zu Basel, so mag er sie wol auffbrechen vnd lesen, vnd biss er kompt, behalten. Das wöllet ihm schreiben."

This communication clears up Kvacala's question as to how Postell's letter was received. Schwenkfeld's letters were returned because Postell had fled from the Inquisition and had gone to Vienna.[17]

We may then consider Kvacala's conjecture as practically confirmed that this is the second letter to Schwenkfeld. Since the Basel manuscript differs slightly from the text as printed both in Mosheim and Kvacala I have thought fit to reproduce the manuscript with the variants at the end of this article.

The Jorist papers reveal further interesting connections with Postell. There are several excerpts from his works copied without any acknowledgement of the source and in one case with a very free reworking. The passage is taken from Postell's *Panthenosia*[18] in which he is pleading for a tolerant attitude not only toward heretics but also toward Jews, Pagans and Ishmaelites. The transcriber dropped such embarrassing company. Postell's tolerance extended even to the persecutors who were actuated by good motives. "Many of the torturers of the martyrs on account of zeal for religion and the public peace may be more highly honored by God than the martyrs themselves." The copyist turns this into, "Many of those called heretics will on account of their zeal for religion be more highly honored by God than their torturers and judges." Again the transcriber is content to let Postell go his own way when he pleads that we should give up all party cries and be known only by the name of Jesus, "Jesuits." Postell uses the form "Jesuani," but it is difficult to suppose that he was not thinking of the society to which for a time he belonged, and toward which he was always friendly.

On a scrap of paper there is a transcription without change and without acknowledgement of a portion of Postell's *Apologia pro Serveto*.[19] Then follows a statement about Schwenkfeld, the

---

[17] *ARG*, XI (1914), p. 224.

[18] Reproduced together with the Jorist transcript at the end of this article.

[19] Universitätsbibliothek, Basel, Joriskiste, IQ. *ACJ* (1915), p. 22 from „Certe nec nomen" to „nec admodum inquisivi". Mosheim, *Anderweitiger Versuch*, p. 470.

source of which I do not recognize. Is this also from Postell? The statement reads, "Quisquis est ille salutari illum meo nomine curabis: et super omnes homines qui sunt in mundo velim foelici animo Dno Gasparis Schwencfeldij. an in uno solo libello de duplici corpore redemptoris superavit omnes Teologos mundi. Si erit occasio illum curabis meo nomine salutari."

Another document[20] throws very interesting light on the dissemination of Postell's works in Anabaptist circles. A correspondent of Blesdyck writes that he has come across several writings of Elias Pandocheus, namely the *Clavis Absconditarum,* the *Ostium Apertum* and the *Candelabrum.* The correspondent suspects that Blesdyck may be the author or that these are excerpts from the *Wonderboeck* of David Joris. The relevant portions are given at the end of this article. The quotation from Postell I had not time to locate when abroad and have not now the means. The *Clavis Absconditarum* is the *Absconditorum à constitutione Mundi Clavis, quâ mens humana, tam in divinis, quàm in humanis, pertinget ad interiora velaminis aeternae Veritatis.*[21] The *Candelabrum* is clearly the *Candelabri Typici, in Mosis Tabernaculo, jussu divino, expressi, brevis, ac dilucida interpretatio,* Venetiis, 1548.[22] The *Ostium Apertum* presents difficulties. In none of the bibliographical works can I find that Postell published a book with that title.[23] Des Billons says that he announced, but never brought out, a work to be entitled *Opus justae magnitudinis, quod inscribitur: Abscondita à constitutione mundi, de Naturae humanae Restitutione in eam conditionem, quam ante peccatum habetat, nunc adfuturâ in inferioribus cum magno foenore, in quo haec continentur: Clavis Scripturarum, quâ ad interiora itur velaminis: Ostium apertum aeterni Mysterii: Septem Sigillorum Libri, ab Agno aperti, reseratio: Evangelion aeternum seu naturae & gratiae*

---

[20] Universitätsbibliothek, Basel, Joriskiste G4.

[21] Des Billons, *Nouveaux éclaircissements sur la vie et les ouvrages de Guillaume Postel.* 1773, No. XI. Sans indication d'année, ni de lieu; mais imprimé sûrement à Basle, chez Oporin, en 1547.

[22] Des Billons, *op. cit.,* No. XIV.

[23] In addition to Kvacala and Des Billons I have consulted G. Weill, *De Gulielmi Postelli vita et indole (Thesis),* Paris, Hachette, 1892, and *Nouveau dictionaire hist. et crit., supplement de M. Pierre Bayle* par Jaques George de Chaufepié (Amsterdam et La Haye, 1753), III, pp. 229ff.

conjugium."[24] Can it be that Postell really did publish a portion of this under the title *Ostium apertum?*

In Joris' own correspondence there are two letters which discuss Elias Pandocheus. Nippold was unable to take proper account of these passages because he was not aware that Pandocheus was a pseudonym for Postell.[25] The first letter is interesting because of the place. Gregory Bussal in Denmark has inquired about Pandocheus, Joris replies,[26]

Aenghaende Pandocheus/ daer weet ick weynich af: want hy heeft het al in Latijn geschreuen/ selfs sold hy een Fransois een Meester in die Universiteyt te Parijs/ Leser geweest sijn: Also dat ick daer soo niet van ghesegghen kan/wyder als Ick ghehoort unde verstaen heb. Hy geeft sich hooch voor/ wilde Godt/ dat het also waer/ 'tsolde my wel lief sijn. Etlijcke dingen staen my wel aen/ heb daer oock ghoet bericht van Godt voor hem ontfanghen: dan als Ick mijn heymelijckste herte openbaren solde/ soo dunckt my/ of Godt sijn meeste eere unde glorie/ Name unde fame deur den mondt der Jongher Kinderkins (Ick meen aen die boosheyt van herten) unde der ghener/ die noch d'onghevalschte Melck suyghen/ groot unde Heerlijck wil maken: na luyt der Gheschrift: Te weten/ deur dat cranck is het stercke (gelijck deur den Dauidt Goliath omghebrocht ward) onder-brengen. So hy (sy wie het dan wil) een van die seluighen is/ unde dat hy van sijn geleertheyt een ongeleertheyt/ mitten armen ellendigen unde crancken simpelen of eenvuldighen holdt/ mach't van hem/ als van anderen wel sijn. Dat is op dese tijdt op 't cortste mijn Antwoort van hem: Godt gheef hem unde ons allen geluck unde heyl/ goeden voortganck/ soo wy recht in of wt dat eenvuldighe ooch der waerheyt Christi begonnen hebben/ Amen. Holdt v vromelijck.

The second letter is of interest because of the date, Jan. 18, 1549.[27] Joris refers to Postell's relations to Joanna, the female Messianic figure with whom Postell became acquainted probably in 1546.[28] His extravagant claims with regard to her redemptive role

[24] Des Billons, *op cit.,* p. 14.

[25] Friedrich, Nippold, "David Joris v. Delft," *Zeitschrift f. d. hist. Theol.* (1864), pp. 570 and 581.

[26] *Sendbrieven,* 1, 2 fol. 55 Copy in the Doopgezinde Bibliotheek at Amsterdam.

[27] *Sendbrieven,* 1, 2, fol. 71*b.* A parallel to Postell's Joanna is found in Guiglielmina of Milan (1270), who was believed to be the incarnation of the Holy Spirit. See Decima Douie, *The Nature and Effect of the Heresy of the Fraticelli* (Manchester, 1932), p. 32.

[28] *ARG,* IX, 1911-1912, p. 328.

were confided to friends only and not published until after her death in 1551.[29] If then Joris' letter is correctly dated his information with regard to her must have come from oral sources. His statement in this letter is as follows:

> Ick laet v dat ten goede heymelijck weten/ dat/ so ghy anders sonder afstaen der conuersatien Mr. Eng. te met by hem comt oder spraeck hebt/ soo holdt hem eenmael voor/ dat daer een groot Meester van twaelf Tongen (villicht weet hy 't wel) opgestaen is/ die wonderlijcke nieuwe dinghen schrijft: secht dat den tijdt der Wederbenginge hier sy/ ja secht mit craft groote dingen/ dat wie hem lase/ uñ onsen grondt bewust ware/ meenen solde/ of 't deur ons beschict wurde: dan nv sijn wy hem algheheel vreemt unde onbekent. Dese meent alleen den grondt of Geest ghevonden te hebben: heet oder noemt sich Elias Pandocheus/ die 't alles wederbrengē sal/ &c. Dit seg ick v maer kinderlijck/ om mit hem so veele te spreken/ so ghy anders ghewoonlijck sijt mit hem te conuerseren/ seg ic/ op of hy des Mans Schriften niet en had/ na staen mochte/ soo het hem ernst waer: want sulcke luyden sien op gheleertheyt unde niet op simpelheyt. Ick heb my wel laten duncken/ of Godt an beyden syden den Mensch so goetlijck voorquame/ dat hy gheen oorsaeck hadde sich t'ontschuldighen/ als hy van hem seluen unde van Joanne betuycht: gelijc haer beyder comst verscheyden was/ d'een in droefheyt unde vasten/ d'ander in blytschap/ eeten unde drincken/ als een ander Mensch: also nv den selfden Geest in een nederighen simpelen/ unde in eenen hooghen vernuftigen geleerden Gheest synen sin daer-stellen wilde. Dan hebt ghy geen conversatie/ so maeckt daer om geen/ holdt het by v alleen/ om die minste clappinge/ dat is mijn hertlijc begeerē/ laet het doch anders niet gheschieden. Mijn gunst sy in den Heere mit v/ Amen. Vale.

There is one further document in the Joriskiste bearing on Postell. David Joris Tractate No. 4 contains a translation from the work of Willem Postello beginning Wt godlicker decreten. This passage also I had no time to relocate when abroad and cannot now.

THE LETTER OF POSTELL TO BAUHIN

The following letter is printed by Kvacala without the superscription in French and the address to Bauhin, *ACJ* (1915), p. 11-13. Kvacala heads the letter . . . „Postell an Schwenkfeld. Wien (?) 1554(?). Anonym in den meisten Abschriften der ‚Apologia Serveti' wie auch in deren Mosheimschen Druck, S. 497ff". The reference is to Johann Lorenz von Mosheim's

[29] *ARG*, XI, 1914, p. 207.

Anderweitiger Versuch einer vollständigen und unpartheyischen Ketzergeschichte (Helmstaedt, 1748). Kvacala follows the text of Mosheim except for a few variants taken, I gather, from a MS copy in the British Museum (MS Sloane 1411, f. 120) of which Kvacala says . . . „doch bilden diese nur abschriften von fremder Hand". *ACJ* (1915) *Postelliana*, p. XIII. The following text is that of the Basel MS, Joriskiste G 10. Passages which appear neither in Mosheim nor in Kvacala are inclosed in brackets. Variants are given in parentheses. The letters M and K stand for Mosheim and Kvacala.

[Domino Suo D. Johannj Boin
  Medico Gallo Basilee.
  A maistre Jehan Boin
medecin tres cher amy
        a Basle.]

       [La souueraine misericorde du Seigneur face son effect en vous et en tout le monde.]
       Charissime frater ut possit latius per linguam pluribus communem Divinum promulgarj beneficium, et Misericordiae infinitus effectus sicuti est etiam possit cognoscj et haberj ad te scribo. Scias itaque mi frater et per te ex nostro ad te scripto, sciat vniuersus membrorum Christj consessus (M & K consensus) Deum esse infinitum in Duabus vijs suis quae sunt Misericordia et Juticia seu Veritas. Vnde ab aeterno, in Virtutis sua (M & K suae) gratia nunquam destituendae exercitio, (K exercitatio) ita posuit vim Justiciae, ut necessario quanto quisque magis esset virtute praeditus, tanto magis et esset et videretur afflictus, et super omnia se Deum Amare in hoc ostenderet, quod in Paupertate Dolore [et Contemptu] sive probro gratum esset illj viuere. Quum autem in hoc et Adam Vetus et Eua Vetus et omnes esse filij defecerint Deumque sit impossibile fraudari sua intentione, opus fuit, ut ipsius Iusticiae seueritas summa, supra Innocentissimum filium Dej, exerceretur, vt nomine omnium compatientium lueret. Alioquj infinitudo Iusticiae viderj non poterat. Sed quid in Arido debuisset fierj (M & K fierj debuisset) sic hoc in VIRIDI? Vt autem videretur Infinitudo Misericordiae diffundi sicut et Iusticiae, opus est omnino ut non tantum, sit omnium eorum quj sunt hactenus prius damnatj quam natj Restitutio, sed ut sit unus (M & K unde, MS un') Misericordiae primogenitus, antea perditissimus damnatissimusque et omnino Antichristus qualis sum Ego, quj ea de re me in Caino occidisse Fratrem, in Sancta Republica per Coreh datan et Abiram contra Moseh fecisse seditionem. In Iudah proditore contra redemptorem procurasse Innocentissimj filij Dej et Patris mej condemnationem, ita ut sim radix et Basis iniquitatis, sicut ille est Iusticiae, [hoc est in summo gradu.] Sed quia placuit illj, pie infinitam hanc Misericordiam, mihi per spiritualem Matris meae Euae nouae (M & K nouam) substantiam concessam, eo quod Iniquitatem meam supra omnes creaturas cognosco, (M & K agnosco) me ad stolae primariae

annulj et vestis nouae receptionem reparauit, ut meo exemplo totus pecca-
torem orbis tanta amaritudine resipiscat et seipsum accuset quanto vult
et cupire debet ut sit ante Deum justior. Hi sunt meae gloriationis titulj.
Summus itaque Iusticiae et Afflictionis neruus in Patrem meum est inten-
sus, ut in me primo Infinitudo misericordiae manifestaretur. Sic me
Beatum fecit, non quod non peccauerim, sed quod remissa mihi (M & K
mihi remissa) sint tertio peccata mea. Beatorum enim sum primus cuj
Remissum est peccatum sub Lege Naturae cuius tectum est peccatum sub
Lege [illud] Aggrauante, cuj non est a Deo imputatum peccatum in Lege
Gratiae, ad hoc solum ut quarto in loco non sit in meo spiritu Dolus. Nam
nec satis est remittj, nec tegi, nec satis non imputarj, nisi in aeternum
aboleatur et nunquam redeat, nunquam detegatur, nunquam imputetur,
quod unum faciet hoc votum, non solum ut non sit dolus, sed ut potius
quam (M qui) fiat a nobis Iniuria proximo, malimus damnarj, et cupia-
mus assidue si Deus hoc concederet ut pro totius mundj salute poenis
aeternis destinemur. Haec est enim votiua et prima conformitas quam
omnes et singulj habere ad filij Dej et Patris Matrisque nostrae coelestis
imaginem debent, et ad hoc sunt omnes predestinatj sicut vult omnes
homines saluos fierj, licet sciat quos elegerit ipse hoc est in summo supra
alios gradu quouis modo constituerit. Ideo non est ipse Iudas adhuc salua-
tus licet sit Restitutus quousque ipse legitime certauerit, postquam non
Impius ut ante, sed pius et bonus per Spiritum fuerit Restitutus. Ideo
etiam ipsimet Apostolj quj alioquj fuere [hominum] perfectissimj sunt (M
& K sint) hic Restituendj, et in sua Restitutione agnoscendj, ut compleant
Judicando 12. tribus Israel quod non potuere per martyria sua. Vt ego
quum Cainus vetus eram fraudauj per meam cupiditatem Deum sua Intentione quoniam occidj fratrem ad temporale mundj Imperium desti-
natum, sic in meo fratre a me occiso et in omnibus bonis pijsque inno-
center occisis Deus est etiam fraudatus sua intentione, vnde et Restituj
in Integrum et cognosci haberjque omnes et singulos homines maxime in
sacrorum libris nominatos opus est, ut non tantum sit, sed etiam habeatur
et probetur in hac vita Deus habere rerum humanarum curam, et sua esse
Infraudabilem voluntate, et omnes in integrum Restituere ad hoc ut possit Iustissime illos iudicare per actualia et nullo modo per originale
peccatum quod opus est omnino ita abolerj, atque omnia eius remedia
praeter Christj corpus passiones et merita, tollj de medio, quod fiet in
omnibus quum seipsos esse peccatum et cognoscent et odio habebunt
fugientque et Deus in illis habitet. Satagite tu vna cum fratribus in Christo
dilectis ut Lux Matris mundj oriatur in animis vniuersi, ut tabulae Resti-
tutionis adsint ab Oporinj typis suj commentarij. Nam sumus (M & K sum)
in mora ipsi Christo donec in sua Inferiorj parte etiam cognoscatur reg-
nare per Spiritum in nobis. Deus vos conservet fratres. Seruate Epistolam.
1553. scriptam ut ad 1556. pareminj sicut in diebus Noe. Valeto.

Vester omnino abiectissimus seruus

Guilielmus Postellus.

An den eersamen Claes Meijer
mijn bijsonder goeden vriendt in eijgh.
der handt.
(Original; Universitätsbibliothek Basel, Joriskiste G4).

... Euen wel na tontfanghen uwer letteren hebbe ick ter plaetse geweest, daer mij in hande ghegeuen is een wonderlick schat ende cleijnoedie
van ghescrift. Dan soe ick nogh vleijschelick bin sijn mij die redenen volle
hoogh om wel te verstaen ende te begrijpen. Maer de scrijuer van dien
(soe hij voer gheeft) spreeckt niet van tgheen dat hij heeft hoeren segghen
ende dat hij als ijet ghelesens ghelooft, maer van tgheen dat hij siedt ende
seker weet, soe dat hij mit Christo hem vermeten soud mogen in Christo
te segghen Quod scimus loquimur et quod vidimus testamur, Ick ver-
moede mijn broeder oft wt v luijder boesem ghecommen magh sijn, doer
v lieffde mij thoe ghewinscht, ende van God bij anderen ghegheuen De
author noemt hem Elias pandocheus, ende this een vereenighing van alle
twist des werlts, niet alleen der Christenen maer oeck der Turcken Joden
ende Mahumethisten oder Ismaëliten etc. De selfde heeft oeck ghescreuen
dat hij noemt Clauem absconditorum, Een ander genaemt Ostium apertum, ende een Candelabrum, behaluen veel anderen. Mij twijfelt wel
half of dit stuxkens mogen wesen ex magno volumine mirabilium, van
welck ick somtijden heb hoeren spreecken. Ick bidde v mij daer waer-
heijdt of te willen laten weten. Ende ist anders, wat ick luttel twijfel of
sijn sin is onder v luijden wel becandt. Sijn woerden om beter gheloof te
vijnden bij den goeden leeser int eerste cap: sijn aldus Quum sua infinita
clementia JESVS dignatus sit me spiritu munifico et principali confor-
mare, ut ipsissimus parentis primi spiritus sit in nobis, adeo ut quae olim
credere, fidéque sola affirmare solebam, illa mihi sint in tanta intellectus
claritate exposita, ut non manifestus mathematum principia aut axiomata
me possint certum facere, quàm mente principio vel incarnationis verbi
Dei, vel sacrosancti Eucharistiae sacramenti mysterium, necessario cogor
ista mundo proponere, ut his legibus discat mundus unicum salutis a
quauis creatura expeti solitae, authorem JESVM ubiuis praesentem repe-
riré, repertum agnoscere agnitum colere et amare Hic enim finis uniuersi
est. Sic ille. Hij wil oeck segghen dat die gheest Christi nu in eenighe
leeden Christi haer soe versterckt ende vercloeckt kenlich, waerlick, ende
sekerlick, als of sij bijnaest selfs Christus JESVS waren. Dat mijn broeder
laet ick mij duncken waer een man die mij van den gheest mijnder despe-
ratien grondlich(?) soud moghen verlossen, als voermaels Christus JESVS
den iongheling deed, an welch alle dapostolen haer raed ten eijnde waren,
soe voer waer alle de werlt mit mij is, ende ick in mijn seluen oeck, wtghe-
nomen dat ick mit den mallaetschen wtsettighe mensch dick in alle mijn
verlatenheijd in goeder gheloeue roep, Heer wilt ghij, ghij moecht mij
reijnighen voer den desperaten ende verblindenden geest mij na v goedt-
heijdt gheuende een salijghen vastheopende ende sienden geest welc mij

alsoe gheuen ende v altijdt meer ende meer vergroeten ende verstercken
wil ons Heer JESVS Christus ghebenedijth ghepresen ende lofwaerdigh
in ewigheijdt Amen.

... Hieren bouen soe leese ick in desen Elia pandoch: (van welck ick
voerwaer veel houde, al versta ick hem niet gans want ick vermerck dareen
sonderling begenadight verstand ende gheest in) van de tijde des restitutijs
daer de scrift rijckelick of betuijght, dat hij hem laet duncken dat hij nu
al gherestitueert is in de selfde staet als Adam was voer de sond, ende dat
het menschlick gheslacht daghelicks nu gherestitueert wordt ende ganslick
in sulcken staet altesamen gherestitueert sullen worden voer den groeten
quaelen dagh des oordels. Voerwaer wat sulcker menschen wesen, doen
ende laten al schandalisatijs ende argernisse in veel der harten soude
commen maken, weet v liefde self beter, dan ick can scrijuen. Soude de
vrijheijdt der kinderen Gods sulx sijn, als men ghemeenlick seijdt dat
Adam gehadt soude hebben voer douertreding, soe most daer in die resti-
tutie noch voerttelinghe ende lustijghe wassing ende vermennichouding
sijn. Ende oeck baring sonder smart of pijn, alsoe men van de baring
Mariae seijdt, wanneer sij JESVM onsen heijland baerde. Ende die an-
wassende kinderen of vruchten mosten voerwaer oeck van eenen anderen
aert sijn (dunkt mij) dan nu ons sondighe aerdts vrucht is, euen wel souden sij blijuen in haer vleijschs lusten ende begheerten, maer eens reijnen
suijueren ende God anghenamen vleijsch, soe dat oeck alle die lusten en
begheerten God souden wesen angenaem.

Dese saken mijn lief broeder sijn mijn verstandt vollen hoogh ende
swaer om to begrijpen, ende betrou mijn verstand in deser saken niet.
Christus IESVS onse eenighe liefhebbende middelaer gunne ons doer sijn
ontbarmende ghenadighe gheest sulcke kennisse als ons saligh ende sij
Godlijcke naem prijselick looflick ende danckelick is, v mit alle Godes
mannen ende des ewijghewaerheijdt liefhebbers in hem, doer hem ende
tot hem versterckende ende meer ende meer tot den ewijghen leuen be-
ghenadighende.

Kleijdt v schuldighe
goedgunstighe dienaer

A passage from Postell's *Panthenosia,* 1547 (Des Billons, No.
XII) pp. 130-131, in parallel columns with the transcription and
reworking in the Joriskiste No. 3.

Postell	Jorist transcriber
Cessent ista anathemata, et ful-mina: donec adsit ille cui omnes ex aequo curae sunt, ante cuius exa-men non est iudicandum, qui illu-minat nunc & illuminabit abscon-dita tenebrarum, & manifestabit	Cessent ista anathemata, et ful-mina: donec adsit ille cui omnes ex aequo curae sunt, ante cuius exa-men non est iudicandum, qui illu-minat nunc et illuminabit abscon-dita tenebrarum, et manifestabit

consilia cordium: & tunc laus erit unicuique à Domino, non uni tantum, aut alteri, sed omnibus & singulis, seu Catholici, seu haeretici, seu Judaei, seu Pagani, seu Ismaelitae.

Mensurat enim IESVS non facta aut contentiones exteriores tantum, sed ipsos affectus, voluntates, desideria, zelos, licet non sint secundum scientiam. Quoniam enim ipse in nobis posuit principia affectuum, non respicit ad errorem, sed ad intentionem & finem: ita ut multi martyrum tortores, sint futuri ob suae religionis & pacis publicae zelum, in maiori apud Deum loco quam ipsi martyres, multo haeretici quam fideles. Has uero intentiones ob zelum proprium non potuimus hactenus considerare. Ideo quum Deus non repulerit populum suum quem praeelegit, sed salutem eius distulit, donec plenitudo gentium intrauerit, quum non possimus assere excommunicationem in Judaeos, qui in ijsdem ueteris Testamenti principijs nobiscum uersantur: quanto minus licet fulmine sacro percellere illos, qui in articulis fidei omnino nobiscum conueniunt. Sistite ô patres, sistite per sanguinem IESV Christi, sistite inquam hunc maledicentiae et imprecationum in fratres nostros fluxum. Ipsi enim habent zelum Dei, de quo solus est iudex. Sistite & uos fratres aquilonares, sistite hanc intemperantiam maledicendi istis, considerate quoniam et uos homines estis: quod de earum possessionum usu quo negligenter uti solebant iudicare uel sanguine uestro potestis. Permittite inter uos, ut unusquisque pro suo ritu uiuat, donec omnes uniat Christus, semo-

consilia cordium: et tunc laus erit unicuique a Domino, non uni tantum, aut alteri, sed omnibus et singulis, seu Catholici seu heretici.

Mensurat enim Jesus non facta aut contentiones exteriores tantum, sed ipsos affectus, voluntates, desideria, zelos, licet non sint secundum scientiam.

Quoniam ipse in nobis posuit principia affectuum, puto enim non sic respicere ad errorem quam ad intentionem et finem: ita ut iuxta meam opinionem ac spem multi hereseos titulo denotati futuri sint ob suae religionis zelum in maiori apud Deum loco, quam eorum tortores aut iudices. Has vero intentiones ob zelum proprium non potuimus hactenus considerare.

Ideo quum Deus teste Paulo apostolo populum Iudaeorum quem praeelegerent [sic], non repulerit, sed eius salutem saltem distulet donec plenitudo gentium intrauerit: quumque assere non possimus Apostolicam ecclesiam excommunicasse Judaeos ob indignissimum et horrendissimum in Christum perpetratum scelus eo quod in eisdem veteris testamenti principiis secum verserentur. Denique quum et hodie illis permittent ut inter nos suo arbitrio et ritu uiuant. Imo ut nostram religionem et qui eam sectabunt, ceu impuram profanam et impiam exercentur: quanto aequius erat non sic percellere sacro fulmine illos qui in omnibus articulis ad salutem necessariis omnino nobiscum conueniunt. Summam salutem in ijsdem quibus et nos collantes rebus, eadem pietatis officia agnoscentes quae et nos. Eadem de Deo ac Domino nostro Jesu Christo,

tis illis dissidijs, quae in sacro ritu uersari solent. Postquam in principijs conuenimus, non potuerit fieri quin & ad uera ueniamus axiomata, & ad finales ueritates. Nullus sit amplius papista, nullus Lutheranus, omnes ab expetita salute de IESV nomen capiamus. Simus omnes Iesuani.

de eius ecclesia, euangelio, sacramentis, et de scriptura sentientes, confitentes, docentes et obseruare studentes.

15. The Anabaptist Contribution to History

The Anabaptist contribution to history is comparable to that of the Norsemen who visited America prior to Columbus. They found what he found and they found it first. Their intrepidity was no less and possibly greater than his. But they do not occupy the same place in history because their deed was without sequel. Not they, but he opened up the trek from Europe to the New World. Similarly, the Anabaptists anticipated all other religious bodies in the proclamation and exemplification of three principles which, on the North American continent, are among those truths which we hold to be self-evident: the voluntary Church, the separation of Church and state and religious liberty. From the days of Constantine to the Anabaptists these principles, to us so cardinal, had been in abeyance. They were not, however, transmitted to us by the Anabaptists, but rather by the Puritan revolution and the French Revolution.

The possibility of Anabaptist influence hinges on the question whether the English free churchmen in exile in Holland learned from the Mennonites. The question is worthy of fuller investigation. But this is plain, that as to the voluntary Church the English sectaries had already made up their minds before ever they went to Holland, and the other two principles were bound to follow. In the present state of research it appears most likely that the English Puritans and the Anabaptists grew from the same sources. One was Zwingli. Anabaptism, as we well know originated in his circle; and English Puritanism was in close touch with Zürich. The other source was the New Testament. A minute examina-

First published in *The Recovery of the Anabaptist Vision*, a sixtieth anniversary tribute to Harold S. Bender, edited by Guy S. Hershberger (Scottdale, Pa., 1957), pp. 317-326.

tion of its contents, with the resolve to restore its pattern, led the Anabaptists to diverge from Zwingli; and this may well have had a like effect in England. On the whole, Anabaptism appears to have been an amazingly clear-cut and heroic anticipation of what with us has come to be axiomatic; but the line is not direct. The discovery had to be made over again.

This is not to say that Anabaptism made no contribution to the rise of religious liberty. The Anabaptists in the sixteenth century were the party *par excellence* of suffering. Their pleas for liberty might be discounted as intended only to relieve their own situation. But pleas on their behalf were made by the champions of religious liberty who were not of their party. Sebastian Franck wrote in his *Chronica, Zeytbuch und Geschychtbibel* a most discriminating account of the Anabaptists and pleaded that they be accorded the freedom of their faith. Only those guilty of overt revolution should be constrained and from none did he fear it so little as from the Anabaptists. To be sure Hans Hut was a revolutionary, but he had been repudiated by the Anabaptists. More on this score, according to Franck, was to be feared from the Pope, the Kaiser and the Turks. Not everything indeed in Anabaptism was to be approved. There was among the Anabaptists a sectarian spirit and too much concern for outward ceremonies. "I have listed them," says Franck, "among the heretics that they may perceive that their church is not the true church, that they may turn to genuine unity in spirit and in truth, but I warn their persecutors not to play the part of Caiaphas and Pilate. The Anabaptists are not entirely right nor is anyone else and from each we should take the best."[1]

Sebastian Castellio likewise, in his *De Haereticis* composed for the immediate purpose of excoriating the execution of Servetus, contained also a protest against the persecution of the Anabaptists. "They were miserably slain," says he, "even those who were not in arms and, what is still more cruel, the suppression was carried on not only by the sword but also in books which reach farther and last longer, or rather forever perpetuate this savagery."[2] At the end

[1] Sebastian Franck, *Chronica, Zeytbuch und Geschychtbibel* (Strasbourg, 1531), ccccxlix-ccclii.

[2] Sebastian Castellio, *Concerning Heretics*, translated and edited by Roland H. Bainton, Columbia University *Records of Civilization* (New York, 1935), 218.

of his life Castellio penned a still more poignant plea. It lay in manuscript until discovered in our own day by Professor Bruno Becker of Amsterdam. The whole has not yet been published. The portions were edited by Etienne Giran in *L'Esprit et la Vie*. Although this defense of the Anabaptists cannot be said to have influenced history, it is worth citing because such thoughts lay behind what Castellio committed to the printed page. In this manuscript, addressing Beza, Castellio says:

"With regard to the Anabaptists I would like to know how you know that they condemn legitimate marriages and the magistracy and condone murders. Certainly it is not in their books and much less in their words. You have heard it from their enemies, but if enemies are to be trusted, then in France it was rumored that Zwingli preached to trees, stones, and beasts, because of the text 'Preach the Gospel to all creatures.' And it was said that Farel had as many devils in his beard as hairs, and that whenever he ate he fed the devils. Beza, would you have us believe such things? I do not believe what you say about the Anabaptists. Those at Münster did not reject the magistrate and they retained Knipperdollinck as magistrate. As for marriage, their enemies say that each had more than one wife. Very well, but that is not having wives in common. There are some persons who certainly are not Anabaptists who testify that in Bohemia the Anabaptists hold marriage in such reverence that if any among them is guilty of adultery he is rigorously excluded from their community. Neither should people be held responsible for a position which they have themselves repudiated, any more than you, Beza, should be reproached for the amatory verses of your youth."[3]

In England Adriaan van Haemstede, pastor of the Dutch congregation in London in the days of Elizabeth, undertook a defense of the Anabaptists when in 1560 the Queen ordered that they should all leave the realm within twenty days. Haemstede protested on the grounds that the Anabaptist doctrine of the flesh of Christ touched only the non-essentials and not the fundamentals of the Christian religion, and ought therefore to be tolerated. When Haemstede himself in consequence was in trouble, a lance on his

[3] *L'Esprit et la Vie, IV*, No. 6 (May 1939).

behalf was broken by the great champion of religious liberty, Jacob Acontius.[4]

These examples are cited to show that the advocates of religious liberty found their prime examples of persecution in the treatment meted out to the Anabaptists. And therefore by their sufferings it may be said that they contributed directly to the ultimate achievement of freedom in religion. Their most direct contribution, however, lies in another area. It is a demonstration of the power of the segregated Church to maintain its identity and continuity over the course of four centuries. This involves three phases. First came the resolve to become a segregated Church. Secondly arose the problem of finding a refuge from extermination; and third was the achievement of internal cohesion.

The resolve to be a segregated community came about largely as a result of circumstance. There is at the outset in early Anabaptist literature an ambiguity, not to say a sharp dichotomy, between the concept of the Church as a remnant and the Great Commission, binding upon every member, to proclaim the faith to all creatures. What was the purpose of the Great Commission? If the Church must always be a remnant the conclusion appears inevitable that the Great Commission was bound to fail. Was this clearly envisaged by those who embarked upon it? Were they not trying to convert, but merely shaking off the dust from their feet as a testimony to increase the condemnation of those who rejected the message? One does not have the feeling in reading the documents that this was the point. There seems rather to have been a genuine hope of conversion. Nor was it fatuous at the time. Anabaptism spread in Switzerland, down the Rhine Valley and in the Netherlands. The documents now in process of publication reveal an amazing dissemination and indicate a real possibility that Anabaptism, if unimpeded by the sword of the magistrate, might have become the prevailing form of the Church in Germany. If that had happened, an infinitude of problems would have confronted the Anabaptists. What then would have happened to the state? Would there have been a theocratic community, with Church and state united, and coercion reduced to the ban and avoidance? But we need not pur-

4 Bainton, *op. cit.*, 113-14.

sue these questions because the dilemmas were never raised. The Great Commission did not succeed. Persecution turned the Anabaptists into the Church of the Remnant.

Then came the problem of survival. There were only two ways: one was the way of accommodation and this way was taken by those of the Mennonites who remained in the Netherlands and by those Hutterites in Austria who accepted the mass in return for liberty in every other respect to retain their pattern of life. The other way of survival was that of migration to a frontier, whether that of the eastern fringe of Europe where feudalism still prevailed and some well-disposed nobleman could grant an asylum without interference from the central government, or else the frontier of the forest primeval in Canada, the Dakotas or Paraguay. Even here survival was conditioned upon participation in the common life of the entire community at one point, namely, the economic. The immigrants were such good farmers that the ruler viewed them as a department of public economy and as contributing to the common effort even in wartime. He could get other people to fight. These pacifists he could use to feed the populace. This observation is not made in scorn. It is part of the dilemma of all pacifism. There is no survival in wartime unless one is prepared to do something which can be regarded as a service useful to those engaged in the conflict.

The next question was that of internal cohesion. Nothing is more amazing than the way these sixteenth century dissenters learned to live with each other. Their genius and their experience lay in opposition. They were masters in the art of obstruction. They would shock the community by baptizing adults in the public fountain or by marching in procession through the streets of Zürich crying "Woe, Woe," and proclaiming that Zwingli was the dragon of the Apocalypse. Some in Holland like the later Quakers went naked as a sign in imitation of the prophet Isaiah. Some like Blaurock would interrupt public worship, and attempt to supplant the minister in his own pulpit. Summoned before a court, they might refuse to answer a word or they might wax denunciatory and call their examiners idolaters and heathen. Banished, the Anabaptists refused to stay away. Tortured, they endured without flinching. Executed, they died with a song. Even among themselves there were clashes because rival prophets claimed divergent inspirations from the Lord. And the ideal of perfection led not only to scrupulous self-criticism but also to censoriousness in regard to others. That people with such a temper should have been able to establish a stable community is indeed an amazing achievement.

Their squabbles often appear petty unless one bears in mind all they had endured and all they were striving to attain. In the Hutterian colony at Austerlitz quarrels at once commenced when Jacob Wiedemann selected husbands for the girls. The maidens murmured in spite of his remonstrance that if they did not consent the men would have to marry heathen girls. There were complaints that the children were being too severely disciplined. Positive schisms occurred because of personal rivalries. Räbel could not endure the leadership of Wiedemann and led a seceding group to Auschwitz. This group had as its head Simon Schützinger, when Jacob Huter arrived. He too was a shepherd and now the community had two shepherds. The confusion was adjusted by making Simon a "shepherd" and Jacob an "apostle" with differentiation of function. But this arrangement was upset when it was rumored that the Schützingers had violated the rule of absolutely no property. Search was made and in their possession were discovered some extra shirts and four pieces of money. Frau Schützinger was consequently a Sapphira and her husband an Ananias. They had to do penance and he was, of course, deposed from the leadership of the community. But a certain Philip suspected that Jacob Huter had engineered this *coup* and therefore seceded. Then Huter received a call from the Lord to go out on the Great Commission which for him ended in martyrdom. Reconciliation was eventually achieved between the Hutterites and the Philipists and under the leadership of Peter Ridemann a spirit of healing prevailed.[5] Such examples are cited not to stigmatize the movement as contentious and petty, but only to show how difficult and how remarkable was the taming of those very qualities which had made the first generation of Anabaptists so stalwart in their opposition to the world.

The subsequent history centers on the efforts of the community to retain its children, and this was done by fencing them off

---

[5] A. J. F. Zieglschmid (Ed.), *Die älteste Chronik der Hutterischen Brüder* (Ithaca, 1943). The relevant portions can be found through the index of names.

from the corrupting influences of the world round about. Persecution at this point is of real assistance, provided it stops short of extermination, and nothing is so disruptive of the pattern of the segregated Church as friendliness from the outside. Therefore, in our own day the Hutterites and the most extreme of the Mennonites, notably the Amish, have sought in every way to make themselves a peculiar people uncontaminated by the ways of the evil world. They object, not so much to mechanization, and are willing to employ whatever is needful in order to compete with neighboring farmers; but they deliberately choose those forms of mechanization which entail the least contact with the world beyond. Gasoline is preferable to electricity because electricity affords the possibility of introducing so many appliances and gadgets like the radio and television which bring the outside world into the very parlor. Riding in automobiles is not forbidden, but only the owning of automobiles, because in that case there will be altogether too much running around and the young people will be hard to retain within the confines of the community. The telephone for obvious reasons is taboo, and without it these people are well able to relay news in an incredibly short time. The most acute area of conflict is education because in this land of the free we require that everyone should be free in precisely the same fashion.

One cannot but admire the loyalty of these groups to their tradition which they believe to be the very will of God. They have demonstrated astoundingly the ability of groups despised and rejected by the world to triumph over opposition from without and disintegration from within and to hold their own children. Yet one may question whether such a way of life is to be deliberately chosen in our present culture. Recently there has been a revival of the Hutterite *Bruderhofs* in England, Paraguay and the United States. A number of our most idealistic and best-trained young people are throwing in their lot with these communities. Such a course appears to me to be justified only on one or two assumptions. The first is that our society is utterly hopeless, that it can never be Christianized nor even ameliorated in a Christian direction. This is an assumption which for myself I am not prepared to make. The very fact that three Anabaptist principles have come to be cardinal for our way of life is itself the demonstration that the world is affected by the Church and that some problems do admit of solution on a large scale and in a Christian way. Much indeed remains, and only with qualification can we speak of our country as a Christian land, yet this example should expel the spirit of utter hopelessness.

The second assumption is that a withdrawal may exert an influence upon society as a whole. This is always possible. Catholic monasticism in the Middle Ages undoubtedly exerted an impact on the whole social fabric. The Hutterites and the Amish in our day, however, do not in my judgment exert such an influence. They arouse interest because they are quaint, and in our stereotyped culture we are glad to discover anything at all different. But this does not mean that we have the least disposition to apply the pattern to ourselves. I greatly question then whether the new *Bruderhofs* will evoke anything more than the interest excited by oddities. If this be true, then the withdrawal in this fashion from the common life, even though the discipline in the societies is rigorous, appears to me to be taking an easy way out of the complexities and dilemmas of our modern society. Living in the midst of the American culture in a world bristling with projectiles is no light assignment for a Christian, but we are not to assume that we are more Christian by disdaining it.

Thus far I have accepted the assignment to speak of the Anabaptists' contribution to history. Let it now be said that the worth of their endeavor is not to be judged in the light of their contribution to history. They took their stand in the light of eternity regardless of what might or might not happen in history. They did not fall into the error of those who treat the way of the cross as if it were a weapon, a political strategy by which to put over a program on the assumption that suffering will melt the persecutor and make him ready to adopt the way of his victim. The persecutor may be melted, but on the other hand he may be hardened, and the cross is not a strategy. It is a witness before God, no matter whether there may or may not be any historical consequences.

For multitudes of the Anabaptists there was not enough of a consequence to let us know even whether they did or did not suffer. We have for example the following list of names of men and women arrested at Augsburg (1528):

"Sebastian Vischgatter, hucker; Jorg Gietler, weber; Mang

Betz, ringmacher; Wolf Coderus, schlosser; Hans Schlund, Hans
Heises, Wilhalm Echsen; Jorg Schweitzer, wallschlager; Jakob
Heises; Hans Hertlin, hucker; Hans Butz, weber; Jos Thoman,
ferber; Hans Fesenmair, weber; Eloi Forster, weber; Thoman Paur,
tagwerker. . . .

"Getraut Heisesin, Afra Schleichin, Anna Berchtoldmairin,
Magdalena Seitzin, Anna Kochin, Elisabeth Wollschlagerin, Mar-
gareth Berchtoldin, Martha Beckin, Maxencia Wisingerin. . . .[6]

Names, just names! Back of every one lay a history and after
every one came a sequel, but we do not know what. Were they imprisoned, banished, beheaded, burned, drowned? The record does
not say. Before God they stand with no notice in the annals of man.

There is in these same documents a letter which I found profoundly moving. It is from a wife to the town council of Regensburg in November or December 1539. She writes:

"Most noble lords, I beg you to look upon my petition with
favor. Gabriel Weinperger was arrested because of *misglauben*. His
case has dragged on for a long time. I am left with my little children without the help of their father and I find it very difficult to
provide daily bread. We would like to live together again and I believe that if I can be permitted to speak to my husband I could
persuade him for my sake and the children to give up these ideas
because he never was a leader and never persuaded any others to
take up these errors, but he simply listened to others. That my children may be supported I beg you to let me talk with him and I will
not cease to pray God that your government may have long life
and good fortune."

At the bottom of the letter is simply written the word "endorsed."[7] If Gabriel Weinperger listened to his wife and renounced
his conviction, he would eat out his heart for the rest of his days as
a renegade; if he rejected her plea and held firm to his confession,
he would eat out his heart with concern for his wife and for his
children. What he did we do not know. If he was faithful to his
conviction, his deed stands not in the annals of history but in the
eternal book of God.

[6] Karl Schornbaum (Ed.), *Quellen zur Geschichte der Täufer V: Bayern,
II Abteilung* (Gütersloh, 1951), 19.
    [7] *Ibid.*, 82-83.

III. Religious Struggles After the Reformation

16. The Struggle for Religious Liberty

A sketch of the struggle for religious liberty during the course of the last four hundred years will be attempted in this paper. Attention will first be focussed on the theories and factors affecting persecution and tolerance on the part of both Catholics and Protestants. Then the administrative aspects of the subject will be considered alike from the broader standpoint of the structure of the Church and of the state and from the more specific angle of the handling of dissent by political authority. Finally brief consideration will be devoted to residual and perennial problems of constraint and freedom.

The age of the Reformation has been taken as our point of departure because this period at once intensified persecution and at the same time opened the door to an ultimate freedom. Let us cast a preliminary glance at the situation as it was in the sixteenth century before proceeding to a consideration of questions of theory.

The Protestant Reformation itself has at times been credited with the rise of religious liberty but such a statement can be made only with distinct reserve. The remark of Gooch that democracy was the child not of the reformers but of the Reformation[1] could be transferred with equal warrant to religious liberty and with equal qualification, for in both cases the outcome was only indirect and eventual. The outstanding reformers of the sixteenth century were in no sense tolerant. Luther in 1530 acquiesced in the death penalty for Anabaptists and Calvin instigated the execution of Servetus, while Melanchthon applauded. The reformers can be ranged on the side of liberty only if the younger Luther be pitted against the older or the left wing of the Reformation against the

The presidential address delivered at the meeting of the American Society of Church History on December 27, 1940. First published in *Church History*, X, 2 (June 1941).

[1] G. P. Gooch and Harold Laski, *English Democratic Ideas* (Cambridge, 1927), 7.

right. Consistent liberals, to be sure, there were such as Franck, Castellio and Acontius, but they were a small and powerless minority. The opinion of the dominant group was expressed with pithy brutality by Theodore Beza when he stigmatized religious liberty as a most diabolical dogma because it means that everyone should be left to go to hell in his own way.[2]

Neither can one say that the Reformation at the outset brought any gain to liberty. Rather the reverse, for Protestantism arrested secularist tendencies and made religion again the pre-eminent concern of men for another century and a half. The spirit of persecution was thereby aroused. A latitudinarian Catholicism was stung by the emergence of a formidable rival into a renewal of inquisitorial rigor. The last portion of the sixteenth century in consequence came to differ vastly in temper from the opening decades when even in Spain the Inquisition, having done its work against the Moors and the Jews, appeared to be on the point of discontinuance. The Alumbrados and Erasmians flourished and in Portugal the humanist George Buchanan could actually secure release from the toils of the Holy Office. Protestant heresy trials commenced in Spain in 1552.

In England likewise Sir Thomas More in his Utopian days had toyed with the idea of a world parliament of religions. In Germany, Reuchlin to all practical intent had won the battle for the freedom of Semitic studies. In France incendiaries like Farel were harbored by a Bishop Briçonnet and Francis I could oscillate in his policy toward heretics depending on whether he was seeking an alliance with the Lutherans, the pope or the Turk. How vast was the change under Henry II when not only the Inquisition and the local clergy became active, but even the civil courts organized special tribunals for cases of heresy such as the notorious *Chambre Ardente* in Paris, which in the year 1548-1549 made 450 arrests and sent 60 to the stake! In Italy, similarly, the early years of the century had seen little system, *poca regola,* in ferreting out unbelief, as the liberal Cardinal Morone testified years after when himself

---

[2] *Epistolarum Theologicarum Theodori Bezae Vezelij, Liber Unus* (Geneva, 1575), 20. *Est enim hoc mire diabolicum dogma, Sinendum esse unumquemque ut si volet pereat.*

under detention.[3] In the first decades Venice refused to close her lagoons to the Lutheran merchants[4] and Naples stoutly resisted the introduction of the Inquisition.[5] The change came here in 1542 with the bull *Licet ab initio,* establishing the Roman Inquisition. Shortly thereafter the implacable Caraffa, the Calvin of the Counter Reformation, became pope as Paul IV and all irenicism between Catholicism and Protestantism was definitely at an end.

Protestantism in the meantime had grown likewise more intransigent as it passed from Lutheranism to Calvinism. The upshot of the conflict between the rival faiths was religious war, first in Switzerland from 1529-1531, then in Germany from 1546-1547, and in France and Holland commencing in the sixties and continuing throughout the sixteenth century. The seventeenth century saw the civil wars in England and the Thirty Years War on the Continent, in both of which religion played no minor role. The bitterness became so intense that the Calvinist Frederick V, the exiled Elector of the Palatinate, when offered restoration to his rule on condition that he tolerate Lutherans, flatly refused. We see then that the struggle for religious liberty had to be waged at the same time against the intolerance of a Catholicism menaced by a new foe and of a Protestantism seeking to preserve itself against the Catholic onslaught to the right and sectarian disintegration to the left.

The battle took place primarily in the field of ideas. Religious persecution was religious and only incidentally social and political. The belief that outside of the Church there was no salvation, that heresy damns souls—this was the root of the matter. Protestants and Catholics at this point were agreed, and the differences between their theories of persecution are slight. Lord Acton was quite mistaken in portraying the Protestant theory of persecution as diametrically opposed to the Catholic on the ground that

---

[3] Cesare Cantù, *Gli Eretici d'Italia* (3 vols., Torino, 1865-66), II, 180.

[4] Georg Martin Thomas, ed., *Martin Luther und die Reformationsbewegung in Deutschland vom Jahre 1520-32 in Auszügen aus Marino Sanuto's Diarien* (Amsbach, 1883), 155. "Quanto alli Lutherani et heretici, el stado e dominio nostro è libero, e perhè non potemo devedarli."

[5] Luigi Amabile, *Il Santo Officio della Inquisizione in Napoli* (2 vols., Città de Castello, 1892), I, 120.

Protestants had nothing left for which to persecute save error, whereas Catholics withstood the disruption of society through dissent.[6] This picture is utterly misleading. Neither Catholic nor Protestant ever persecuted mere error but only obstinate error. Both persecuted heresy as heresy, and both believed that heresy, if unchecked, would disintegrate society. Both were driven by the exigencies of the situation to suppress dissent. That was the theory of *cuius regio eius religio,* which conceded to princes of rival faiths the right to establish each his own religion and to expel dissenters; and the Anglican settlement was based precisely on latitude toward error and severity toward non-conformity.

There are a few differences between the Catholic and Protestant theories, but they are not great and they go in diverse directions. Luther took a faltering step toward liberty when he made the object of suppression not heresy but blasphemy. The actual gain in his own practice, however, was slight because he simply treated heresy as blasphemy. Calvin declined to avail himself of this subterfuge and burned Servetus outright as a heretic.[7] At several points Calvin intensified the Catholic theory of persecution; first by accentuating the feudal conception of sin, according to which the enormity of an offense depends on the rank of the person against whom it is committed. When then God was exalted by Calvin to a dizzy transcendental eminence, heresy as an insult to His majesty became a crime of infinite depravity. In consequence the Catholic proviso that only a relapsed heretic should be put to death was abandoned. On no pretext could Servetus be regarded as relapsed. The other great difference was that the doctrine of predestination necessarily altered the purpose of persecution which could not be to save souls since they were saved or damned already but could only be for the glory of God. Of this, more later.

The greatest difference lay in the legal basis for persecution. For Catholics this was the canon law which was jettisoned by the Protestants. For it were substituted the Bible and the Roman law. In the long run this shift made for liberty, because the Bible pro-

---

   [6] John Emerich Edward Dalberg-Acton, *History of Freedom* (London, 1922), Chapter V, "The Protestant Theory of Persecution."
   [7] George L. Burr, "Anent the Middle Ages," *American Historical Review,* XVIII (1913), 721-22.

vides but an insecure basis for the persecution of heresy, and the Roman law, while explicit enough, was to enjoy only a temporary vogue. The difficulty in the case of the Bible is that although the Old Testament is severe in its penalties, they are directed not against heresy but only against idolatry and apostasy, whereas the New Testament, though mentioning heresy, is mild in its treatment of the offender. The Protestant persecutors had to combine the offense of the new with the penalty of the old Covenant, a combination which the liberals were not slow in prying apart.

The Roman law was more explicit both with regard to the offense and the penalty.[8] The two heresies penalized by death in the *Codex Justinianus* were a denial of the Trinity and a repetition of baptism. The former offense was menaced with dire though unspecified penalty, the second was proscribed by death. This ancient legislation directed against Arians and Donatists was revived in the sixteenth century and applied to anti-Trinitarians and Anabaptists. Luther, Melanchthon and Calvin all appealed to the imperial law. Joris, Gentile and Servetus, and the Anabaptists as a whole, suffered under its terms. In fact, the very name Anabaptist, meaning re-baptizer, was invented in order to subject to the im-

---

[8] *Codex Justinianus* I, I: *De Summa Trinitate-Codex Theodosianus* XVI, 1, 2. *Codex Justinianus* I, 6, 2, *Ne Sanctum baptisma iteretur-Codex Theodosianus* XVI, 6, 6. Cf. George L. Burr, "Liberals and Liberty," *Proceedings of the Unitarian Historical Society*, II (1933), part 2. For the charge of Donatism against the Anabaptists see *CR* (Melanchthon) IV, 739 and III, 199. For the charge of Manicheism *ibid.*, III, 201. Servetus was accused of Manicheism *CR* (Calvin) VIII, 463 and 773. The Roman law played a prominent part in Protestant heresy trials, for example in the case of Servetus. Here the claim has been made that not Calvin but Servetus appealed to the Roman law and that the plea was promptly rejected because Geneva recognized only the Old Testament. (Walther Köhler, *Reformation und Ketzerprozess*, p. 40). On the contrary it was merely Servetus' interpretation of the law which was rejected, in that he averred the maximum penalty under Constantine to have been only banishment (*CR* VIII, 762). The procurator replied that the death penalty had been exacted from Constantine to Justinian, and that Servetus was guilty of various offenses enumerated in the imperial codes (p. 771f). Servetus upbraided Calvin for relying on Justinian (p. 797f). For Joris see my "David Joris," *ARG*, Ergänzungsband VI (1935), p. 11. On the case of Gentile consult Trechsel, *Die Protestantischen Antitrinitarier* (1884), II, 328. Melanchthon frequently appealed to the Theodosian code (*CR.*, II, 18 and 712), though he considered the penalties too severe (III, 242; IX, 1004; XII, 143). Luther signed the two memoranda against the Anabaptists which relied on the code (*ibid.*, IV, 739: III, 199).

perial laws those who preferred to call themselves simply Baptists. They would never admit that they baptized over again, for infant baptism was to them no baptism, but rather a "washing in the Roman bath." The prevalence of the imperial code goes far to explain why anti-Trinitarianism and Anabaptism were the two heresies visited with the severest penalties in the sixteenth century. Significantly, the last infliction of the death penalty for heresy in England under James I was for just these offenses. Roman law, however, was destined to succumb in favor of national codes and a policy of persecution resting on no deeper legal basis than the old imperial laws could not indefinitely survive.

Differences, then, there are between the Catholic and Protestant theories of persecution, but they are comparatively trivial. When one turns to the theory of liberty the case is different, for Protestantism can be tolerant on more grounds than Catholicism, which cannot relinquish so many of the requisites for persecution. Of these there are three: the persecutor must believe that he is right; that the point in question is important; and that coercion will be effective. Catholicism can relax only on the third of these conditions, but Protestantism on all three.

The Catholic can never admit any uncertainty as to the cardinal affirmations of the Church. Neither can he concede that a wilful denial of an article in the ecumenical creeds is a venial offense, since it will certainly entail damnation. The only ground for tolerance is expediency; but this is a larger ground than the word at first connotes, for expediency may be ecclesiastical, political or religious. The Church can argue from the ecclesiastical point of view that persecution will recoil upon Catholics and do the Church more harm than good. This has been the situation in the United States. If any Church had been established it would not have been the Catholic and if any churches were persecuted the Catholic would not have been exempt. Leading American Catholics have clearly recognized this situation and commonly have wholeheartedly endorsed the American system of toleration. Archbishop Ireland, speaking in 1913, declared: "Would we alter if we could the constitution in regard to its treatment of religion, the principles of Americanism in regard to religious freedom? I answer with an emphatic no. . . . Violate religious freedom against Catholics: our swords are at once unsheathed. Violate it in favor of Catholics against non-Catholics: no less readily do they leap from the scabbard."[9] In similar phrase, Cardinal Gibbons declared: "American Catholics rejoice in our separation of church and state, and I can conceive of no combination of circumstances likely to arise which would make a union desirable to either church or state. . . . Other countries, other manners. . . . For ourselves we thank God we live in America. . . . The question arises, which is the best arrangement, the official union of church and state or the mutual independence of both? I have nothing to say in regard to other countries, but our own friendly relation of church and state without official union is best for us."[10]

Again, expediency may be conceived in political terms. Persecution is then regarded as indiscreet because it wrecks the state. Here is the program of the French *Politiques*. As a Catholic, Henry IV promulgated the Edict of Nantes and as a Catholic, Joseph II established the Decree of 1781. He was actuated by distress over the impoverishment and depopulation of the land through the expulsion of wealthy Protestants. As a corrective, toleration was granted openly to Lutherans and Calvinists and tacitly to Hussites, though not to Deists who presumably mattered less.[11]

Finally, expediency may be religious. From this point of view, persecution is ineffective because incapable of engendering that heartfelt adherence which alone the Church can regard as adequate. Such a feeling presumably lies behind the repeal in the latest edition of the canon law[12] of every penalty for heresy save excommunication. The preface of Cardinal Gasparri's edition declares that the sources of the present provisions will be found in the notes, but agreement between the text and authorities need not be expected. The discrepancy will be particularly marked in the section on penalties. Then one turns back to the penalties for heresy and discovers that all of the frightful stipulations by which the Inquisi-

[9] Cited from the speech of August 11, 1913 in John Augustine Ryan and Moorhouse F. X. Millar, *The State and the Church* (New York, 1922).

[10] Allen Sinclair Will, *Life of Cardinal Gibbons* (New York, 1922), collects these and other passages in I, chapter XVII.

[11] Hermann Meynert, *Kaiser Josef II* (Vienna, 1862).

[12] *Codex Iuris Canonici* (Rome, 1919), Praefatio xlii-xliii and Lib. V, Pars iii, Tit. xi.

tion was supported are relegated to the bottom of the page. Protestants expiate the intolerance of their forbears by expiatory monuments, Catholics by footnotes.

In saying, however, that Catholics can be tolerant only on grounds of expediency one must not forget that Catholicism has nurtured three movements which made for tolerance, especially when transferred to Protestant soil. Namely, mysticism, humanism and sectarianism. Mysticism contributes by diverting attention from dogma to experience and by equating the way to God with the way of suffering which comports more readily with martyrdom than with persecution. Humanism demands freedom for investigation in a limited area; and sectarianism, as in the case of the Spiritual Franciscans, places obedience to God, or to the founder of the order or to the Holy Spirit above obedience to the pope. Such movements, to be sure, were restricted or suppressed by Catholicism, but none the less served in a measure to check dogmatic intolerance within Catholicism and proved a powerful solvent when transmitted to the Reformation.

Protestantism has made for liberty in much more varied ways, because it has been able to attenuate all three reasons for persecution. Certitude with regard even to the most cardinal doctrines and with regard to the authority of the Church and the Bible has wavered in the face of attack on Protestant soil. And this despite the fact that Protestantism at first produced a more audacious theory of knowledge than that ever claimed by Catholics. Calvin, by basing religious certitude on Scripture confirmed by the testimony of the Holy Spirit, brought the assurance of the medieval Augustinians to its apex and went beyond them in equating faith with knowledge.[13] Against this citadel of certainty the attack was launched from the Protestant ranks, notably by Sebastian Castellio, who like Aquinas differentiated knowledge and faith, assigning to the latter a lower grade of certainty. His own theory of religious knowledge was derived from the Stoic epistemology of Cicero for whom knowledge is derived only from sense experience and rea-

---

[13] *Instit.* III, ii, 2-14, *Cal. op.* II, 399-410. Cf. Peter Brunner, *Vom Glauben bei Calvin* (Tübingen, 1925), and Karl Heim, *Das Gewissheitsproblem in der systematischen Theologie bis zu Schleiermacher* (Leipzig, 1911).

son.[14] To this the Christian added revelation as contained in the Bible, itself in turn subject to reason which practically takes the place of the *testimonium Spiritus Sancti,* and the "reason" in question is not that of a close-knit intellectual system after the manner of Aquinas but is rather akin to common sense. This sort of rationalism was to run through Locke and the Deists until shipwrecked on the skepticism of Hume, but in the meantime such tenets as the Trinity, the real presence, and Biblical miracles had been irreparably damaged.

The second prerequisite for persecution, that the point in question be regarded as important, was demolished in part by a shift of interest within the realm of religion itself and in part by a secularism which diverted attention from religion as a whole. We shall look at both approaches, though only the former is relevant to a discusion of Protestant attitudes.

Within the sphere of religion the importance of the dogmas supported by the sword of the magistrate was minimized in favor of the mystical and ethical elements. The one elevated inner experience, the other right conduct as more significant than correct opinions. In Protestantism the ethical attack was the more prevalent. The argument was that in the eyes of God deeds count for more than creeds and creeds themselves must be subject to ethical tests. Just as the medical theories are judged by the cures which they effect, so, too, must theological affirmations be evaluated in terms of the correction of sins. Creeds are even ethically conditioned, for correctness of opinion is valueless apart from sincerity of conviction. From this position the step was easy to the assertion that sincerity is to be esteemed even though the opinions held be incorrect. The reason why Castellio was so incensed over the execution of Servetus was that the victim, however mistaken, could not be accused of insincerity and died precisely because of a staunch avowal of those convictions by the denial of which he might have been saved. Here then we have an enunciation of the rights of error

[14] Castellio's *De Arte Dubitandi* was published by Elizabeth Feist (Hirsch) in *Per la Storia degli Eretici Italiani,* Reale Accademia d'Italia (Rome, 1937). Cicero's views are found in his reply to the Academics, *Lucullus* II, 7. Cf. Ludwig Stein, *Die Erkenntnislehre der Stoa* (Berlin, 1889) .

as a stage in the quest for truth. Error is not the goal, but honest error is nearer to the truth of religion than dishonest correctness.[15]

On this basis alone does conscience acquire any rights. The dominant reformers of the sixteenth century scoffed at any conscience save a right conscience. *Conscientia,* they claimed, means nothing apart from *Scientia; Gewissen* must be based on *Wissen.* Heretics have only a fictitious conscience. One recalls how Knox scoffed at Queen Mary's appeal to her conscience. The plea for conscience becomes relevant only when moral integrity is prized above dogmatic impeccability.[16]

Another way of minimizing the importance of the points over which persecution raged was to make a distinction between one dogma and another. In this way fundamentalism arose. It was an attempt to segregate the fundamentals from the non-essentials in the interests of liberty. This type of thought has a long history. The *Devotio Moderna* had deprecated theological speculation to the point that Wessel Gransfort declared no ampler theology necessary for salvation than that of the penitent thief who was admitted to Paradise on very minimal terms.[17] In the same vein Erasmus upbraided those who dissipated their energies on arid trivialities. The mediators between the Lutherans and Zwinglians relegated the sacramentarian controversy to the periphery.[18] Castellio consigned the Trinity and predestination to the non-essentials because the publicans were saved in ignorance of these tenets. This line of thought was definitely formulated by Acontius who reduced the creedal issues to those points distinctly stated in Scripture as both necessary and necessary to be known for salvation. The fundamentals then boiled down to two points: belief in Christ as the Son of God and in justification by faith alone. The first requirement would exclude the Sabellians, with whom perhaps some Antitrini-

---

[15] See my article on Castellio in the Burr *Festschrift* listed in the bibliography at the close of this article.

[16] This question is well handled by Johannes Kühn, *Toleranz und Offenbarung* (Leipzig, 1923), and again by Heinrich Hoffman, *Reformation und Gewissensfreiheit* (Giessen, 1932).

[17] E. W. Miller and J. W. Scudder, *Wessel Gansfort, American Society of Church History Papers* (2 vols., New York, 1917), II, 101-102.

[18] Walther Koehler, *Die Geistesahnen des Acontius,* Festschrift für Karl Müller (Tübingen, 1922).

tarians of the sixteenth century might have been identified; the second ruled out the Catholics. The only penalty was excommunication.[19]

An obscure Lutheran theologian, Petrus Meiderlinus, gave to the program of Acontius a formulation which became the classic slogan of English latitudinarianism. *In necessariis unitas, in non necessariis libertas, in omnibus caritas.*[20] Locke summed up a long tradition when he compared religious controversies to complaints that a pilgrim to the heavenly Jerusalem was not equipped with buskins, ate meat on the journey, avoided bypaths and the company of those who appeared to him unduly frivolous or austere, and attached himself to a guide clad or not clad in white and crowned with a mitre. These of course are non-essentials which "breed implacable enmities among Christian brethren who are all agreed in the substantial and truly fundamental part of religion."[21]

This approach, however, had its limitations and pitfalls. So long as there were any fundamentals someone might always be left out, and the penalty might well exceed excommunication. Or, if this possibility were excluded by reducing the fundamentals to practically nothing, what then became of Christianity as a religion? The Enlightenment left very little.

Furthermore, the distinction between the essentials and non-essentials readily became a boomerang. The established Church and the government could very well argue that the individual subject ought not to be a stickler for points which by common consent do not imperil salvation. In such matters let him relinquish his preferences in the interest of seemliness and public order. The argument was succinctly put by Agricola in defense of the Augsburg

[19] *Jacobii Acontii Satanae Stratagematum libri octo,* ed. Walther Koehler (Munich, 1927). On the essentials, 58 f; on the specific requirements, 186-187; on the exclusion of Sabellians, 69, 244-246; on Catholics, 109, 183, 185, 187, 188. There is now an English translation by Charles O'Malley, *Satan's Stratagems,* (2 vols., Sutro Branch, California State Library, San Francisco, English Series, May, 1940), V, 2.

[20] A. Eekhof, *De Zinspreuk In necessariis unitas . . .* (Leiden, 1931). Meiderlinus was known to Baxter under the pseudonym *Rupertus Meldenius.* Karl von Müller in his *Kirchengeschichte,* II², traced the thread of what he called the *Acontiusgeist* through Dutch and English thought in the seventeenth century. He well points out that Laud himself was in this tradition (p. 460).

[21] *Works,* III, 15 (London, n. d.).

Interim. "Inasmuch as the Interim, thank God, includes the main points of the Christian teaching and religion, the Elector of Brandenburg does not know what better advice he can give than that everyone is obligated to obey the emperor.... No one has reason to say that he is not at liberty to hold the true faith, since the essentials of the true religion are freely conceded. In ceremonies and outward practices every one is bound to obey the government.... This serves public order and does not infringe upon liberty. One is not saved if one does these things, nor damned if one does not. Therefore the regulation of such matters belongs to the government."[22]

Just the same type of reasoning was employed in defense of the Anglican settlement. Said Whitgift in his reply to Cartwright: "In things indifferent private men's wills are subject to such as have authority over them; and therefore they ought to consent to their determination in such matters, except they will show themselves wilful; which is a great fault and deserving to be punished."[23]

This was again the position of Laud. In matters of doctrine he was a latitudinarian, loath even to formulate the fundamentals, "for to whomsoever God hath given more, of him shall more be required." The only doctrinal requirement which he could discover in Scripture was belief that "God is and that he is a rewarder of them that seek Him" (Heb. 1:6). The line should not be drawn so narrowly as to shut even the meanest Christian out of heaven.[24] But that was no reason why he should not be shut out of the Church of England, if he would not do what he was commanded in matters not imperiling salvation. Because the Church may be wrong it does not follow that she is not to be obeyed.[25] Laud thus combined latitude in dogma with rigidity in discipline as to the adiaphora.

Jeremy Taylor had the same program and is not to be regarded as basically more tolerant than Laud because he was spared the onus of carrying it out. Said Taylor, "A man may be a good Christian though he believe an error not fundamental. Neverthe-

---

[22] See Sebastian Castellio, *Concerning Heretics*, transl. and edited by Roland H. Bainton, 64.

[23] *Works*, Parker Society (1852), II, 571.
[24] *Works*, II, 402-403.
[25] *Ibid.*, II, 286-287.

less his opinion may accidentally disturb the public peace. In that case he is to be dealt with."[26] The distinction between fundamentals and non-essentials having thus become a tool of repression, some of the champions of liberty in the seventeenth century pronounced the whole concept unworkable since the Protestant sects were divided as to the fundamentals and the magistrate was not in a position to decide.[27]

Thus far we have been moving in the religious sphere in considering the ways in which the importance was minimized of the grounds for persecution. At the same time non-religious factors were operative for Protestants and Catholics alike. The economic factor affected the reluctance already noticed of Venice to close her lagoons to the Lutheran heretics. The *Fondaco dei Tedeschi* was too profitable an institution to suppress. William of Orange protested that the banishment from Holland of a "vast body of Reformers, even if it be carried out without resorting to force, would strip the country of its best workers and chief traders—our country which is 'the market of Christendom.' "[28]

His advice in the end was taken and the example of Holland was not lost upon England. Roger Williams pointed out that there had descended upon Holland a "confluence of the persecuted" which drew "boats, drew trade, drew shipping, and that so mightily in so short a time that shipping, trading, wealth, greatness, and honor . . . have appeared to fall as out of heaven in a crown of garland upon the head of this poor fisher town."[29]

Another historical example was cited by Henry Robinson, namely the great economic gain to Turks and Barbary pirates in the expulsion of Moors and Jews from Spain and equal detriment to Christendom. "Oh let not the like befall England with her manufacturors."[30] Early in the reign of James, the Baptist Leonard

---

[26] *Liberty of Prophesying*, XVI, 4.

[27] John Owen, *Works* (London, 1851), VIII, 198 (Tract of 1649). Robert Greville asserted that nothing is indifferent. William Haller, *Tracts on Liberty* (New York, 1934), II, 57.

[28] Frederic Harrison, *William the Silent* (New York, 1924), 68-69.

[29] The bloody tenent yet more bloody, *Publ. Narragansett Club*, IV (1870), 9. Cf. Jordan, III, 503.

[30] "Liberty of Conscience," 1643, facsimile, Haller, *Tracts*, III, 123; reprint in *Temple of Religion and Tower of Peace* (Sutro Branch, Cal. State Library, July 1940), 89.

Busher reminded him of the "great benefit and commodity which
would redound to your majesty and to all your subjects . . . by the
great commerce, in trade and traffic, both of Jews and all people;
which now, for want of liberty of conscience, are forced and driven
elsewhere."[31] In our own land the last straw which broke the back
of the establishment in Massachusetts was the industrialization of
the state and the consequent need for cheap labor which at that
moment happened to be Irish Catholic.[32]

In this connection, too, may be mentioned economic imperialism. The Hohenzollerns facilitated annexations of territory by
demanding no religious changes on the part of newly acquired subjects. In England Harrington commended British imperialism as
a religious duty in order to provide a "sanctuary of the afflicted"
for "oppressed peoples." If the question is raised "whether it be
lawful for a commonwealth to aspire to the empire of the world, it
is to ask whether it be lawful for it to do its duty, or to put the
world into a better condition than it was before." Divine aid in
such an enterprise can be confidently assumed, "for if the cause of
mankind be the cause of God, the Lord of Hosts will be your Cap-
tain and you shall be a praise to the whole earth."[33]

Nationalism again eclipsed religion for those who came to
feel that the unity and security of the nation were of more importance than the victory of a single religion. To this party in France
was given the appropriate title of the *Politiques*. Their leader,
Michel de l'Hôpital, was grieved to see his beloved France ravaged
by Spanish and Italian mercenaries in the pay of the Catholics, or
English and German mercenaries in the pay of the Huguenots.
Better toleration than desolation.[34] Such considerations induced

[31] *Religion's Peace* (1614), reprinted from the edition of 1646 in *Tracts on Liberty of Conscience*, Hanserd Knollys Soc. (London, 1846), 62.

[32] Joseph Francis Thorning, *Religious Liberty in Transition* (Diss., Washington D. C., 1931), 83.

[33] *Oceana*, 199-200 in the 3rd ed., of John Toland (London, 1737), but 193-194 in the edition of S. B. Liljegren, "James Harrington's Oceana," *Skriften utgivna av Vetenskaps-Societeten i Lund* IV (1924).

[34] Henri Amphoux, *Michel de L'Hopital et la Liberté de Conscience au XVIe siècle* (Paris, 1900). Etienne Pasquier has commonly been regarded as a leader of the *Politiques* because of the attribution to him of the *Exhortation aux princes et seigneurs of* 1561. His authorship is contested by Albert Chamberland, "Etienne Pasquier et l'intolérance religieuse au XVIe siècle," *Revue d'his-*

Henry IV both to embrace Catholicism and at the same time to accord comparative liberty to the Huguenots. Queen Elizabeth in England had a similar outlook. In the American colonies one cannot exactly speak of nationalism as a factor, yet the desire for military security accelerated the toleration of dissident groups. In Virginia where the Anglican Church was established, Huguenots, Germans and Presbyterians were settled on the frontier "to awe the straggling parties of northern Indians, and be a good barrier for all that country."[35] The Baptists in Virginia first obtained toleration in the army, when the need for a united front against England in 1775 led to a concession to dissenting ministers to exhort and celebrate worship for "scrupulous consciences" among the recruits.[36]

At the same time internationalism deliberately diverted attention from religious controversies in order to secure a stable ground for the relations of the new national states. After the collapse of the universal Church and the universal empire, where could a solid basis for internationalism be discovered? The canon law would not do because it was rejected by Protestants. The Roman law would not do because it was not conceived in terms of international relations. The Bible would not do because both vague and controverted. The answer was discovered by Hugo Grotius in the theory of natural law, but a new kind of natural law it was, no longer identified with the law of God as formulated in the Pentateuch, but secularized and thereby rendered immune to religious division; grounded in experience and nature like Locke's theory of knowledge; valid even if there were no God; accessible to the understanding of the natural man. This type of natural law was not altogether new. Its origins lay in the Nominalism of the late Middle Ages which separated faith and reason and

toire moderne et contemporaine, I (1899), 38-49, where it is shown that in the genuine works Pasquier regarded two religions in the same place as a "meslange et pesle-mesle et desbauche." The suppression of the Huguenots was, however, limited for him by practical and legal considerations. Consult the more recent discussion by D. Thikett, "Bibliographie des oeuvres d'Estienne Pasquier," *Travaux d'Humanisme et Renaissance,* XXI (Geneva, 1956).

[35] Henry R. McIlwaine, *The Struggle of Protestant Dissenters for Religious Toleration in Virginia* (1894), 37.

[36] Charles F. James, *Documentary History of the Struggle for Religious Liberty in Virginia* (Lynchburg, 1900), 53.

put natural law on the side over against faith. The revival of this secularized version of the concept explains why the seventeenth and eighteenth centuries could use the law of nature as a ground for religious liberty, whereas the sixteenth century had employed what appeared to be the same language in favor of persecution. Melanchthon could say that the execution of heretics is grounded in natural law and by that he meant the code of Deuteronomy, whereas Grotius and Pufendorf could declare, on the contrary, that variety in religion is the law of nature, by which they meant the visible order of society which in their day had come to exhibit religious diversity. The main point, however, is that an interest in a stable international order had taken precedence over the dominance of any religious group.[37]

We return now to the Protestant treatment of the premises for persecution. The third is the belief that persecution is of some good. Here the Protestant was compelled to inquire, "Good for what?" The Catholic would have had an immediate answer, for the obvious purpose of persecution for him would be to save souls. But the Protestant, if he were a Lutheran or more particularly a Calvinist, as we have noted, could never say this, because according to the doctrine of predestination the salvation of souls is predetermined by God. The purpose of persecution is not to alter His decrees but to vindicate His honor. To this the liberals replied that for this purpose also persecution is ineffective since God is quite able to look out for Himself. Neither can His honor be vindicated by burning men, for He takes no delight in holocausts. Here of course the attack is being leveled at the whole picture of God involved in the theory of predestination. Over against the Calvinist deity is set the Erasmian, who is "slow to anger and plenteous in

[37] I have dealt briefly with this subject in "The Appeal to Reason and the Constitution" in *The Constitution Reconsidered,* ed. Conyers Read (New York, 1938). The basic discussions are those of Otto Gierke, *Johannes Althusius* (Breslau, 1880), and *Natural Law and the Theory of Society, 1500-1800,* tr. Ernest Barker (Cambridge, Eng., 1934). Cf. Hildegard Doer, *Thomasius Stellung zur landesherrlichen Kirchenregiment* (Bonn, 1917). The secularized natural law did not preclude the suppression of atheism as subversive of society. So Christoph. Matthaei Pfaffii ... *commentationes* ... *ad Verba Christi* ... *Compelle ad intrandum* ... *De Zizaniis* ... (Frankfurt, 1753). Cf. Francesco Ruffini, *La Libertà Religiosa* (Torin, 1901), 233-257.

mercy." Erasmus' tract on the "Immense Mercy of God" was very influential on this type of thought and inspired another treatise with a similar title by Curio on the "Amplitude of God's Mercy." From these writers the line runs through Castellio to the Arminians, Remonstrants and Universalists.[38]

The champions of liberty, while hammering at the notion that persecution either should or can glorify God, at the same time drew from the predestinarian arsenal in order to batter the Catholic position that persecution can be of any avail in saving souls. The doctrine of predestination at this point became a weapon of liberty on the ground that if man's salvation depends wholly on God then constraint is futile. Here we see why the theory of predestination cuts both ways. On the Godward side it means indifference to the fate of the damned, but on the manward side it means impotence to alter matters by coercion. The particular determinist slogan on which the liberals fastened was a phrase from the Apostle Paul which in the Vulgate reads: *Gratia enim estis salvati per fidem, et hoc non ex vobis: Dei enim donum est* (Eph. 2:8). Whence the formulation *fides donum Dei,* which naturally became a favorite text for all the predestinarians from Augustine to Calvin.[39] The first to use it in the interests of liberty, to my knowledge, was Luther in his tract "On Civil Government," where he asserted that "Faith is a free work to which no one can be forced. It is a divine work in the Spirit. Let alone then that outward force should compel or create it."[40] Thereafter the Protestant liberals, even though themselves inclined to free will and Universalism, appropriated the slogan for their cause. The Swiss used it.[41] The Bohemians used

---

[38] I have referred to the subject in my Castellio, *Concerning Heretics*. The thought of Curio is now well treated by Delio Cantimori, *Eretici Italiani del Cinquecento* (Florence, 1939). The treatise of Erasmus has been translated by Charles O'Malley and published by the Sutro Branch of the Cal. State Library (May, 1940).

[39] Augustine, *Enchiridion*, XXXI; Calvin, *Institutes*, III, ii, 33 = *Calvini opera*, II, 426 and Catechismus, *Calvini opera*, V, 334.

[40] *WA* XI, 264, 1523.

[41] Mandate of the Town Council of Basel, Feb. 29, 1528. "Diewil der gloub ein gab gottes... darumb es unbillich, das ein burger unnd nachpur vonn des glouben wegenn, der doch inn keins mennschen gwalt, den andern hassenn, sonnder vil mer ein anndernn duldenn..." Paul Roth, *Aktensammlung zur Geschichte der Basler Reformation* (Basel, 1937), III, 50.

it;[42] the Dutch used it;[43] and the Hungarians in the first official edict of toleration promulgated in 1568 decreed that no one should be imprisoned or discharged because of his belief, *denn der Glaube ist Gottesgeschenk.*[44]

Because, however, the liberals in general were not themselves predestinarian in their thought, they preferred to give the determinist argument a different slant and shifted it from the soul to the mind. There is a determinism of the intellect. No more can the mind assent to that to which it does not assent than can the eye see as red that which it sees as blue. Constraint will not mend matters. In some cases this determinism is absolute. A moron never can grasp an argument; but in other cases the point is simply that apperception is slow and impeded by many obstacles. To effect conversion we must then master the art of persuasion. The greatest hindrances to clear sight are passion, pride and prejudice, and these are only accentuated by vainglory and arrogance on the part of the one who is seeking to persuade. Humility and obvious devotion above everything else to the truth are the prime requisites for winning converts. No one better enunciated this point of view than Acontius. Beneath the argument of course lies a confidence in the ability of truth to command assent in the long run. Lessing thus justified his publication of the Reimarus fragments on the ground that he had greater confidence in Christianity than his opponents because he was persuaded of its capacity to stand up under any attack.[45]

Thus far we have been considering the problem of liberty in religion from the point of view of ideas. We have observed that the Catholic and Protestant theories of persecution do not seriously differ but that the theory of liberty is capable of much greater flex-

---

[42] Professor Odložilik calls my attention to a letter of Jan of Pernstein to Ferdinand, Dec. 2, 1539, in which protest is made against religious persecution. *Fides autem, rex clementissime, donum est Dei, et cui a Deo non datur, ab hominibus minime potest dari. Archiv Český,* XX (1902), 86.

[43] *Want het geloof is'n gave Gods.* A. A. Van Schelven, "De Opkomst van de Idee der Politieke Tolerantie in de 16e eeuwsche Nederlanden," *Tijdschrift voor Geschiedenis,* XLVI (1931), 344.

[44] Frederich Teutsch, *Geshichte der evangelischen Kirchen in Sieben-bürgen* (2 vols., Hermannstadt, 1921-22), I, 284.

[45] *Sämtliche Schriften,* XIII (Leipzig, 1897), 142.

ibility in Protestantism. Now the problem must be considered from the institutional point of view both as to the theory of the Church and as to the theory and administration of the state.

Christian history exhibits two main theories of the Church. They are sometimes distinguished by calling the one the Church type and the other the sect. In England the terminology has been more frequent of the "parish" versus the "gathered" Church. They differ markedly in their attitude to religious liberty. The Church type is based on a sacramental theory of salvation in which force is more appropriate because the sacrament can be regarded as a "medicine of immortality" which will benefit the recipient whether he likes it or not. The sacrament of baptism is administered to babies. In a Christian land the Church is then considered to include all those born and baptized into the community. Alliance with the state becomes more natural because both Church and state comprise the same persons. Salvation outside the Church is impossible because the Church, even the visible Church, is like the ark of Noah outside of which no souls were saved. To be in the ark one must receive the sacraments, subscribe to the doctrines and obey the officers. Achievement of the moral demands is not so imperative because the unclean beasts were allowed in the ark. They are the tares to be left until the harvest. The heretics are not the tares. To them applies the text, *Compelle intrare,* for they are comparable to Noah's wife in the mystery plays, who, incredulous of the flood, refused to board the ship until picked up bodily and shoved up the gangplank by her sturdy sons, whose place in the Christian commonwealth is taken by the secular arm. This theory of the Church fits in with the ideal of comprehension and latitudinarianism. The way to heaven is not to be made narrower than necessary and as many as possible are to be induced to walk therein.

The sectarian theory of the Church looks upon the institution less as an ark of salvation than as a city set upon a hill to save itself and the world by an example of righteousness. The emphasis is ethical rather than sacramental. The tares are the heretics who must be left outside and not compelled to come in lest they sully the purity of the community. The moral offenders are not the tares and may be rooted out by excommunication. Babies are not to be baptized and Church membership depends on mature conversion. This the state cannot effect by the sword of the magistrate. All constraint in religion is renounced and commonly any alliance with the state is repudiated, since the state is instituted by God because of sinners and is to be administered only by sinners. This view of the Church makes it exclusive. The ideal of comprehension is rejected and liberty is demanded to form small purist groups. The slogan of this party is:

> We are the choice elected few:
> Let all the rest be damned:
> There's room enough in hell for you.
> We won't have heaven crammed.[46]

An attempt at the combination of these two types was made by Calvin, who tried to achieve a Church coterminous with the community and at the same time comprising none but the saints. This could be done only by excluding the unworthy both from the Church and from the community. Excommunication and banishment thus tended to coincide. In Geneva this was easy because it was a select community due both to expulsions and to a numerous increment of refugees. In England, Scotland and New England, where the population was larger and less select, the problem was not so simple. In England a theocratic minority attempted to impose its will upon the land. In Scotland the inner cleavage manifested itself in the use of the token to distinguish those who were worthy to receive the sacrament from those who were broadly included in the national establishment. In New England the small frontier communities endeavored to recover the pattern of Geneva, in part by excommunication and banishment, but more largely by a restriction of the franchise. Only Church members could vote. Church and state thus became one, but not the Church and the community. In the New Haven Colony in 1649 the estimate is that out of 144 planters only 16 were free burgesses.[47] The Half Way Covenant was a move in the direction of the parish theory of the

---

[46] Michael Freund, *Die Idee der Toleranz*, 119. On the whole subject compare my article, "Religious Liberty and the Parable of the Tares," in Series I of this work, pp. 95-121.

[47] Louise M. Greene, *The Development of Religious Liberty in Connecticut* (Boston, 1905), 62.

Church, in that the children of non-Church members of respectable conduct and opinions were received to baptism. Stoddardism made a further step in the same direction by extending the Lord's Supper to the less worthy in the hope of their conversion. The Great Awakening sought to redress the balance and to give reality to the theory of a comprehensive community of the saints by converting everybody. The result was rather to divide the churches into New Lights and Old. This situation, together with growing secularism, eventuated in the separation of church and state.[48]

With regard to the form of the state, whether one is more congenial to liberty than another, is difficult to say. Protestantism and Catholicism alike have made every manner of political alliance depending on which government at the moment would grant the maximum of recognition. Catholicism has been Carlist in Spain, legitimist in France, particularist in Italy, and democratic only in the United States.[49] Protestantism in the sixteenth century allied itself with the German princes and cities against the Empire, in France and Poland with the feudal nobles against the crown, in Switzerland with the popular fronts in the cantons, in England with the Tudor monarchy, in Hungary and Transylvania with the Turk rather than the Hapsburg. In the light of the outcome all one can say is that it does not pay to be on the losing side. The alliance with feudalism in Poland and France ended in disaster. The alignment with English monarchical nationalism proved successful.

As to the forms themselves, democracy is not, as we sometimes assume, of itself any guarantee of liberty. In Cromwell's days toleration could be achieved only by dictatorship. Cromwell could accord liberty to the Anglican Church, as he was disposed to do, only by flouting Parliament, which he was not disposed to do.[50] On the other hand, religious restrictions were progressively removed under enlightened despots like Frederick the Great. The democratic form of the state means most for religious liberty in those cases where the Church seeks to influence political issues. Such activity will be tolerated only by a state which grants a simi-

[48] I have discussed these theories of the church in "Congregationalism—the Middle Way," *Christendom* (Summer number, 1940).

[49] Albert Houtin, *L'Americanisme* (Paris, 1904).

[50] W. K. Jordan, *Religious Toleration*, III, 251.

lar liberty to various groups within its structure, like trade unions. The totalitarian state will concede freedom to those churches alone which confine themselves strictly to divine worship. Hence we may say that although the democratic state need not be tolerantly disposed, nevertheless in no other state is there so wide a scope for the activity and influence of the churches.

As an administrative problem, the policy to be adopted by the state to dissident groups is conditioned only in part by its own constitution. Much more depends on the number and the temper of the groups themselves. Only if they are willing to live and to let live can the state drop the matter. If they are not so disposed, some measure of control becomes inevitable. Three solutions have been tried: territorialism, comprehension and complete religious liberty. The formula of the first is *cuius regio eius religio*. The slogan of the second is *in necessariis unitas, in non necessariis libertas,* and the caption for the third is *pax dissidentium*. The first two methods were tried when the sects were intolerant of each other. The third became possible only as their temper changed.

Territorialism was rooted in the view which went back to antiquity that the state must be supported by a religion and that a single established religion is the best guarantee of the security and unity of the people. Such a motive led to the adoption of Christianity as the most favored religion of the Roman Empire. The division of Christendom occasioned by the Reformation was far from shattering the ideal. Since it could no longer be realized on a universal scale, the attempt was made to conserve it in many miniatures. The welfare of the state was still the determinative factor and the prince was permitted to decide which religion should prevail in his domains. No other religion should be tolerated. Dissenters could be banished. The system of the union of Church and state, of the fusion of religion and the community, was thus conserved by an exchange of populations, and that was the point at which the system of *cuius regio* enshrined liberty of a sort. Extermination was displaced by emigration.

This solution was adopted in Europe at the Peace of Augsburg of 1555 which recognized, however, only the Catholic and Lutheran churches. The Peace of Westphalia of 1648 was conceived after the same pattern but added the Reformed. And the American

Constitution of 1787 was still cast in the same mould. Though no religion was to be established by the federal government, the states were free to retain or introduce any or none. The colonies had naturally grown up on the principle of territorialism. The Congregationalists gravitated to Massachusetts and Connecticut, the Baptists to Rhode Island, the Presbyterians to New York and New Jersey. The Catholics went to Maryland, the Quakers and Pietist sects colonized Pennsylvania, and the Anglicans predominated in the South. Established churches prevailed everywhere save in Rhode Island and Pennsylvania, which latter presented the anomaly of religious disabilities without an establishment. The federal Constitution interfered with none of this. Certain prerogatives of the Episcopalians in Virginia lasted until 1802.[51] The establishment of Congregationalism continued in Connecticut until 1818 and in Massachusetts until 1833. In New Hampshire civil disabilities against Jews and Catholics prevail to this day.[52]

As a matter of fact territorialism was nowhere so compatible with liberty as in the American colonies because the *ius emigrandi* was not too difficult of realization so long as the frontier remained open. When Hugh Peters, on his return to the old country, declared that the New England way of handling dissenters was to put them over the river,[53] he scarcely regarded such treatment as illiberal, for the land on the heterodox side of the stream was no worse than that on the orthodox bank. If Rogers Williams was unacceptable in Massachusetts, after all, there was Rhode Island to which he could go.

Unhappily, a practice once not incompatible with liberty has since passed into political theory and has become a pretext for stifling criticism of American institutions. The theorists of the social contract availed themselves of the *ius emigrandi* to bridge a serious gap in their scheme. For why should those merely born into

---

[51] James, *Documentary History*, 142.

[52] Joseph Francis Thorning, *Religious Liberty in Transition* (Diss., Washington D. C., 1931). Stephen M. Wheeler, Acting Attorney General, State of New Hampshire (Nov. 29, 1943) writes that the decision in the case of Hale *vs.* Everett construes the law as directive rather than prohibitive of the employment of Catholic schoolteachers. Hale *vs.* Everett 53 N.H.I.

[53] William Haller, "The Puritan Background of the First Amendment," in *The Constitution Reconsidered*, ed. Conyers Read (New York, 1938), 134.

a community be bound to a compact contracted by their remote ancestors? This is the political counterpart of the ecclesiastical problem of why those baptized as babies should be held accountable for the Apostles Creed. The answer was that non-removal from the community implies tacit consent. Those who do not subscribe may leave.[54] This theory has been carried over from the frontier churches and colonies and applied to the United States, and now political criticism is silenced by the retort, "If you don't like it you may leave."

If today such advice is thoroughly unrealistic in a world without a frontier, at no time was the formula genuinely satisfactory. To pull up with goods and kin was never easy, and for that reason governments had recourse to another expedient for solving the problem through a system of comprehension, which sought to satisfy as many as possible in the community by latitude as to their most cherished tenets. These being conceded, they were then asked to subscribe in other matters to a scheme of uniformity. The recusants on the fringes to the right and the left were subject to one penalty or another. The Augsburg Interim which Charles V endeavored to impose on Germany was cast in this mould and only after it failed did he have recourse to the territorialism of the Peace of Augsburg. The failure of this method in Germany is explicable in terms of the deep religious conviction of the Lutheran populace and the resentment aroused by the enforcement of the Interim at the hands of the Spanish troops.

The English settlement was built on the same theory and succeeded. The reasons for the failure of comprehension in Germany and the success in England are a matter of speculation, but some differences are obvious. Charles V tried to reconcile the Catholics and Protestants. Elizabeth attempted comprehension only within the Protestant frame. Charles was half Spanish. Elizabeth was English and Tudor. And the date was later. England was already wearied by change and persecution from Henry through Edward and Mary. The disastrous effects of the religious wars on the Continent had given dramatic reenforcement to the theories of the *Politiques*. Besides, Erastianism from the outset had been deeply

[54] For the employment of this expedient in political thought see J. W. Gough, *The Social Contract* (Oxford, 1936), 90 and 130.

rooted in England. This, by the way, was not the doctrine that the state might introduce any religion it chose, but that in a Christian community the king held the two keys rather than the pope. Here we have the culmination of medieval imperialistic thought transferred to the head of one of the new national states.[55] Perhaps deeper than any other reason is the closer continuity of the Reformation with the Renaissance in England than in other lands. The comprehensive philosophy of the Florentine Academy with its candles for Plato as well as for Christ suggested chapels for diverse cults beneath the one dome of the universal temple. The incursion of the Arminians further reinforced universalist tendencies. The system of comprehension, however, succeeded only relatively in England, since the champions of the narrow way refused either to comprehend or to be comprehended and were able in time to win for themselves an unmolested place outside of the establishment.

The same thing happened in the American colonies, for if our federal Constitution is an instance of territorialism, the individual colonies, whatever the religion established, displayed the same basic pattern as that of England. The rigidity of the first settlements soon moved in the direction of comprehension. Witness the Half-Way Covenant and Stoddardism, which we have already instanced as tending to the parish system. At the same time the dissenters on the fringe gained an increasing footing: Baptists, Quakers and Presbyterians in Virginia; Episcopalians, Baptists and Quakers in Connecticut; and these, plus Unitarians, in Massachusetts. The process was arrested at this stage in England, but in America passed on to the third solution of the problem, that of a complete religious liberty in which the dissidents agree to differ.

The *pax dissidentium* had its first exemplification, I believe, in Poland, where this very title was applied to the settlement of 1573, where those who frankly differed in religion covenanted to preserve the peace among themselves, to shed no blood, impose no penalties and confiscate no goods because of diversity in faith and practice.[56] This peace, however, was made only between Protestant groups and was soon upset by the Counter Reformation.

[55] Edward Allen Whitney, "Erastianism and Divine Right," *Huntington Library Quarterly*, II, 4 (1939), 373-398.
[56] Ruffini, *La Libertà religiosa*, 461. Dr. Halecki informs me that an ex-

The next great attempt at this type of settlement was made by Oliver Cromwell who abandoned the concept of the Christian commonwealth, with a single form of religion established by the state, in favor of a limited state exercising a benevolent patronage to a group of churches on equal footing.[57] The intolerance of the sects themselves wrecked his plan, and the establishment in England remains to this day, though combined with a system of complete toleration. The separation of Church and state was a phenomenon in many lands of the nineteenth and twentieth centuries with varying degrees of friendliness or hostility in the process.[58]

The historical steps by which this culmination has been reached may now be briefly reviewed. Obviously the process has been slow. Very roughly I would say that the sixteenth century was characterized by the death penalty, the seventeenth by banishment, the eighteenth and early nineteenth by civil disabilities, and the last century by complete emancipation. There are, of course, exceptions and the pattern is truer for England than for other countries. Two developments in that country during the course of the seventeenth century are worthy of special note. The first in the field of law was the defeat of the death penalty even for blasphemy in the case of the Quaker, James Naylor. He had been guilty of messianic pretensions and was therefore not a heretic but by common consent a blasphemer. Luther's formula that not heresy but blasphemy should be punished would have sent him to the block. But he did not go. That point was settled.

The other notable change was in the area of Church theory and is marked by the abandonment on the part of the sectaries of the ideal of a united Christendom. The Protestants of the sixteenth century had lamented the rending of the seamless robe of Christ

---

tensive discussion has taken place among Polish scholars in recent years as to whether the *pax dissidentium* completely excluded the territorial principle. The nobles were free, but was the same liberty extended to the peasants on their estates?

[57] Ernest Barker, *Oliver Cromwell and the English People* (Cambridge, 1937).

[58] The documents on the separation of church and state are assembled and reprinted by Zaccaria Giacometti, *Quellen zur Geschichte der Trennung von Staat und Kirche* (Tübingen, 1926).

and did their best to mend the rents among themselves.[59] But the sectaries of the seventeenth century definitely abandoned the ideal of unity and regarded diversity and competition as wholesome and stimulating,[60] after the analogy of *laissez faire* in trade. The Baptist, Samuel Richardson, in 1647 asked the rhetorical question: "whether it be not better for us that a patent were granted to monopolize all the corn and cloth, and to have it measured out unto us at their price and pleasure, which yet were intolerable, as for some men to appoint and measure out unto us, what and how much we shall believe and practice in matters of religion?"[61] Similarly Henry Robinson argued: "In civil affairs we see by experience that every man most commonly understands best his own business, and such as do not, but rely upon the managing and foresight of others . . . in a few years run out at heels, to the utter undoing of themselves and whole families; besides we think it a most gross solecism, and extravagant course in any State which did make Laws and Statutes, that the Subject might not go about and dispatch his wordly business, save in one general prescript form and manner, as a thing most irrational and inequitable . . . Besides, as our Saviour in the Parable . . . said, Is it not lawful for me to do what I will with mine own? So we know that every man is desirous to do with his own as he thinks good himself . . . but in spiritual matters it holdeth much stronger."[62]

Such passages ring the knell of *Corpus Christianum*. The analogy with trade, however, may explain why civil disabilities could survive even after liberty of worship had been achieved. For though competition of religions might be stimulating to religion, dissension might nevertheless be detrimental to trade. Therefore, let all religions worship, but permit only one to govern.

This brief survey reminds us how slow has been the gain and how insecure, but definite gain at certain points and in certain lands is at any rate observable, enough at least to inspire valor.

Now we come to the residual and perennial problems. The

[59] John T. McNeill, *Unitive Protestantism* (New York, 1930).

[60] Jordan, *Religious Toleration*, III, 366 and 373.

[61] *Tracts on Liberty of Conscience*, Hanserd Knollys Society (London, 1846), 258.

[62] William Haller, *Tracts on Liberty*, III, 153-156.

whole question of tolerance is reopened with tragic insistence in our own day by the emergence of opinions which do damn souls and the more sincerely they are held the more dangerous do they become. They cannot be met by round-table discussions, since one side will not discuss. They cannot be overcome by any halfhearted and mildly sceptical attitude toward truth, nor will an appeal to ethics apart from theology offer stable ground. The ethics of love, mercy, and humanity are spurned and unless they can be shown to be grounded in the very structure of life, unless there be after all a natural law which is a divine law, then morality too goes by the board. Fanaticism can be overcome only through deep conviction. Whether there must also be a clash of body against body is a problem which must deeply agitate all those who have been nurtured in the liberal and pacifist tradition.

Again, in relation to the state, the problem of conscience has become acute. The rights of conscience have gained recognition on non-political questions, but can conscience claim immunity at the hands of the state if conscience imperils the security of the state? The problem was raised in the sixteenth century by Theodore Beza, who inquired whether the government could tolerate a conscientious objector to military service or a conscientious tyrannicide.[63] The view that even an erroneous conscience must be followed is double-edged, for it applies not only to the subject but also to the magistrate. If conscience must always be obeyed, the only possible outcome is a clash in which the magistrate suppresses and the objector suffers. Pierre Bayle, to my knowledge, was the first to formulate this political theory of inescapable conflict. The conscientious tyrannicide, he asserted, is bound to try to kill the ruler whom he esteems a tyrant and the conscientious magistrate is bound to do his best to stop him.[64]

The manner, however, in which such clashes are conducted must be influenced by the recognition that that which justifies each in his intransigeance is a common loyalty to truth. Neither contestant can yield that which he now sees to be true until he is brought to see otherwise. Yet since truth is one, both sides in a controversy

[63] See Sebastian Castellio, *Concerning Heretics,* transl. and edited by Roland H. Bainton, p. 107.

[64] *Oeuvres diverses de Mr. Pierre Bayle* (Hague, 1727), II, 432-433.

cannot be equally right and each should recognize that he may be mistaken and should concede to the other the duty of following his own lights. Conscience then has only a relative *ius divinum*. It is not an absolute guide to truth, but only an arbiter of action in that we can arrive at no ultimate truth save by loyalty to our present convictions. The recognition that each side in a controversy is equally bound by the claims of conscience will serve not to end conflict but to inspire respect. Let the objector, then, not rail against the magistrate, nor the magistrate revile the objector. Samuel Johnson remarked, "The only method by which religious truth can be established is by martyrdom. The magistrate has a right to enforce what he thinks; and he who is conscious of the truth has a right to suffer. I am afraid there is no other way of ascertaining the truth but by persecution on the one hand and enduring it on the other."[65] This, however, is true only in a crisis and even in a crisis the asperity of the clash will be mitigated if the constrainer and constrained are bound by the common constraint of the quest for truth.

[65] *Boswell's Life of Johnson* (Oxford ed., London, 1904), I, 511 under 1773.

Selected Bibliography

General:

BATES, M. SEARLE, *Religious Liberty an Inquiry* (New York, 1945), the widest treatment in scope.

CARILLO DE ALBORNOZ, A. F., *Roman Catholicism and Religious Liberty* (World Council of Churches, Geneva, 1959), illuminating as to contemporary opinion.

KÜHN, JOHANNES, *Toleranz und Offenbarung* (Leipzig, 1923), a penetrating analysis of the ideas of Protestant groups.

LECLERC, JOSEPH, *Histoire de la Tolérance au Siècle de la Réforme* (2 vols., Paris, 1955), the best summation of the sixteenth and seventeenth centuries.

RUFFINI, FRANCESCO, *La Libertà religiosa* (Turin, 1901), English *Religious Liberty* (London, 1912), a survey stressing the contribution of Italian rationalism.

The following studies are less comprehensive:

BAINTON, ROLAND H., Castellio's *Concerning Heretics* (New York, 1935). The introduction deals briefly with the early Church and with a number of Reformation figures.

—"Academic Freedom in the light of the Struggle for Religious Liberty," *Proceedings of the Middle States Association of History Teachers*, XXXIII (1935), 37-44. A very brief sketch, largely incorporated in the present article.

BORNKAMM, HIENRICH, article "Toleranz" in *Die Religion in Geschichte und Gegenwart*, 3rd ed.

BURR, GEORGE LINCOLN, *Persecution and Liberty, Essays in Honor of* (New York, 1931), contains essays by Ernest W. Nelson on "The Theory of Persecution," Austin P. Evans, "Some Aspects of Medieval Heresy," Wallace K. Ferguson, "The Attitude of Erasmus toward Toleration," and by myself on "Sebastian Castellio and the Toleration Controversy of the Sixteenth Century."

—"Anent the Middle Ages," *American Historical Review*, XVIII (1913), 710-726.

—"Liberals and Liberty Four Hundred Years Ago," *Proceedings of the Unitarian Historical Society*, II (1933), Part 2.

GARRISON, WINFRED ERNEST, *Intolerance* (New York, 1934).

MATAGRIN, AMEDEE, *Histoire de la Tolérance Religieuse* (Paris, 1905).

SCHAFF, PHILIP, "Progress of Toleration as shown in the history of Toleration Acts," *Papers, Am. Soc. Church History*, I (1889).

Germany and Switzerland in the Age of the Reformation:

HERMELINK, HEINRICH, "Der Toleranzgedanke im Reformationszeitalter," *SVRG*, XCVIII (Leipzig, 1908).

KOEHLER, WALTHER, *Reformation und Ketzerprozess* (Tübingen, 1901).

MURRAY, ROBERT HENRY, *Erasmus and Luther: Their Attitude to Toleration* (London and New York, 1920).

PAULUS, NIKOLAUS, *Protestantismus und Toleranz im 16. Jahrhundert.* (Freiburg i. Br., 1911), Catholic, very thorough as to facts.

VÖLKER, KARL, *Toleranz und Intoleranz im Zeitalter der Reformation* (Leipzig, 1912).

For the literature dealing more specifically with Luther see the article on Luther's attitude on religious liberty in this volume.

Spain and Portugal in the Sixteenth Century:

LEA, HENRY C., *History of the Inquisition in Spain* (New York, 1922), III, 411-479, gives a brief summary of the treatment of Protestantism in Spain. He drew heavily and avowedly on

MENENDEZ Y PELAYO, "Historia de los heterodoxos españoles," 2d ed. in the *Obras completas* (Madrid, 1911-33).

BELL, AUBREY F. G., "Liberty in Sixteenth Century Spain," *Bulletin of Spanish Studies*, X, 37 (1933), 164-79 gives a brief summary.

BATAILLON, MARCEL, *Erasme et L'Espagne* (Paris, 1937), is splendid for the treatment of the Alumbrados and Erasmians.

SCHAEFER, ERNEST, *Beiträge zur Geschichte des spanischen Protestantismus und der Inquisition im 16. Jahrhundert* (3 vols., Gütersloh, 1902), covers the trials of Protestants before the Inquisition.

AITKEN, JAMES M., *The Trial of George Buchanan before the Lisbon Inquisition* (Edinburgh, 1939), gives the documents and a good discussion.

Italy:

AMABILE, LUIGI, *Il Santo Officio della Inquisizione in Napoli* (2 vols., Città di Castello, 1892).

BUSCHBELL, GOTTFRIED, "Reformation und Inquisition in Italien um die Mitte des XVI Jahrhunderts," *Quellen und Schriften ... Görresgesellschaft,* XIII (1910).

France:
Sixteenth Century:
MÜNZER, GEORG FLORIAN, *Franz I und die Anfänge der französischen Reformation* (Diss., Freiburg i. Br., 1935).
WEISS, NATHANAEL, *La Chambre Ardente* (Paris, 1889).
Later Periods:
BONET-MAURY, GASTON, *Die Gewissensfreiheit in Frankreich vom Edikt von Nantes bis zur Gegenwart* (Leipzig, 1912).
PUAUX, FRANK, *Les Précurseurs français de la Tolérance au XVIIe siècle* (Paris, 1881).

Holland:
VAN SCHELVEN, A. A., "De Opkomst van de Idee der Politieke Tolerantie in de 16e eeuwsche Nederlanden," *Tijdschrift voor Geschiedenis,* XLVI (1931), 235-47, 337-388.

England:
BANNER, HYPATIA BRADLAUGH, *Penalties upon Opinion* (London, 1934), deals with the quite recent period.
FREUND, MICHAEL, "Die Idee der Toleranz im England der Grossen Revolution," in *Deutsche Vierteljahrsschrift für Literaturwissenschaft und Geistesgeschichte,* XII (Halle, 1927), gives a very illuminating discussion of the religious ideas.
JORDAN, WILBUR KITCHENER, *The Development of Religious Toleration in England* (4 vols., Cambridge, Mass., 1932-1940). Unsurpassed for a thorough survey of the literature, but better for the discussion of political than religious ideas.
LYON, THOMAS, *The Theory of Religious Liberty in England, 1603-39* (Cambridge, Eng., 1937); useful as revealing some pattern in the welter.
MEYER, ARNOLD OSKAR, "Der Toleranzgedanke in England der Stuarts." *Historische Zeitschrift,* CVIII (1912), 255-94; protests against laying the stress on secular factors.
MULLET, CHARLES F., "Some Essays on Toleration in Late Eighteenth Century England," *Church History,* VII (1933), 24-44 reveals that when persecution had narrowed down to civil disabilities the arguments against it were no different from those of the sixteenth century.
ST. JOHN, WALLACE, *The Contest for Liberty of Conscience in England* (Chicago, 1900).
SCOTT, NANCY ELNORA, *The Limits of Toleration within the Church of England from 1632-1642* (Thesis, Univ. of Pa., 1912).
SEATON, A. A., "The Theory of Toleration under the Later Stuarts," in *Cambridge Historical Essays,* XIX (Cambridge, 1911).

The United States:
COBB, SANFORD H., *The Rise of Religious Liberty in America* (New York, 1902).
THORNING, JOSEPH FRANCIS, *Religious Liberty in Transition* (Diss., Washington, D. C., 1931).

Connecticut:

COONS, PAUL WAKEMAN, *The Achievement of Religious Liberty in Connecticut* (New Haven, 1936).

GREENE, LOUISE M., *The Development of Religious Liberty in Connecticut* (Boston, 1905).

PURCELL, RICHARD J., *Connecticut in Transition 1775-1818* (Washington, D. C., 1918).

Virginia:

JAMES, CHARLES F., *Documentary History of the Struggle for Religious Liberty in Virginia* (Lynchburg, 1900).

MCILWAINE, HENRY R., *The Struggle of Protestant Dissenters for Religious Toleration in Virginia*. Johns Hopkins Studies, XII (1894).

17. St. Ignatius Loyola's Methods of Religious Teaching

The greatest educational work of Ignatius Loyola was the *Spiritual Exercises,* if education be taken to mean the formation of the whole man. The *Exercises* developed out of his own process of spiritual maturity which needs first to be sketched. This father of the Jesuit order began his career as a knight in the service of the Queen of Spain. The fortress which he defended was besieged by the French. Ignatius persuaded the older officers to refuse to surrender and himself led the defense until his leg was shattered by a cannon ball, the bravado of chivalry rendered ridiculous by the impersonal machine of modern warfare. Loyola, to regain his shapely limb, had the bone rebroken, sawn and stretched. During the long convalescence he called for romances, but was given the lives of the saints and of Christ, by which his thoughts were turned from the Queen of Spain to the Queen of Heaven, from the garrison of Pamplona to the militia of Jesus.

The first undertaking of the new life was penance, from which he learned to discountenance extreme asceticism. Mortification of the flesh is but a means. Here is the distinction between means and ends, which no one previously had drawn so sharply, and which was to serve as the basis of the teaching later attributed to his order that the end justifies the means. Next came a pilgrimage to the Holy Land. Here Ignatius visited the Mount of Olives and saw in the stone from which the Savior ascended to heaven the very imprint of his feet. On leaving the garden Ignatius could not remember which way the imprints pointed, and bribed the Turkish guard for another look. Here we discover that pictorial sense which plays so large a part in the *Spiritual Exercises.* Loyola returned to

First published in the *International Journal of Religious Education,* December 1932.

Spain and started his education from the bottom. During the course he gave himself to the cure of souls for abandoned women and hilarious students. The reform of the Catholic Church came not from popes and committees, but from the saints who commenced with individuals. At the University of Paris Ignatius would play billiards on condition that if his opponent lost he should take the *Spiritual Exercises*. Of these we shall speak in a moment. By relentless luring Loyola won a student band which was to become the militia of Jesus, the Jesuits.

The order grew. Loyola was made general. Then he became too busy for that personal attention which had characterized the beginnings. A recent biographer[1] suggests that this may explain the difficulty in recovering his likeness. The saint had refused to have his portrait painted. As soon as he lay in death the disciples called in a great painter to recapture the man in the few hours of light before the burial. The features were reproduced, but the saint proved illusive. An attempt from the death mask was equally unsuccessful. Then it came to light that some years previously a smuggled artist had worked from the saint in sleep and had failed. Was it because the true Ignatius had disappeared sometime before, lost in a mass of decisions and correspondence?

Whether or no, the *Spiritual Exercises* continued to fashion men according to his hope. This is one of the great books of devotional literature. Or should it be called a book? It is a manual, a soldier's manual, bare and austere, uninspiring of tears, laughter and reasoned reflection like the *Confessions of St. Augustine*. The effect was produced not by the reading of the book but by the practice of the drill.

The success depends in part upon flexibility, in part upon rigidity. The *Spiritual Exercises* call for a contemplation of the entire drama of redemption in the course of four weeks. Five meditations, each of an hour, are allotted to each day. But there is great elasticity. The director—the *Exercises* are not to be taken alone— may shorten or lengthen the time and in other ways temper the cure to the malady. This is probably why such liberties have been taken with the *Exercises* in modern editions that it is difficult to

---

[1] René Fülöp-Miller, *The Power and Secret of the Jesuits* (1930).

obtain them in their original form. This freedom, too, has permitted the introduction of banalities which the saint rigorously excluded. I have, for example, an edition in which there is a meditation on the state of man after death when the worms are crawling through the sockets of the eyes, and so on, long beyond *ad nauseam*.

But with flexibility is combined rigidity. The time may vary and to some extent the content, but not the logical sequence. Sin, death, hell, the life and passion of Christ must all precede his glorification and man's redemption. The terror of the impressions is not to be lightened by any anticipations of the release to come. In fact during one week the candidate is not to know what is in store for the next. There is nothing of our cafeteria education. And we may observe that the *Exercises* were effective. Men love authority, as do children who grow utterly weary of having always to choose the hymn and the number of verses and of deciding every time whether to stand up or sit down to sing. What a relief to have some one settle all that and let them sing! But, we are told, they must learn to make decisions whether they like it or not. O! As Lord Northcliffe said, "America is the land of the free and the home of the brave where each man does as he likes and if he doesn't, you make him."

The *Spiritual Exercises* depend for their success in large measure upon ability to stimulate the imagination. Not for nothing had St. Ignatius gone back to fix in his mind the direction of the imprint of the Savior's feet. In just such concrete and vivid detail he would now lead the candidate to relive the drama of redemption. Every scene should be reconstructed with the aid of all the five senses, "to taste and smell the infinite fragrance and sweetness of the Godhead" (second week, fifth contemplation). As an aid to the memory of our sins we are to recall ourselves in the midst of our associates. In this total setting shame will overtake us for faults which otherwise might have eluded remembrance. After the contemplation of sin comes that of hell with the "smell of smoke, brimstone, refuse, and rottenness." St. Ignatius is very restrained here, however, in comparion with contemporary literature.

Next comes a survey of the life of Christ. The candidate is to imagine himself as actually present at all the scenes, listening to the conversations. "The exercitant must taste the loaves and fishes with which Jesus feeds the multitude; he must smell the Magdalene's ointment, and with her must anoint the Savior's feet, wipe them, and kiss them." Except that these are the words of a modern commentator.[2] Loyola is very sparing in his directions, and much more prosaic, or shall I say, less obvious? The direction is to consider the road from Bethany to Jerusalem whether it is wide, whether it is narrow, whether it is flat, and the rest, and likewise the Garden of Gethsemane whether wide, whether large, whether of one style, whether of another. Just these little suggestions start the process of imagination and with astonishing reserve the candidate is then left to himself. There is room for authority in education, but St. Philip Neri well remarked, "If you want obedience do not give commands."

It would be interesting to know what shape the life of Christ assumed for those who abandoned themselves to their imaginations. Loyola gives them only a little skeleton of the Gospels to work from, and very occasionally an extra detail. Christ appears first to his mother, but we are distinctly told that this is not in the Gospels. Jesus indignantly overthrew the tables of the wealthy money-changers, but spoke gently to the poor who were selling doves. These are almost the only embellishments. Ignatius showed severe restraint in the omission of the many imaginative touches of the devotional literature with which he was familiar. In one of these works Mary is preparing broth for Joseph when the angels inform her that her son is hungry in the wilderness. She thereupon supplies the food with which they minister unto him. Another writer knows the exact number of wounds of Christ, 5,490 symbolizing perfection. None of this in Ignatius! Yet quite probably his disciples, when left to themselves, would revel in the details which appealed to the taste of the times. Doubtless the gory would be prominent. Children love it. I find with my own that, if I make a slip in my dexterous skipping about the Old Testament and inadvertently hew someone to pieces, interest immediately picks up. Doubtless, too, the disciples of Ignatius would reconstruct the Gospel in local colors. Tissot had not yet introduced the vogue of portraying Christ in a Palestinian setting. In that day the nativity at

[2] *Ibid.,* p. 10.

Venice took place near the Grand Canal, at Florence with the background of Fiesole, in Spain beside the foothills of the Pyrenees. To introduce an example from the Old Testament, there is at Basel a fountain in stone above which a Teutonic Samson sprawls over the lap of a Teutonic Delilah, neither of the cinema type, while she prepares to hack his hair with an implement resembling modern tin shears. The Prodigal was German for Dürer, as the Madonna was Italian for Raphael or Filippo Lippi.

And why not? We do the same thing with our lives of Christ to the despair of some who say that if there are so many pictures it is because no one knows what Jesus is like. Ought we not to say that if the pictures were uniform it would be because he had ceased to stir? Jesus, even in outline, kindles the creative and lives by assuming ever varied forms. But is there not also a recognizable likeness in all the types? The real Jesus is, after all, inescapable. The lilies of the field may wither, but the cross always reappears.

The strength of the *Exercises* lies partly in the very fact that all the means are subordinate to the end, and the end is the glory of God and the propagation of the faith. This is a manual for the soldiers of the cross, who are to overcome not only themselves but also the heretics and the infidels. To Germany, to India, to China and to the New World they were to go, indelibly stamped with the imprint of those four weeks. With St. Ignatius they had learned to pray, "Take, O Lord, and receive all my liberty, my memory, my understanding, and all my will, all I have and possess: Thou hast given it me; to thee, Lord, I return it; all is thine, dispose of it entirely according to thy will. Give me thy love and grace, because that is enough for me."

18. Congregationalism and the Puritan Revolution from the Just War to the Crusade

The Congregationalists during the Puritan revolution, like all Christians in time of war, were confronted with the ethical problem of reconciling the precepts of the Sermon on the Mount with the inevitable violence and hate customary in war. Little that was new could be said in the 1640s because all the answers compatible with Christian presuppositions had been voiced long before the Protestant Reformation. Three main attitudes had emerged. The first is an attitude of non-participation, pacifism; the second an attitude of reluctant participation, the just and mournful war; the third an attitude of hearty participation, the crusade. Broadly speaking these three positions appeared in chronological order. The early Church was prevailingly pacifist. The Christian Roman Empire developed the doctrine of the just war. The Middle Ages added the crusade.

The pacifism of the early Church need not detain us since there is no hint of it among the Congregationalists of the Puritan revolution. Their thought was to shift from the just war to the crusade. These two types, therefore, call for a measure of elucidation.

The theory of the just war was elaborated in the Christian Roman Empire in the period between Constantine and the barbarian invasions. Chief among the formulators was St. Augustine. The sources for the idea of the just war were primarily classical. To be sure Biblical confirmation was found in the New Testament in the verses in Romans 13: "The powers that be are ordained of God . . ." The ruler "beareth not the sword in vain, for he is a minister of

Given as the Southworth Lecture in 1942. First published in the *Andover Newton Bulletin*, XXXV, 3 (April 1943).

God, a revenger to execute wrath upon him that doeth evil." This description of the police power of the state could be extended to war only if war were itself regarded as a form of policing. In the Old Testament a code for the conduct of the just war was discovered in Deuteronomy 20. Yet the primary source was classical. The concept had been built up from Plato to Cicero. In the classical picture the just war had to be just as to its object, which was to vindicate justice and restore peace; just as to its conduct in that the war must be formally declared, good faith observed with the enemy, prisoners and hostages respected, non-combatants spared and violence restrained within the limits of military necessity. Such conditions could be fulfilled by both sides at once and the war could thus be reciprocally just. The authority of the state, as embodied in the will of the ruler, was also requisite.

This classical theory was in several respects modified and amplified by St. Augustine. For him the war could be just only on one side at a time. He is the father of the war guilt theory. The determination of the justice fell to the ruler. Hence, the war was fought not only under his authority but, one might almost say, under his conscience. The common soldier was ordinarily relieved of responsibility for a judgment as to the justice of the cause. To the just object and the just conduct, St. Augustine added the just intention which is love for the enemy. This does not exclude killing his body since the destruction of a mortal body cannot harm an immortal soul. The pacifism of the early Church was conserved by a graded ethic. The prince and the soldier are pacifist not in act but in disposition. The private citizen must be completely non-resistant in his own behalf. The clergy and the monks are entirely exempt from military service because of dedication to other tasks. In one other respect a feeling for the earlier pacifism is retained in that the mood of the warrior must be mournful. The prince and the soldier like the magistrate, all sinners themselves, must undertake the task of restraining other sinners only with a heavy heart.

The theory of the just war survived throughout the Middle Ages to become the essential position of the Catholic Church to this day. A certain modification crept in with regard to the Augustinian contention that the war could be just on one side only. In the sixteenth century the theory began to crumble in the hands of

Vittoria who could conceive of justice on both sides in the New World where the Spaniards were justified in fighting the natives who interfered with the natural right of freedom of travel, and the natives by virtue of their invincible ignorance were at the same time justified in resisting the Spaniards.

The crusade which originated in the Middle Ages differs from the just war in several respects. The cause is more than just, it is holy. The object is the vindication of religion or of something invested with all the sancity of religion. The authority of the prince is not necessary. The war may be fought under the authority of God or of His representatives on earth, presumably the Church. The common soldier fights not at the behest of the prince but volunteers by taking the cross. The restriction on exempted classes breaks down. The clergy and even the monks participate. The Crusades saw the formation of monastic military orders such as the Templars and Hospitalers. Support for the crusading idea was found to a minor degree in the New Testament: in the indignation with which Jesus expelled the money-changers and the zeal with which St. Peter defended his Lord. The first Christian poem in the German tongue celebrates the mighty deeds of that doughty knight St. Peter who wielded his broadsword and clave clean the high priest's servant's ear. For the Middle Ages St. Peter took over the role of Jehovah of Hosts. The details of the crusading idea were drawn primarily from the Old Testament which had known two wars of religion—the conquest of Canaan and the revolt of the Maccabees. Crusaders have always been disposed to canonize Joshua, Gideon, Deborah and Jael, and have been fond of such texts as "Curse ye Meroz" (Jud. 5: 23), and "Cursed be he that holdeth back his sword from blood" (Jer. 48: 10).

The Protestant Reformation saw a distribution of the three attitudes. Pacifism was espoused in the sixteenth century by the Anabaptists, in the seventeenth by the Quakers. The just war, minus the exemption of monks, was taken over by the Lutherans and the Anglicans. The crusading idea intrigued the Lutherans momentarily, only to be dropped and taken up subsequently by the Calvinists. The reason was in part that Calvinism took a more positive attitude toward the state than Lutheranism and looked upon the ruler as ordained of God not merely to restrain sin, but also to erect Christ's kingdom. Yet the shift from the just war to the crusade was largely a matter of circumstances depending upon whether Protestantism was driven to revolution for the sake of survival. Only for a brief time in the Schmalkald war was Lutheranism confronted with this menace, but Calvinism faced the threat for more than a century in France, Scotland and England.

A revolution is very difficult to square with a just war because the just war is fought under the authority of the prince, whereas a revolution is directed against the person of the prince. There are three possible harmonistic devices. One is to say that the war is not against the prince but only against the evil counselors of the prince, from whom he is to be emancipated. This was the contention of the Huguenots when they sought to deliver the king from the Guises. The second way out is to say that the king, if he be a tyrant, ceases to be a king and may be dealt with as a private citizen. This argument had already been used in England by the Marian exiles.[1] The third solution involves a theory of constitutional government and a distribution of sovereignty. One branch of the government can then restrain another. The idea was developed by Luther with the aid of the jurists who pointed out to him that the Holy Roman Empire was a constitutional monarchy. If the emperor were faithless to the conditions of his election oath he might be restrained by the princes in the role of inferior magistrates. Calvin took up the argument pointing to the Ephors in Sparta and the Tribunes in Rome as inferior magistrates who could vindicate the rights of the people. Concretely, the doctrine that the inferior magistrate might restrain the superior meant in Germany that the princes might resist the emperor, in France that the nobles might withstand the crown, in England that parliament might curb the king.

This whole background of ideas lay behind the Congregationalists when they were anew confronted with the problem of defending "laws, liberties and religion" against the crown. Having come from the body of Anglicanism they were steeped in the theory of the just war. As Calvinists they had all the presuppositions of the

---

[1] Christopher Goodman, *How Superior Powers ought to be obeyed*, Facsimile Text Society (New York, 1931), p. 119. John Ponet, *A Shorte Treatise of Politike Power*, facsimile in Winthrop S. Hudson, *John Ponet* (Chicago, 1942), p. 104 of the tract and p. 158 of the book.

crusade, and circumstances drove them in that direction after having first exhausted all the harmonistic devices. This very transition
was a part of the process of the emergence of Congregationalism, or
Independency as it was then called, for it was the Independents
rather than the Presbyterians who became the definite spokesmen
of the crusading idea. In the opening years of the struggle, when all
were trying to conserve the formula of the just war, Congregationalism was amorphous and no specifically Congregational theory
can be isolated. In fact, one has difficulty in saying precisely who
were the Congregationalists. One can, of course, take certain individuals later distinguished as Independents, but they did not form
a party in 1640. One can take as definitely Congregational those
who were so insistent on the gathered Church and the congregational choice of the minister that they could not suffer themselves
to be comprehended under the establishment. The Separatists were
undoubtedly Congregationalists. But Perry Miller has made us
aware[2] that there were also non-separating Congregationalists, who
were willing that the clergyman should be presented to the parish
by the bishop provided the congregation ratified the appointment.
And if Congregationalism could thus be accommodated to episco-
pacy why not also to presbyterianism? Hexter has shown us that
there were those who might be called Presbyterian Congregationalists,[3] for though later marked as Independents they were not un-
willing during the Presbyterian ascendency to serve on the local
presbyteries. We cannot, then, speak of clearly demarked parties
in 1640. Presbyterianism emerged in England because of the Scot-
tish alliance in 1643. The Independents grew into a self-conscious
opposition and took the lead after the break between the army and
the parliament in 1647.

Nor was the attitude toward the war at first a matter of religious affiliation. Hexter discovers three parties with reference to
the war: those who would negotiate with the king but keep their
powder dry, the moderates; those who would negotiate with powder wet, the appeasers; and those who with powder dry would not
negotiate, the implacables. Presbyterians were found in all three

---

[2] *Orthodoxy in Massachusetts* (Cambridge, Mass., 1933).
[3] "The Problem of the Presbyterian Independents," *American Historical
Review*, XLIV (1938), pp. 29-49.

camps.[4] One may doubt whether the Independents were similarly divided, for in the main they tended to side with the implacables, yet a layman among them, Henry Robinson, could wish that the quarrel might be settled by accommodation.[5]

Men scarcely knew themselves at first where they belonged. Witness the dilemma of a Francis Quarles, a Puritan when it came to personal manners and churchly reform, and yet so imbued with the sinfulness of rebellion against the authority of the prince ordained of God that for want of a better alternative he allied himself with the party of the king.[6] Or take the case of Christopher Love who was so devoted to the monarchy that he could indeed prosecute the war against a tyrant king and then lose his head for conspiring to bring in the king's son.

In general, then, up to 1643 there is no great point in trying to isolate the Congregational from the general parliamentary ethic of war, nor from 1643 to 1647 in isolating the Congregational from the Presbyterian. For the first we may study in general the utterances of the clergy on the parliamentary side; for the second phase the Presbyterians and the Independents together; and only in the third phase the Independents apart.[7]

---

[4] J. H. Hexter, *The Reign of King Pym* (Cambridge, Mass., 1941), p. 97.

[5] Preface to *Liberty of Conscience* (1644), facsimile in William Haller, *Tracts on Liberty* (New York, 1934), vol. III, and in modern script in *Pamphlets on Religion and Democracy*, Sutro Library Project (July 4, 1940).

[6] Gordon S. Haight, "Francis Quarles in the Civil War," *Review of English Studies*, XII, 46 (April 1936), pp. 1-18.

[7] The persons referred to and cited in this article may be classified as follows. Those who ended with the Independents are credited to them. Members of the Assembly of Divines who were not later members of the Savoy conference are listed as Presbyterian. Independents: William Ames, William Bridge, Edward Bowles, Jeremiah Burroughs, Edmund Calamy, John Canne, Joseph Caryl, John Goodwin, Philip Hunton, John Milton, Matthew Newcomen, John Owen, Henry Parker, Hugh Peters, John Price, Henry Robinson, John Robinson, Obadiah Sedgwick, Peter Sterry. Judging by their utterances William Hussey and John Redingstone belong here, but I cannot otherwise identify them. Wildman and Lilburne were Levelers who sided with the Independents in the quarrel with the Presbyterians. Presbyterians: Richard Baxter, Thomas Case, Francis Cheynell, Samuel Gibson, Charles Herle, Richard Heyricke, Thomas Hodges, John Ley, Christopher Love, Stephen Marshall, Herbert Palmer, Samuel Rutherford, John Strickland, Francis Taylor, Richard Vines, George Walker, John White, Thomas Wilson. Anglicans: H. Ferne, Thomas Fuller, Joseph Hall, Francis Quarles. Erastian: Thomas Coleman.

All religious parties approached the struggle with a sound grounding in the theory of the just war. The position had been well summarized by the non-separatist Congregationalist, William Ames.[8] War, he declares, is always an evil because there cannot be a just war without an unjust war on the other side. Here, he is thoroughly Augustinian and quite untouched by the concession of Vittoria on the double justice in the wars of the New World. But although war is always an evil, continues Ames, it may nevertheless be waged by Christians. The authority of the prince is necessary, who, along with the officers of high rank, is responsible for the determination of the justice. The common soldier must serve at their behest unless he knows the war to be manifestly unjust. The innocent will undoubtedly suffer but they are to be hurt as little as possible. Thus far one recognizes the familiar Augustinian lines. At two points only is there any divergence. In private life self-defense is allowed, and the exemption of monks automatically drops from a Protestant treatise.

This traditional view was the common heritage of all parties in the Puritan struggle. The Anglican Thirty-nine Articles affirm that "it is lawful for Christian men to weare weapons and serve in warres." The Westminster Confession of the Presbyterians asserts that "it is lawful for Christians . . . to wage war upon just and necessary grounds" (1647). The Savoy Declaration of the Independents took over this article without change (1658). The Presbyterian John Ley, addressing the Commons in 1643 on *The FVRY of WARRE* set forth the customary conditions of the just cause, the just intention, the just conduct and the lawful authority.[9] John Owen, the Independent, expected "the blessing of God upon a just and lawful war" such as the one waged by Abraham in his capacity of sovereign prince.[10]

[8] *Conscience with the Power and Cases Thereof* (London, 1643).

[9] April 26, 1643 (London, 1643), p. 15.

[10] *Works* (Philadelphia, 1870), XIV, 316; (Edinburgh, 1875), XXII, 316. Further examples among the Anglicans may be found in the section on "The Good Souldier" in Thomas Fuller's *The Holy and Profane State* (1642), and in Joseph Hall's *Resolutions and Decisions of Divers Practicall Cases of Conscience* (London, 1649), Decade II, section 9, "Whether, and how farre a man may take up armes in the publique quarrel of a war." The treatment is thoroughly Augustinian. The same may be said of the discussion by the Presbyterian Richard Baxter in his *Christian Directory*.

But at just that point came the Puritan dilemma. So long as they were fighting against the king where was the authority of the Prince? The first harmonistic device employed was the one formerly used by the Huguenots, to claim that the war was not directed against the prince but rather against his evil counselors, the Malignants. To be sure, the king was in their midst and issuing commands on their behalf. His commands must be resisted, even his will must be resisted. Yet his authority would not be resisted, since the war was directed to liberating alike his person and his mind from malign influences.

The theory, never too tenable, continued to be used long after it had ceased to be plausible. Many examples can be given from the sermons of the period. Take for example the sermon before the Commons on May 31, 1643 by Francis Cheynell on *Sions Memento, and Gods Alarum,* where he declares: "If a King of the Protestant Profession should give his strength and power to his Queene a Papist, and she give it to the Jesuits, to the Beast, it is neither Rebellion nor Treason to fight for the King, to recover his power out of the hand of the Beast; I say, for the King, that the *power* being regained may be setled upon the Kings Royall person, and posterity."[11] To be sure parliament is going against the king's express command, but did not the ass do the like to save Balaam?[12] "The Parliament may be called the Kings Physitians."[13] After all, who is to say what it is to serve the king? Shall parliament, which is the Great Council of the kingdom, determine, or the wicked counselors that have usurped their office? "Must the State and those that hold with them, learne of Delinquents that have deserved death, how to be for the King? Or of perfidious Covenant-breakers, to whom an oath of God is no more than a collar to a Monkey, that he can slip at pleasure? . . . Must they learne of damne-swearers, that familiarly sweare themselves into hell? or of Papists, who are pleased so long as the King serveth their turne, but would blow him up with powder if they could, if he should execute the lawes against them? Or of the *wild Irish,* & other *Irish* murtherers, that

[11] (London, 1643), p. 10.
[12] Richard Vines, *CALEBS INTEGRITY,* Sermon before the Commons, November 30, 1642 (London, 1642), p. 26.
[13] John Robinson, *The Peoples Plea* (London, 1646), p. 4.

first kill a hundred thousand of the Kings *Protestant* subjects in *Ireland*, and then come and offer their service to him in *England*, with a desire to do as much here, if they can?"[14]

William Bridge assured the volunteers: "There is much difference between taking up of Armes against the Kings Person, and taking up of Arms for the defence of the Kingdom, without the Kings command," as David fought not Saul but the Malignants about him.[15] Jeremiah Burroughes proclaimed: "Wherefore that which is now done, is not against the King; though it be against the *personall command* of the King, yet it is not against the *Legall power* of the King: when we speake of a King, we mean such a man invested with a Regal power by the lawes and constitutions of that country he is the King of. Now if nothing be done against this power that the laws & constitutions of our countrie invests him with, then nothing can be said to be done against the King." They are mistaken who do not distinguish between a man in authority and the authority of that man.[16] Parliament, according to an anonymous tract, acts under the "king's juridicall authority though his personall pleasure be withheld."[17] The Earl of Essex was encouraged by John Price with the assurance: "You fight for his [the king's] Authority which is greater than his *personall Commands*. . . . You will not destroy the Kings lawfull Authority by submitting yourselves to his unlawfull commands? . . . You fight for the recovery of his Royall Person out of the hands of those miscreants."[18]

Scriptural warrant for respect to the king's person coupled with resistance to his entourage was found in the example of

[14] Samuel Gibson, *The Ruine of the Authors and Fomentors of Civill Warres*, Sermon before the Commons, September 24, 1645 (London, 1645), pp. 22-23.

[15] *A Sermon Preached unto the Voluntiers of the City of Norwich* (London, 1642), p. 17.

[16] *The Glorious Name of God* (London, 1643), p. 28.

[17] *Touching the Fundamental Lawes* (London, 1643), p. 9.

[18] *A Spirituall Snapsnacke for the Parliament Souldiers* (London, 1643), p. 8. Compare: Herbert Palmer, *Scripture and Reason pleaded for Defensive Armes* (London, 1643), p. 37. Philip Hunton, *A Treatise of Monarchie* (London, 1643), p. 51. Matthew Newcomen, *The Craft and Cruelty of the Churches Adversaries*, Sermon before the Commons, November 5, 1642 (London, 1643), p. 36. In March, 1642 Milton held the "Malignant" theory. Don M. Wolfe, *Milton in the Puritan Revolution* (New York, 1941), p. 209.

David's conflict with Saul. Appeal to this example raised the inevitable question whether the example of David might be regarded as valid for a later time. Everyone recognized that the patriarchs were not to be imitated in all instances, as in the practice of polygamy. This, and similar outmoded practices were commonly explained as having been permissible in the olden time because God granted a special dispensation in the form of a direct revelation. This hoary device for obviating an Old Testament example was employed by the Royalist apologist Dr. Fern in his *The Resolving of Conscience*.[19] The Independent William Bridge countered by affirming that whatever extraordinary command and special instinct may have been vouchsafed to David—the record mentions none—is equally available to us.[20]

Yet in the end the contention that the king's authority could be used against his will amounted to this: that the king's will is not the will of the king, but the constitution of the kingdom to be interpreted by parliament. There are better ways of saying that. The King pointed it out. To regard the resistance offered to him as an act of "loyalty and affection," said he, was of a piece with the assumption that he was actually surrounded by Papists and Turks.[21] Very well then, argued some on the parliamentary side, if the king disavows the shifting of responsibility from himself to his counselors, let him have it. "If it be stood upon, that his Majesty scornes any such evasion, and, as he hath already been perswaded to doe, take all upon himself, why should wee endanger our selves by a solicitude for the reparations of that honour, which they, whom it most concernes, are not at all [?]"[22]

Although, then, the "Malignant" theory might continue to do service it was manifestly a fiction. The claim that parliament should declare the mind of the king already implied a theory of constitutional government. Recourse was early taken to the second device for conserving the theory of the just war under princely authority by distributing authority among the several organs of the

[19] (London, 1642), p. 8.
[20] *The TRUTH of the Times Vindicated* (London, 1643), pp. 34-35.
[21] J. W. Allen, *English Political Thought 1603-1660* (London, 1938), p. 409.
[22] Edward Bowles, *Plaine English* (London, 1643), p. 11.

state. Stress was laid by Stephen Marshall on the plural *powers* in
Romans 13, which in the case of England was taken to mean the
king *and* parliament.[23] For such a view of the constitution there
was already precedent in English thought. *The Case of SHIP-
MONY briefly discoursed* in November 1640 referred to the king
as "potent in Parliament"[24]and this language but echoed the words
of James Whitelocke in 1610: "The power of the king in parliament is greater than his power out of parliament and doth rule
and control it."[25]

The exigencies of the parliamentary struggle elicited a more
precise formulation of constitutionalism when in 1642 the British
government came to be described as a mixed monarchy. The idea
was old but as a theory of the British constitution it came into
prominence first in the civil war. Both sides for a time found it useful, in as much as the king posed as a defender of the constitution
quite as much as parliament. If they could argue that he was not
supreme without them, he could argue just as well that they were
nothing without him. The first enunciation of the doctrine of
mixed monarchy came from the king's side in the reply to *The
Nineteen Propositions* in which parliament was claiming not so
much a mixed constitution as sovereignty for itself in the control
of the militia. The king, through the pen of Sir John Colepepper,
answered that this would be to leave him but the "Style of Majestie" with hand-kissing and maces, crown and sceptre, "but as to
true and reall Power We should remain but the outside, but the
Picture, but the signe of a King."[26] This would be a violation of
the British constitution. "There being three kinds of government
amongst men, Absolute Monarchy, Aristocracy and Democracy. . . .
The experience and wisdom of your ancestors have so moulded this
out of a mixture of these, as to give to this kingdom . . . the con-
veniences of all three, without the inconveniences of any one, as

[23] *A Plea for Defensive Armes* (London, 1643), p. 14.

[24] (London, 1640), p. 38.

[25] Cited by J. H. Hexter, *The Reign of King Pym* (Cambridge, Mass.,
1941), p. 214.

[26] *HIS MAIESTIES Answer to the XIX Propositions* (Oxford, 1642),
pp. 13-14.

long as the balance hangs between the three Estates."[27] The conclusion is that the existing checks on monarchy were sufficient and
nothing more should be conceded.

In the meantime parliamentary thought was moving in precisely the same direction. The king's *Declaration* appeared in June.
In October of the same year John Goodwin came out with his *Anticavalierisme* in which he declared that no government is of specific
divine ordination. Any form may be chosen by a people, for "all
formes of government are lawfull and just, whether they be simple,
as the three commonly known by the names of Monarchy, Aristocracy, Democracy; or whether they be mixt, having somewhat of
two, or all of these simples in them, are equally and indifferently
from God."[28] Goodwin did not further pursue the point in these
terms.

But before the year was out a preacher on the parliamentary
side, Charles Herle, had taken the argument of the King's answer
over into the opposite camp:

Before we judge of what a Parliament can doe in England, it will
be needfull to know what kinde of Government this of Englands is: We
are therefore to know, that Englands is not a simply subordinative, and
absolute, but a Coordinative, and mixt Monarchy; This mixture, or Coor-
dination is in the very supremacy of power it selfe, otherwise the Monarchy were not mixt: all Monarchies have a mixture, or composition of
subordinate and under-officers in them, but here the Monarchy, or
highest power is it selfe compounded of 3. Coordinate Estates, a *King*,
and two *Houses* of Parliament; unto this mixt power no subordinate authority may in any case make resistance . . .

This mixture the *King's* Majesty himselfe is often pleased in his
Declaration to applaud, as by a mutuall counterpoise each to other, sweet-
ning and alaying what ever is harsh in either, the Treatiser himselfe doth
no lesse, calling it that excellent temper of the three Estates in Parliament, confessing them (there) to be the fundamentalls of this Government, and if fundamentalls, what subordination (I pray) can there be in
them, . . . ?

But you'l say, what, is not the Parliament subordinate to the King?

[27] Ibid., p. 22. Compare Stanley Pargellis, "The Theory of Balanced Government," in *The Constitution Reconsidered*, edited by Conyers Read (New
York, 1938).

[28] Reprinted in facsimile in William Haller, *Tracts on Liberty*, II, 225.

and are they not all Subjects? I answer; the Parliament cannot properly be said to be a Subject, because the *King* is a part. . . .

It was the consent of both *King* and people, in the first coalition or constitution of the Government, that makes them in their severall Houses coordinate with his Majesty, not subordinate to him, how else were the Monarchy mixt more than that of Turky? . . .

They are a *coordinative part* in the *Monarchy,* or highest principle of power, in as much as they beare a *consenting* share in the *highest office* of it, the *making of Lawes.*[29]

The theory once voiced became very popular on the parliamentary side and was echoed in sermons and tracts. Henry Parker, the following year in his *A Political Catechism*[30] replied point by point to the king's *Declaration.* Taking up the words: "The experience and Wisdom of your Ancestors hath moulded this Government out of a mixture of these," and the concession that the State of England is a "regulated monarchy" he concluded: "If this Government be a mixture of all these, and a Regulated Monarchy; then it is a fond thing with us to talk of an Absolute Monarchy." Philip Hunton in his *A Treatise of Monarchie* of the same year asserts: "The Authority of this land is of a compounded and mixed nature in the very constitution thereof. . . . It is acknowledged to be a Monarchy mixed with Aristocracy in the house of Peeres, and Democracy in the house of Commons . . . that Monarchy, in which three Estates are constituted, to the end that the power of one should moderate and restrain from excesse the power of the other, is mixed in the root and essence of it."[31] The tract *Touching the Fundamentall Lawes* similarly finds England a "mixed regiment."[32] Samuel Rutherford testified: "A limited and mixed Monarchy, such as in Scotland and England, seeme to me the best government."[33] Christopher Love in 1645 complained that a "mixed monarchy is ayming at an absolute Tyranny,"[34] and the *Remonstrance*

[29] *A Fuller Answer to a Treatise written by Doctor Ferne* (London, 1642), pp. 3-4.

[30] Ordered printed May 20, 1643 (London, 1643).

[31] Pages 30-40.

[32] (London, 1643), p. 5.

[33] *Lex, Rex* (London, October 6, 1644), p. 387.

[34] *Englands Distemper* (London, 1645), p. 36.

from Fairfax to the Commons in November 1648 still refers to England as a "mixed state."[35]

The question of resistance to the king was not settled, however, by a mere theory of mixed government. From this theory one could deduce that if a coordinate member disturbed the balance the others might interpose in some fashion, but to justify recourse to the extreme of war, the old Protestant doctrine was more specifically relevant that inferior officers might resist superiors. This was the main plea of John Goodwin in his *Anticavalierisme*. The same argument was employed by Jeremiah Burroughes[36] and by Samuel Rutherford.[37]

Yet it was a theory which had originated under other circumstances and did not well suit the English situation. It did not even square with the concept of mixed government according to which all of the parts were coordinate and none inferior. Much less was the picture of the inferior magistrate applicable to the claim of parliamentary sovereignty being advanced by men like Parker and Hunton. Some more satisfactory basis was needed to justify parliament in taking up arms against the king.

A more defensible claim was this, that parliament constituted a supreme Court of Judicature, competent to summon even the king himself. Force might be used to bring culprits before the tribunal. Ordinarily if the miscreants were few constables would suffice. If they were many the militia would have to be used for the purpose. This, then, was the ground on which parliament claimed jurisdiction over the militia. The argument was not entirely fantastic, for in some sense parliament was a court.[38] That it was a court having jurisdiction over the king even to the point of taking his life was highly contestable. Further to bolster the claim, parliament was portrayed not only as the "chiefest court" but also as the representative body for the kingdom. Sovereignty then was shifted to the people and their safety became the highest law. *Salus populi suprema lex*. The law of necessity was held to supersede all others.

---

[35] *Old Parliamentary History, XVIII* (November 16, 1648), p. 176.

[36] *The Glorious Name of God* (London, 1643), p. 127.

[37] *Lex, Rex* (London, 1644), p. 159.

[38] For Coke's recognition of parliament as in some sense a court see Francis D. Wormuth, *The Royal Prerogative* (Ithaca, 1935), p. 66.

Milton's none too coherent manipulating of these arguments is well expounded by Wolfe in the work already cited. Abundant examples point by point can be discovered in the minor pamphlets and sermons. The following proclaim parliament to be the chief court. *A Disclaimer and Answer* affirms that "The House of Commons is absolutely intrusted with our persons and estates, and by our Lawes invested with power to dispose of them as they shall thinke meet, not onely by making new Lawes, but also as they are the Great Court above all ordinary Courts, to governe us, and to determine of all things proper and the power and jurisdiction thereof in all things tending to the conservation of the Commonwealth and of our Religion, Laws and Liberties."[39] According to John Canne, Parliament is "the supreamest Judicatory and Soveraign power in the Kingdom: for in this High Court, the Kings Person is no other than another subject."[40] William Bridge argued that parliament as a court might assume charge of the militia because when the culprits to be brought before the "highest Court" numbered 10,000 the ordinary machinery of justice was inadequate to bring them in.[41] Fairfax referred to parliament as "the supreme Judicatory," and as "the supreme council and representative body of the people."[42] Henry Parker called parliament "a representative court."[43] The same language appears in Stephen Marshall,[44] Edward Bowles[45] and John White.[46] For Edmund Calamy parliament was so thoroughly the representative of the nation that the reformation of the one was equivalent to the reformation of the other.[47]

The shift to popular sovereignty and the law of necessity is apparent in a sermon of Richard Heyricke where Queen Esther is commended for overstepping the law. "The observation of Laws is

[39] (London, 1643), p. 2.

[40] *The Golden Rule* (London, 1649), p. 5.

[41] *The TRUTH of the Times Vindicated* (London, 1643), p. 20.

[42] "A Remonstrance presented to the House of Commons from Lord Fairfax, November 16, 1648," *Old Parliamentary History*, XVIII, pp. 211 and 175.

[43] *A Petition or Declaration* (London, 1642), p. 6.

[44] *A Plea for Defensive Armes* (London, 1643), p. 9.

[45] *Plaine English* ([London], 1643), p. 11.

[46] *A Few Propositions shewing the Lawfulnesse of Defence against the injurious attempts of outragious violence* (London, 1643), section 19.

[47] *Englands Looking-Glass* (London, 1642), p. 45.

very commendable, but when exigencies are so violent, when confusion hath turned all upside down, when the State is disturbed, when wicked men are combined, when all Order is perverted, then men are to look to the main chance, then to sollicite the principal businesse, and so much the more zealously, as Esther did, by how much there is less possibility of compassing it in the ordinary way. When necessity is so urgent that it makes the observing of the Laws impossible; Nature, Reason, Laws, Religion, all instruct us to betake our selves to that which is most necessary: Prerogative, Privilege, Liberty, all must be laid aside.... The Parliament shall ever be famous, they have not onely followed presidents but made them."[48]

Again William Hussey declared that so far parliament had fought for right and liberty and the king for prerogative, both pleading law. If now parliament, sword in hand, went on to new principles, God stood over her. She had the proper authority because, though subordinate judges may not, yet the supreme judge may judge by the universal law of *Salus populi suprema lex.*[49] If highway robbers should set upon a village, inquired Herbert Palmer, and the constables were in collusion should we not resist? "Necessity hath no Law.... Ordinary laws for setled times, give way to present pressing necessities."[50]

However pertinent such theories may have been to the actual state of affairs they were more and more difficult to square with the ethic of the just war fought under the authority of the prince. The case was doubly difficult when parliament, dominated by the Presbyterians, recoiled from extreme measures against the king whose person according to the Solemn League and Covenant was to be held sacrosanct; whereas the army, prevailingly Independent, was resolved to bring to account "that man of blood, Charles Stuart." To pretend to be still fighting under the authority of the king while cutting off his head taxed the most inventive imagination, and the theory of mixed government was more comfortable to the British constitution when the three forms of monarchy, aristocracy and

[48] *A Sermon Preached,* before the Commons (May 26, 1646), p. 6.
[49] *The Magistrates CHARGE, for the Peoples Safetie,* sermon before the Peers, May 26, 1647 (London, 1647), pp. 16 and 40.
[50] *Scripture and Reason Pleaded* (London, 1643), p. 19.

democracy were represented by the King, the Peers and the Commons than after the triad had come to be the king, the parliament and the army. The devices previously used by the parliament to justify its rebellion against the king had now to be used by the army in support of disaffection toward both king and parliament. Older theories were more than stretched when made to cover a system verging on military dictatorship.

But they were used. First came the claim that the army had as much right to resist parliament as parliament had to resist the king. Parliament, said Wildman, has become a menace in "endeavouring to make a new warre, or to bring in the King, upon most unjust, unsafe, and unconscionable tearmes."[51] A tract entitled *New Propositions from the Armie to the Presbyterians and Independents within the City of London* affirmed that "Whereas the Lawes of God, Man and Nature justifie the people in opposing, fighting against, and imprisoning of Kings, who act contrary to their Oaths, and the trust imposed on them by the people; and that the same Lawes as much justifie them in opposing the power of Parliament, when they betray their trust, in pleading the interest, justifying the cause of such princes, joyn with them to levy war against the poor people, whose Trustees they are only, and by whose Votes and Election they sit in Parliament."[52]

Here the Army is vested with authority as the body representing the people of England. When it was objected that as a matter of fact the army did not represent the people of England, the reply was similar to that which had been used when parliament was made the interpreter of the king's mind against his will. In like fashion the army became the interpreter of the mind and the custodian of the welfare of the people of England even though they might be otherwise minded. When the pilot is drunk inferior mariners may take over, asserted John Goodwin. That the army had no formal commission from the people was no more held to invalidate their act than a similar lack for many of the acts of parliament. To have waited for a formal call would have prevented giving the relief required by the situation. But if it be said that the people did

[51] *A Cal to all souldiers of the Armie* (London, 1647), p. 4.
[52] (London, 1648), p. 1.

not regard the acts of the army as tending to their relief the answer
was that the physician to persons suffering from distempers cannot
wait for their consent. If the people are incapable of "the things of
their peace" then those who are capable must act on their behalf.
This is in accord with the law of nature.[53]

There were simpler and more defensible expedients than the
pretense that the army was the physician of a distempered people.
Some had recourse to the third of the harmonistic devices for reconciling rebellion with the just war. This theory centers not so
much on building up an authority against the king as upon denud-
ing the king of any authority at all. If he is a tyrant then he is not a
king. He forfeits his prerogative and becomes but a private citizen
amenable to any tribunal in the land. Those rulers who oppress
the people cease *ipso facto* to be rulers, declared John Robinson.[54]
John Canne affirmed, "Howsoever Kings ruling according to Law
are publick Ministers of State, nevertheless degenerating into Ty-
rants, and acting against Law, they are in such case, no more then
private men."[55] Even more explicit is John Redingstone: "Therefore what Ruler soever wilfully and publikely perverts the Law, introducing an arbitrary, tyrannicall and unjust cause, acting against
the publicke good and safety, to the ruine of the People, loseth his
power and ceaseth to be a Ruler, and ought to be declared & pro-
ceeded against for such a one." "The King is wholly elapsed in his
splendor, dignity, honour, Kingly power, Majestie, and stands
guilty of all the precious blood, rapines and ruines of millions of
People in these three Kingdomes, and hath disobliged the Parliament, Army and People of their allegiance to him."[56]

Against the charge of tyranny was levelled the plea by the
Royalists that the king had acted in no more arbitrary a manner
than the kings of Israel. Such a rejoinder might have been expected
to be a poser for the Biblicism of the Puritans. Rather than be en-
snared some of them frankly repudiated the Biblical model for the

---

[53] *Might and Right Well Met* (1649), reprinted in A. S. P. Woodhouse,
Puritanism and Liberty (London, 1938), pp. 215-216. Compare p. 122 where
Ireton says the same thing.
[54] *The Peoples Plea* (London, 1646), p. 6.
[55] *The Golden Rule* (London, 1649), p. 2.
[56] *Plain English* (London, 1649), pp. 1-2.

British constitution. "There is a wide difference betwixt what Israel did then, and what we do now. . . . The Kings of Israel were more absolute Kings, then are the kings of England, they ruled mostly by their *Prerogative* Royall (i.e.) by *meere power*. Our kings ought to rule by the known Laws of the Land. We have these Lawes to warrant our proceedings, *Israel* not so to warrant their revolt."[57] "Why," exclaimed Francis Taylor in a sermon before the Commons, "doe not our kings as *David* and *Solomon* did, when an offender appeares worthy of death, never try him by a Judge, nor execute him by a Sheriffe, but say to one standing by, Goe and fall on him and kill him?" Because "examples . . . of an unlimited Monarchy are not applyable to the Government of such states, as by the fundamental laws have set bounds, and fixed limits."[58]

But once again the question comes up of the compatibility of all these theories, however defensible, with the just war. Aware of the weakness of the case, thinkers began to veer in two directions. Some abandoned any Christian theory whatsoever and moved straight over into a secular war. Such was the expedient of John Lilburne who in *Jonah's Cry Out of the Whale's Belly*[59] declared that when the army defied parliament by seizing the person of the king, England was then dissolved into a state of nature in which the army could make a fresh start at the constitution of a government by choosing their own representatives. Even so religious a man as Jeremiah Burroughes began to seek secular grounds for the war and went so far as to claim that the war was not for religion but only for the civil right which guaranteed religion. "For wee have not onely a right to our Religion, by the Law of God, but wee have a Civill right to this our Religion, that other Christians have not had, and therefore there can be no scruple in this."[60]

The final answer was the crusade because it requires no authority save the authority of a holy cause and a righteous God. Herbert Palmer, as early as 1643, saw that it might come to this. "If it should ever happen," he wrote, "that a Parliament should

---

[57] *Powers to be Resisted* (London, 1643), p. 23.
[58] *Gods COVENANT the Churches Plea*, sermon before the Commons, October 29, 1645 (London, 1645), p. 19.
[59] Cited in Wolfe: *Milton*, p. 447.
[60] *Foure Speeches*, October 6, 1643 (London, 1646), p. 33.

joyne with a King to cast out the true Religion, and bring in Popery, yet might we resist."[61] Oliver Cromwell grew impatient with the quest for the authority of the prince as a guarantee for the justice of the cause. How can the prince determine the justice of a holy war? If it is holy, it is holy no matter what prince, parliament or people may say to the contrary. All of these quibbles about the seat of authority may be but "fleshly reasonings." The Lord Himself has given the answer. "Let us look unto providences; surely they mean somewhat. They hang so together; they being so constant, so clear and unclouded."[62] The crusading theory in these words is complete.

But if the formulation had waited thus long the mood had been present for some time in the sermons of the parliamentary divines and the despatches of the parliamentary leaders. The crusading idea requires that the cause shall be holy, and no cause is more holy than religion, that the war shall be fought under God and with His help, that the crusaders shall be godly and their enemies ungodly, that the war shall be prosecuted unsparingly. Examples of all of these points are abundant.

The cause is holy because religious. Whether or no the preachers were realistic at this point is irrelevant. The schools of modern thought divide over this as over every war. Some look to social and economic causes, some to the force of ideas including the religious. The contemporary preachers recognized both and not uncommonly declared that they were fighting for religion, liberty and laws. Take for example the title of the tract, *The Declaration of the Kingdomes of England and Scotland Ioyned in Armes for the vindication and defense of their Religion, Liberties and Lawes, against the Popish, Prelaticall, and Malignant party.*[63] Some of the preachers went further and insisted that religion was a primary factor in the struggle. Heyricke, for example, exclaimed, "Religion is the very Nerves and sinews of the Common-wealth, the very heart and prime fountain of life and livelihood, the Crown, the glory of a Nation, the beauty, the strength, the perfection, the

---

[61] *Scripture and Reason Pleaded* (London, 1643), p. 51.

[62] Thomas Carlyle, *The Letters and Speeches of Oliver Cromwell*, ed. S. C. Lomas, 3 vols. (London, 1904), I, 396.

[63] London, 1643.

Spirit, the soul of a Kingdome; in Religion is Embarqued the publicke safety; when that is aimed at, the danger is dreadfull, the losse
beyond recovery."[64] Edmund Calamy, urging upon the Commons
the summoning of the Scots in October 1643, defended himself that
as a minister he appeared to plead for war. Did not the priests in
the Old Testament blow the silver trumpets? "And certainly, if this
were the way of God in the Old Testament, certainly much more
in such a Cause as this, in which Cause Religion is so entwin'd and
indeed so interlac'd, that Religion and this Cause, they are like
Hippocrates his twins, they must live and die together."[65] Obadiah
Sedgewick on the same occasion maintained the cause to be the
cause of God, the cause of Christendom, "for if this Cause be car-
ryed against us, certainly the Protestant Cause throughout all of
Europe, will fare the worse for it."[66]

The war is fought under God. "The Saints receive their commission from the great King, King of Kings, to have a two edged
sword in their hands, to execute judgment upon the Heathen, and
punishment upon the people; *To binde their Kings with chaines,
and their Nobles with fetters of iron;* to execute upon them the
judgment written, *This honour have all the Saints.* Hence then we
see what a type of Holy Writ lies upon our Parliament and Army,
to execute judgement upon the King and his wicked Adherents."[67]
God may be trusted to scatter His enemies. So George Walker
preached before the Commons in 1644,[68] and did not Oliver Cromwell pause with his army at St. Abb's Head to sing the sixty-eighth
psalm, "Let God arise, Let His enemies be scattered"?[69] Victory
was regarded as the Lord's doing and the manifest proof of His approval of the cause. Cromwell referred to his success as "an un-
speakable mercy,"[70] and emphasized the disparity of the forces in

[64] *A Sermon Preached*, before the Commons May 27, 1646 (London, 1646),
p. 8.

[65] *Foure Speeches* (London, 1646), p. 21.

[66] Ibid., pp. 15-16.

[67] John Redingstone, *Plain English* (London, 1649), p. 3, referring to
Psalm 149.

[68] *A Sermon*, January 29, 1644 (London, 1645).

[69] Carlyle, ed. Lomas, II, 100.

[70] *A Great Victory God hath vouchsafed by the Lord Generall Cromwels
Forces against the Scots* (London, 1651), p. 5.

order that divine assistance might be the more apparent. "Sir, this is nothing but the hand of God. Praise onely belongs to him."[71] At Marston Moor "God made them as stubble to our swords."[72] Addressing the Speaker of the House the general exclaimed, "Sir, what can be said to these things? Is it an arm of flesh that doth these things? Is it the wisdom, and counsel, or strength of men? It is the Lord only. God will curse that man and his house that dares to think otherwise."[73]

The preachers likewise celebrated Cromwell's victories as works of the Lord. Hugh Peters is reported to have sent his despatch from the massacre at Drogheda: "Sir, the truth is Drogheda is taken, 3,352 of the enemy slain, and 64 of ours. . . . Ashton the governor killed, none spared. . . . I came now from giving thanks in the great church. . . . Dublin, September 15, 1649."[74] Similarly Peter Sterry preached a Thanksgiving sermon before parliament entitled, *The Coming forth of Christ . . . being a publicke Thanksgiving for the Victories obtained by the Parliaments Forces in IRELAND, especially for the taking of Droghedah.*[75]

The deduction of divine favor from victory was highly precarious for what then in case of defeat? The query was all too pertinent in the early years when the parliamentary forces suffered so many reverses. Here the preachers availed themselves of the device employed by the prophets of ancient Israel who interpreted discomfiture as a chastisement for infidelity to the covenant. The moral was not so much to fight harder as to couple fighting with days of public humiliation and more strenuous effort in the work of Reformation. So Herbert Palmer in his sermon, *The Necessity and Encouragement of Utmost Venturing for the Churches Help.*[76] The author of the *Ancient Boundes* warned, however, against the whole equation of success and divine favor. "Successe alone is not a rule for wise men to goe by."[77]

[71] *A Full RELATION of the Great Victory* (London, 1648), p. 7.

[72] Carlyle, ed. Lomas, I, 176.

[73] Ibid., p. 511.

[74] T. B. Howell, *A complete Collection of State Trials* (London, 1816), V, pp. 1116-1118.

[75] November 1, 1649 (London, 1650).

[76] June 28, 1643 (London, 1643), p. 47.

[77] (London, 1645), p. 55.

The corollary of the crusading idea was that the crusaders should be godly and their opponents esteemed ungodly. There can be no question that the parliamentarians were men of religion. Even the army of Essex, though recruited increasingly by impressment, was kept going more by religious zeal than by military training, [78] and the New Model is noted for its concern for religion.[79] But godliness meant more than prayer meetings. It meant discipline and ungodliness meant debauchery. Many were the claims that the saints were truly saints and their enemies unblushing sinners. The Roundheads were said to oppose "their profanenesse with our holinesse of life, their desperate and *God damne-me Oathes* and execrations, with our making scruple of conscience of an Oath."[80] The parliamentary soldiery were exhorted to be as virtuous as those picked men whom Joshua selected to oppose the Amalekites. Let their motto be *Militia sine malitia.*[81]

The Cavaliers were said to consist of "dissolute Gentry."[82] *A True and Perfect Relation of the Barbarous and Cruell passages of the Kings Army* recounts all the depradations of pillaging bands.[83] *The Remonstrance and Protestation, of the GENTRY and Commonalty of Buckingham, Bedford and Hartford and Cambridge* complains that the Royalists are a "blasphemous and impious Crew," who indulge in "cruell slaughter" even during a truce.[84] Thomas Hodges, preaching before the Commons on *A GLIMPSE of Gods Glory,* spares not the "foule-mouthed swearers, abominable blasphemers, prophane Sabbath-breakers, lewd and wicked professors."[85] John Price piles up the tart adjectives. They are "a most Idolatrous, Superstitious, Delinquent, Prophane, Hypocritical generation,"[86] and the pseudonymous Margarey Mar-

[78] Geoffrey Davies, "The Parliamentary Army under the Earl of Essex," *English Historical Review,* XLIX (1934), pp. 32-54.

[79] C. H. Firth, *Cromwell's Army* (London, 1902, 3d ed., 1921).

[80] *Equitable and Necessary Considerations* (London, 1642), p. 8.

[81] William Bridge, *The TRUTH of the Times Vindicated* (London, 1643), Preface.

[82] Edward Bowles, *The Mysterie of Iniquity* (London, 1643), p. 25.

[83] London, November 25, 1642.

[84] (London, December 9, 1642), p. 2.

[85] September 28, 1642 (London, 1642), p. 32.

[86] *Spirituall Snapsnacke for the Parliament Souldiers* (London, 1643), p. 13.

prelate blows a blast of Biblical imprecations. They are "the troublers of Israel, the firebrands of hell, the *Korahs*, the *Balaams*, the *Doegs*, the *Rabshekahs*, the *Hamans*, the *Tobiahs* and *Sandballats* of our time."[87]

The degree to which and the violence with which the Independents espoused the crusade is a matter of some debate. There can be no question that they pressed for the life of the king when the Presbyterians recoiled. On that point contemporary historians of all stripes are agreed. Clarendon affirmed that "the Independent party . . . feared and abhorred all motions toward peace."[88] Thomas Hobbes inquired what greater crime there could be than killing God's anointed, "which was done by the hands of the Independents."[89] The tract *Independency Stript & Whipt*, even before the execution, said of the Independents: "And first they fought for King and Parliament, only to bring Him from His evill councellers. . . . Now . . . they begin to publish their intents to the world to take away His life."[90] Milton frankly boasted that "The Independents, as they are called, were the only men that, from first to last, kept to their point, and knew what use to make of their victory."[91]

Yet the degree to which the preachers on the parliamentary side might in general be described as firebrands was controverted even in their own day. Clarendon said, "The Puritan clergy were the chief Incendiaries, and had the chief influence in promoting the Civil War."[92] Baxter retorted, "It is not true that they stirred them up to War (except an inconsiderable Number of them, one perhaps in a County, if so much.)"[93] In the early years of the eighteenth century Zachary Gray came to Clarendon's defense with citations from nearly thirty sermons, most of them incontestibly inflammatory.[94] The quotations are not, however, altogether repre-

---

[87] *The Lawfulnesse of our Expedition into England Manifested* (London, 1640), p. 6.

[88] *History of the Rebellion*, VIII, 190-197.

[89] *English Works* VI, 357.

[90] ([London], 1648), p. 13.

[91] "A Defense of the People of England," *Prose Works*, I, 193.

[92] *History of the Rebellion*, I, 302.

[93] *Reliquiae Baxterianae* (London, 1696), p. 34.

[94] *An Impartial Examination of the Second Volume of Mr. Daniel Neal's History of the Puritans* (London, 1736), p. 389.

sentative of Puritan preaching. The Yale library has a single collection of one hundred and sixty-eight sermons preached before parliament in the 1640s, many of which are simply appeals to don sackcloth.

A few examples may be given of the incendiary sort as well as of the general type of appeal designed to maintain the morale of the parliament and the army. Thomas Coleman, on the occasion of the taking of the Covenant in 1643, affirmed that God had more adversaries to overthrow. "His Sword hath not eaten flesh enough."[95] Joseph Caryl inquired: *"How can we be quiet seeing the Lord hath given us a charge against Askelon? ... may this Sword and Bow of all the upright in heart be like the bow of Jonathon, and the Sword of Saul, not turning backe nor returning empty, from the blood of sinne slaine, and from the fat of our mightiest corruptions both in Church and Commonwealth."[96]*

Any who showed a disposition to softness were reminded of all those instances in the Old Testament where implacability was enjoined. Charles Herle compared the House of Lords to the mariners in the ship with Jonah who could not manage the vessel till the fugitive prophet had been cast out. "Certainly while these *Amalekites are spared* and suffered to *come forth thus briske and confident with Agag ... the Kingdome is a departing.* (O consider) the blood that *Ahab spar'd in Benhadad* cry'd as loud against him, as that which he *spilt in Naboth.*"[97] John Strickland reminded the Lords that God required of Ahab not merely "thy life for his life," but "thy people for his people." Let them beware then of the calamities which would fall on all England if the Malignants were spared.[98] *A WARNING-PEECE to WARRE* expostulated: "And shall the blood of so many thousands of men, women and children bought and purchased by the precious blood of the sonne of God, be shed and powred out like water upon the earth in unexampled and unheard of wayes of more than barbarous cruelty cry up to

[95] *The Hearts Ingagement ... preached at St. Margarets Westminster* (London, 1643), p. 34.

[96] *THE WORKES of Ephesus Explained,* April 27, 1642 (London, 1642), p. 50.

[97] *DAVID'S SONG,* June 15, 1643 (London, 1643).

[98] *IMMANUEL,* sermon preached before the Lords, November 5, 1644 (London, 1644), p. 26.

heaven for vengeance against those cursed Rebels in *Ireland* . . . ?
*Cursed be he that . . . keepeth backe his hand from sheding of
blood,"* Jer. 48.[99]

Two tracts composed for the army well illustrate how the
zeal of the recruits was fanned. *The Souldiers Pocket Bible* compiled by Edmund Calamy in 1643 manfully disposed of the Sermon
on the Mount by placing together the following verses: "Matthew
5: 44. But I say unto you, Love your enemies. 2 Chronicles 19: 2.
Wouldst thou help the wicked and love them that hate the Lord?
Psalm 139: 21-22. Do not I hate them, O Lord, that hate Thee? . . .
I hate them with an unfeigned hatred as they were mine utter enemies." The summary is that the soldier must "love his enemies as
they are his enemies, and hate them as they are God's enemies."

The Souldiers Catechisme composed by Robert Ram in 1644
sets forth among others these queries and answers:

Q. What Profession are you of?
A. I am a Christian and a souldier.
Q. Is it lawful for Christians to be souldiers?
A. Yea doubtlesse: we have Arguments enough to warrant it. . . . 1. God
calls himself a man of war, and Lord of Hosts. 2. Abraham had a Regiment of 318. Trained men. David was imployed in fighting the Lords
battels. . . . 7. The New Testament mentioneth two famous Centu-
rions . . .
Q. What side are you of? . . .
A. I am for King and Parliament: or in plainer terms: I fight to recover
the King out of the hands of a Popish Malignant Company, that have
seduced His Majesty with their wicked Counsels, and have withdrawne
him from his Parliament. 2. I fight for the Lawes and Liberties of my
Countrey, which are now in danger to be overthrowne by them that
have long laboured to bring into this Kingdome an Arbitrary, and
Tyrannicall Government. 3. I fight for the preservation of our Parliament. . . . 4. I fight in defence and maintenance of the true Protestant
Religion. . . .
    Almighty God declares himselfe a friend to our Party. . . . God
now calls vpon vs to avenge the blood of his Saints. . . .
Q. Who do you thinke were the Authors, and occasioners of this unnat-
urall Warre?
A. The Jesuits . . . 2. The Bishops . . . 3. The Delinquents. . . .[100]

[99] London, 1642.

[100] A satire on this work was issued with the same title by Thomas Swadlin
at Oxford about January 24, 1645, described by Falconer Madan, *Oxford Books,*
II, *Oxford Literature 1641-50* (Oxford, 1912).

Two of the preachers most upbraided for unbridled zeal were Hugh Peters and Thomas Case. With regard to neither is the evidence altogether trustworthy. The most inflammatory utterances attributed to Peters came from the testimony of those seeking his life after the Restoration.[101] Even the report of the sermon preached on December 22, 1648 sounds credible only in part. He is said to have compared Fairfax to Moses. "The Design," he told them, " was to lead the People out of Egyptian Bondage; the Manner of effecting which was to be by rooting up Monarchy, both here and in the Kingdoms round about, the Lord having a great Work to finish throughout Christendom by Means of this Army."[102] That Hugh Peters at that moment actually contemplated casting down the kings all over Europe taxes credulity.

A source likewise hostile affirmed that Thomas Case, "Chaplaine" to the Lord Mayor of London was "growne to such an height of blasphemous frenzie, that at a late administration of the Sacrament he began it thus, *All you that have contributed unto the Parliament come and take this Sacrament to your comfort;* denouncing damnation unto such as should presume to receive it, and had not contributed."[103]

His printed sermons do not go beyond *Gods Rising His Enemies Scattering,*[104] or the *Solemn Thanksgiving unto God for His several mercies to the Forces of the Parliament in divers parts of the Kingdome.*[105] *The Root of Apostacy*[106] gives thanks for the victory vouchsafed to Sir William Waller.

Nevertheless, even after the more flamboyant utterances ascribed to the Independents are discounted, they must still bear the major responsibility for turning the just war into a crusade.

---

[101] T. B. Howell, *A Complete Collection of State Trials* (London, 1816) V, 1116-41 on October 13, 1660.

[102] *Old Parliamentary History,* XVIII, 477.

[103] *Mercurius Aulicus* (February 19, 1643), p. 92.

[104] London, 1644.

[105] August 22, 1645.

[106] London, 1644.

Selected Bibliography of
Roland H. Bainton

1922 "Church History and Progress," in *Education for Christian Service,* by Members of the Faculty of the Divinity School of Yale University (New Haven, Yale University Press, 1922), pp. 243-266.

1923 "Basilidian Chronology and New Testament Interpetation," in *Journal of Biblical Literature* XLII (1923), pp. 81-134.

1925 "What is Calvinism?" in *Christian Century* XLII (March 12, 1925), pp. 351-352.

1929 "The Development and Consistency of Luther's Attitude to Religious Liberty," in *Harvard Theological Review* XXII (1929) pp. 107-149.

1930 *Debtors to God,* Westminster Departmental Graded Materials. Teacher's Edition (Philadelphia, Westminster Press, 1930), 64 pages. Pupil's edition (Philadelphia, 1930).

"The Immoralities of the Patriarchs According to the Exegesis of the Late Middle Ages and of the Reformation," in *Harvard Theological Review* XXIII (1930), pp. 39-49.

1931 "Sebastian Castellio and the Toleration Controversy of the Sixteenth Century," in *Persecution and Liberty,* Essays in Honor of George Lincoln Burr (New York, Century, 1931), pp. 183-209.

"The Smaller Circulation: Servetus and Colombo," in *Sudhoffs Archiv für Geschichte der Medizin* XXIV (1931), pp. 371-374.

"William Postell and the Netherlands," in *Nederlandsch Archief voor Kerkgeschiedenis* XXIX (1931), pp. 161-172.

1932 "Methods of Great Religious Teachers," in *International Journal of Religious Education* IX (1932), September, pp. 7-8; October, pp. 6-7; November, pp. 6-7; December, pp. 19-20.

"The Parable of the Tares as the Proof Text for Religious Liberty to the End of the Sixteenth Century," in *Church History* I (1932), pp. 57-89.

"The Present State of Servetus Studies," in *Journal of Modern History* IV (1932), pp. 72-92.

1935 "Academic Freedom in the Light of the Struggle for Religious Liberty," in *Proceedings of the Middle States Association of History Teachers* XXXIII (1935), pp. 37-44.

Bibliography of the Continental Reformation: Materials Available in English (Chicago, The American Society of Church History, 1935), 54 pages. (Monographs in Church History, No. 1.)

Concerning Heretics, by Sebastien Châteillon: Now First Done into English, by Roland H. Bainton (New York: Columbia University Press, 1935), xiv, 342 pages. (Records of Civilization.)

1936 "Changing Ideas and Ideals in the Sixteenth Century," in *Journal of Modern History* VIII (1936), pp. 417-443.

"Servetus and the Genevan Libertines," in *Church History* V (1936), pp. 141-149.

1937 *David Joris, Wiedertäufer und Kämpfer für Toleranz im 16. Jahrhundert* (Leipzig: M. Heinsius Nachfolger, 1937), vi, 229 pages, (Archiv für Reformationsgeschichte. Texte und Untersuchungen. Ergänzungsband, VI.)
Ulrich von Hutten and the German Reformation, by Hajo Holborn, translated by Roland H. Bainton (New Haven: Yale University Press; London, H. Milford, Oxford University Press, 1937), viii, 214 pages. (Yale Historical Publications. Studies, XI.)

1938 "New Documents on Early Protestant Rationalism," in *Church History* VII (1938), pp. 179-187. Review of *Per la Storia Degli Eretici Italiani del Secolo XVI in Europa,* Testi Raccolti da D. Cantimori e E. Feist (1937).
"Refugees of Other Days," in *Bulletin of the Story Behind the Headlines* II (December 13, 1938), pp. 14-20.
"Servet et les Libertins de Genève," in *Bulletin Société de l'Histoire du Protestantisme Français* LXXXVII (1938), pp. 261-269.
"Straightforward Speech," in *Yale Divinity News* XXXIV (May 1938), pp. 1-3.
"Technology and Pacifism," in *Christian Century* LV (May 18, 1938), pp. 618-619.
"Unity, Utrecht and the Unitarians," in *Christian Century* LV (October 5, 1938), pp. 1189-1190.

1940 *Bernardino Ochino, Esule e Riformatore Senese del Cinquescesto,* 1487-1563, Versione dal Manoscritto Inglese di Elio Gianturco (Firenze: G. C. Sansoni, 1940), x. 213 pages. (Biblioteca Storica Sansoni, Nuova Serie IV.)
"Christian Conscience and the State," with Robert L. Calhoun, in *Social Action* VI (October 15, 1940), pp. 4-42.
"Congregationalism: The Middle Way," in *Christendom* V (Summer 1940), pp. 345-354.

1941 *The Church of Our Fathers* (New York: Charles Scribner's Sons, 1941), vi, 248 pages. Also, an English edition; a special edition for Sunday Schools by the Westminster Press; translations into Spanish, Japanese, Siamese, Hebrew and Chinese.
"The Left Wing of the Reformation," in *Journal of Religion* XXI (April 1941), pp. 124-134.
"The Struggle for Religious Liberty," in *Church History* X (June 1941), pp. 95-124.

1942 "Christian Views of Human Destiny," in *Religion in Life* XI (Winter 1941-1942), pp. 96-105.
"A Communication for a More Explicit Declaration of Peace Aims," in *Christian Century* LIX (September 16, 1942), pp. 1122-1124.
"Individualism, Christian and American," in *Vital Speeches of the Day,* VIII, No. 19, pp. 590-592.
"Teaching Church History," in *Journal of Bible and Religion* X, 2 (1942), pp. 103-107.

1943 "Bossuet and Leibnitz and the Reunion of the Church," in *The Chronicle* (Protestant Episcopal); XLIII (February 1943), pp. 102-103.
"The Churches Shift on War," in *Religion in Life* XII (Summer 1943), pp. 1-13.
"Congregationalism: From the Just War to the Crusade in the Puritan

Revolution," in *Andover Newton Theological School Bulletin* XXXV (April 1943), Southworth Lecture Number, pp. 1-20.

George Lincoln Burr: His Life, by Roland H. Bainton; Selections from His Writings, edited by Lois Oliphant Gibbons (Ithaca, N.Y., Cornell University Press; London, Oxford University Press, 1943), xi, 505 pages.

"Reconciliation and Reality," in *Fellowship* IX (December 1943), pp. 208-210.

1944 "The Christian and the War," in *Christian Century* LXI (May 3, 1944), pp. 559-561.

Pacifism Under Fire. *The Historic Church and Modern Pacificism,* by Umphrey Lee. Review by R. H. Bainton in *Fellowship* X (June 1944), pp. 113-114.

1945 "The Amistad," in *Highroad* (September 1945), pp. 4-6, 47.

"The Churches and Alcohol," in *Quarterly Journal of Studies on Alcohol,*" VI (June 1945), pp. 45-58.

"The Churches and War: Historic Attitudes Toward Christian Participation," in *Social Action* XI (January 15, 1945), pp. 5-71.

"The Cohesive Power of Protestantism," in *The Intercollegian* LXII (January 1945), pp. 8-9.

1944, 45 *The Panorama of the Christian Church in Kodachrome Slides* (Boston, Pilgrim Press, 1944, 1945).

1946 "Early Christianity as a Youth Movement," in *Highroad* (February 1946), pp. 35-37.

"The Early Church and War," in *Harvard Theological Review* XXXIX (July 1946), pp. 189-212. Reprinted without notes in *The Church, the Gospel and War,* ed. Rufus Jones (New York, Harper, 1948), pp. 75-92.

"Our Debt to Luther," in *Christian Century* LXIII (October 23, 1946), pp. 1276-1278.

"Eyn Wunderliche Weyssagung, Osiander—Sachs—Luther," in *Germanic Review* XXI, 3 (October 1946), pp. 161-164.

1947 "Dürer and Luther as the Man of Sorrows," in *The Art Bulletin* XXIX (December 1947), pp. 269-272.

"Let's Agree on the Reformation," in *Christian Century,* LXIV (1947), pp. 237-239.

"*Road to Reformation,* by Heinrich Boehmer," in *Church History* XVI (September 1947), pp. 167-176. Book review.

1948 "The Churches and Alcohol," in *Social Progress* XXXIX (November 1948), pp. 13-15, 18-19. Reprinted.

"Luther's Struggle for Faith," in *Church History* XVII (September 1948), pp. 193-206. Printed by mistake in advance of its appearance in the *Festschrift für Gerhard Ritter* (Tübingen, 1950), pp. 232-243.

"Marriage and Love in Christian History," in *Religion in Life* XVII (Summer 1948), pp. 391-403.

The Martin Luther Christmas Book, with Celebrated Woodcuts by His Contemporaries; translated and arranged by Roland H. Bainton (Philadelphia, Westminster Press, 1948), 74 pages.

"Our Protestant Witness," in *The Pulpit,* XIX (December 1948), pp. 272-274.

1949 "Christianity and Russian Communism," in *Journal of the Industrial and*

Social Order Council of the Society of Friends VI (March, April 1949), pp. 6-11.

"Christmas in 1949," in *American German Review* (December 1949), pp. 3-4. (Philadelphia, Carl Schurz Memorial Foundation, 1949.)

"Luther and the *Via Media* at the Marburg Colloquy," in *The Lutheran Quarterly* I (November 1949), pp. 394-398.

"The Puritan Theocracy and the Cambridge Platform," in *The Minister's Quarterly* V, 1 (February 1949), pp. 16-21. Also in: *The Cambridge Platform of 1648*, Tercentenary Commemoration (Boston, 1949), pp. 76-86.

"Sebastian Castellio and the British-American Tradition," in *Het Boek* XXX, 4 (1949-1951).

"Die Stellung der Quäker zu Krieg und Frieden," in *Der Quaeker*, Monatshefte der deutschen Freunde, 23. Jahrg. 1949 (January, February 1, 2), pp. 1-7.

"Without Despairing of the World, The Quaker Attitude Toward Peace and War," in *Friends Intelligencer* 106, 7 (Second Month 12, 1949), pp. 87-89.

1950   "The Genius of Protestantism," in *The Minister's Quarterly* VI (February 1950), pp. 13-18.

Here I Stand; a Life of Martin Luther (New York, Abingdon-Cokesbury Press, 1950), 422 pages. Reprinted (New York, New American Library of World Literature, 1955), 336 pages. Paperback. Translated into German, Greek, Italian, Japanese, Spanish and Swedish. Portions of this book have been delivered as the Nathaniel Taylor Lectures at the Yale Divinity School (1946-1947), the Carew Lectures at the Hartford Seminary Foundation (1949), and the Hein Lectures at the Wartburg Seminary and Capital University.

1951   "Ernst Troeltsch—Thirty Years Later," *in Theology Today* VIII, 1 (April 1951), pp. 70-96.

"Michael Servetus and the Pulmonary Transit of the Blood," in *Bulletin of the History of Medicine* XXV, 1 (January-February 1951), pp. 1-7.

"The Querela Pacis of Erasmus, Classical and Christian Sources," in *Archiv für Reformationsgeschichte* XLII (1951), pp. 32-48.

"Sebastian Castellio, Champion of Religious Liberty, 1515-1563," in *Castellioniana: Quatre Études sur Sébastien Castellion et l'Idée de la Tolérance*, par Roland H. Bainton, Bruno Becker, Marius Valkhoff et Sape van der Woude (Leiden, E. J. Brill, 1951), pp. 25-79.

The Travail of Religious Liberty; Nine Biographical Studies (Philadelphia, Westminster Press, 1951), 272 pages. The James Sprunt Lectures (1950). Also, an English edition and Harper Torchbooks (paperback).

1952   "Documenta Servetiana," in *Archiv für Reformationsgeschichte*, XLIV (1953), pp. 223-234; XLV (1954), pp. 99-108.

"Forschungsberichte und Besprechungen," in *Archiv für Reformationsgeschichte* XLIII (1952), pp. 88-106.

"Luther in a Capsule," in *Bulletin of the American Congregational Association* III (May 1952), pp. 1-9.

The Reformation of the Sixteenth Century (Boston, Beacon Press, 1952), xi, 276 pages. Also, Beacon paperback and translations into Italian and Hebrew.

1952-53 "Christianity and Sex, an Historical Survey," in *Pastoral Psychology* III, 26 (September 1952), pp. 10-26, 82; IV, 21 (February 1953), pp. 12-29. Reprinted in *Sex and Religion Today* (New York, Association Press, 1953), pp. 17-96.

1953 "The Beginnings of Anabaptism," in *Mennonite Life,* five articles commencing in 1953.

"Burned Heretic: Michael Servetus," in *Christian Century,* LXX (1953), pp. 1230-1231.

Hunted Heretic; the Life and Death of Michael Servetus, 1511-1553 (Boston, Beacon Press, 1953), xiv, 270 pages. Reprinted 1956, Beacon paperback; translated into German. For French see below.

"Man, God and the Church in the Age of the Renaissance," in *Journal of Religious Thought* XI (1953-1954), pp. 119-133. Issued also in mimeographed form in *The Renaissance. A Symposium* (New York, Metropolitan Museum of Art, 1953), pp. 41-62a.

"Michael Servetus and the Trinitarian Speculation of the Middle Ages," in *Autour de Michel Servet et de Sébastien Castellion; Recueil,* ed. Bruno Becker (Haarlem, H. D. Tjeenk Willink, 1953), pp. 29-46.

Michel Servet, Hérétique et Martyr, two editions within a few months (E. Droz, Geneva, 1953), the first with inadequate correction to be in time for the commemoration, the second with care as *Travaux d'Humanisme et Renaissance* VI, 148 pages.

They Built for Eternity, by Gustav-Adolf Gedat, translated by Roland H. Bainton (New York, Abingdon-Cokesbury Press, 1953), 175 pages.

"War and Christian Ethic," in *The Church and Social Responsibility,* ed. J. Richard Spann (New York, Abingdon-Cokesbury Press, 1953), pp. 201-219.

1954 *The Covenant in the Wilderness* (1954).

"Friends in Relation to the Churches," The Ward Lecture, Guilford College (November 12, 1954), 16 pages.

"Man, God, and the Church in the Age of the Renaissance," in *The Journal of Religious Thought* XI (Autumn-Winter, 1953-1954), pp. 119-133.

"Protestant-Catholic Relations in the U.S.," in *Advance* CXXXXVI (October 18, 1954), pp. 13-24.

"What About Catholic-Protestant Relations in the U.S.A.?" in *Messenger* XIX (October 1954), pp. 14-17.

1955 "Freedom, Truth, and Unity; Reflections on the Renaissance," in *Theology Today* XII (April 1959), pp. 85-96.

"Freedom's Religious Foundations," in *Christian Century* LXXVI (January 26, 1959), pp. 106-109.

"Patristic Christianity," in *The Idea of History in the Ancient Near East,* ed. Robert C. Dentan (New Haven, Yale University Press; London, Geoffrey Cumberlege, Oxford University Press, 1955), pp. 215-236.

"The School of Divinity," in *A Study of A Generation in Transition* (1955).

"This Grand Errand," in *Yale Alumni Magazine* (October 1955), pp. 22-23.

1956 *The Age of the Reformation* (Princeton, N.J., Van Nostrand, 1956), 192 pages. An Anvil Original paperback.

"The Ministry in the Middle Ages," in *The Ministry in Historical Per-*

spectives, ed. by H. Richard Niebuhr and Daniel D. Williams (New York, Harper, 1956), pp. 82-109.

"Religious Biography," in *Writing for the Religious Market*, ed. by Roland E. Wolseley (New York, Association Press, 1956), pp. 185-191.

"Yale and German Theology in the Middle of the 19th Century," in *Zeitschrift für Kirchengeschichte*, Bd. 65, Heft III.

1957   "The Anabaptist Contribution to History," in *The Recovery of the Anabaptist Vision*, ed. by Guy F. Hershberger (Scottdale, Pa., Herald Press, 1957), pp. 317-326.

"Luther's Simple Faith," in *Luther Today* (Decorah, Iowa, Luther College Press, 1957), pp. 1-33. (Martin Luther Lectures, 1.)

"The Universal Ministry of All Believers," in *Encounter* XVIII, 2 (1957), pp. 131-140.

What Christianity Says about Sex, Love and Marriage (New York, Association Press, 1957), 124 pages. (An Association Reflection Book.)

Yale and the Ministry; a History of Education for the Christian Ministry at Yale from the Founding in 1701, Line drawings by the Author (New York, Harper, 1957), xiii, 297 pages.

Vignettes of Men Memorialized in the Buildings of the Yale Divinity School; with Drawings by the Author (1957), 11 pages. Condensed from *Yale and the Ministry*.

1958   "Christian Pacifism Reassessed," in *Christian Century* LXXV (July 23, 1958), pp. 847-849.

"The Making of a Pluralistic Society—A Protestant View," in *Religion and the State University*, ed. by E. A. Walter (Ann Arbor, University of Michigan Press, 1958), pp. 42-57.

Pilgrim Parson, the Life of James Herbert Bainton, 1867-1942 (New York, Nelson, 1958), 166 pages.

"Probleme der Lutherbiographie," in *Lutherforschung Heute*, Hrsg. von Vilmos Vajta (Berlin, Lutherisches Verlagshaus, 1958), pp. 24-31. Internationaler Kongress für Lutherforschung, Aarhus, 1956.

"Sex and Religion," in *Ladies Home Journal* LXXV (August 1958).

"Thomas Hooker and the Puritan Contribution to Democracy," in *Bulletin of the Congregational Library* X, 1 (October 1958).

"Total Abstinence," in *Christianity Today* II, No. 20 (July 7, 1958), pp. 3-6.

1960   "Alexander Campbell and Church Unity" (pp. 81-94) and "Alexander Campbell and the Social Order" (pp. 117-129), two articles in *The Sage of Bethany; a Pioneer in Broadcloth*, by Perry E. Gresham (St. Louis, Bethany Press, 1960).

"The Bible and the Reformation," in *Five Essays on the Bible* (New York, 1960), pp. 20-29. Paper read at 1960 annual meeting of the American Council of Learned Societies Devoted to Humanistic Studies.

Christian Attitudes to War and Peace: an Historical Survey and Critical Re-evaluation (New York, Abingdon Press, 1960), 299 pages.

Constantine and Religious Liberty, by Hermann Dörries, translated by Roland H. Bainton (New Haven, Yale University Press, 1960), 141 pages. (The Terry Lectures.)

Early Christianity (Princeton, N.J., Van Nostrand, 1960), 192 pages. An Anvil Original paperback.

1961   *El Alma Hispana y el Alma Sajona* (Buenos Aires, Argentina), 143 pages.
1962   *Collected Essays,* volume one in this series.
       The Medieval Church (Princeton, N.J., Van Nostrand, 1962), 192 pages.
       An Anvil Original paperback.

INDEX